Work and Vocation

A Christian Discussion

Work and Vocation

A Christian Discussion

EDITED

AND WITH AN INTRODUCTION

BY

JOHN OLIVER NELSON

HARPER & BROTHERS PUBLISHERS

NEW YORK

Library of Congress catalog card number: 54-5856

CONTENTS

5

PREFACE

IN THE postwar years, notably in Europe, fresh understanding of the vocation of the Christian has arisen in the churches. All accounts agree that much of the power of this awakening derives from its awareness of a deep connection between everyday work and the calling of God.

At the First Assembly of the World Council of Churches in 1948, upon the specific request of the churches, attention was given to the problem of a Christian doctrine of work and vocation adequate to the contemporary scene. One result of the Assembly's discussion was to commission the Study Department of the World Council to initiate an international study among the churches on this matter. The present book is the result of the American study and it is offered as a contribution to the international discussion as well as for whatever value it may have within the American scene.

The book has been prepared over a period of three years by a group appointed by the USA Study Committee of the World Council. From the outset, it was recognized that three streams of thought and experience would be needed. The first is Biblical thought; the second is the theological formulation of Biblical thought; the third is the experience of those immersed in contemporary industrial life. Accordingly, Biblical scholars, theologians, and laymen have served as members and consultants. The group has thus included Old and New Testament scholars from seven theological seminaries representing half a dozen denominations; leaders in labor, industry, personnel management, and philanthropy; and theologians of different traditions and fields of inquiry. The group and its consultants are as follows:

9

John Oliver Nelson, Chairman
Robert S. Bilheimer, Secretary

Members	*Consultants*
Chester Barnard	John Beardslee
Millar Burrows	David Burgess
Robert L. Calhoun	A. Bryan Clark
Samuel T. Cushing	Clarence T. Craig
Cameron P. Hall	Georges Florovsky
Martin J. Heinecken	Harold Letts
Sherman E. Johnson	James Muilenberg
John Knox	C. A. Simpson
Howard T. Kuist	Thelma Stevens
Elmer A. Leslie	
Stewart Meacham	
Bruce M. Metzger	
Robert S. Michaelsen	
Richmond P. Miller	
Paul S. Minear	
Bertha Paulssen	
Harry King Tootle	

The group proceeded with its work by three stages. First, general discussion served to open up the subject, locate issues and reveal points of view. Second, an extensive series of papers—contributed by fifteen different members and consultants—served as the basis for criticism, further refinement of the various points of view, and further clarification of the field of inquiry. Third, the patterns of the present book beginning to emerge, the structure of the book was determined by the group as a whole, and the chapters assigned to individuals. First drafts of chapters underwent criticism by the entire group; second drafts by an editorial committee appointed for the purpose; and third drafts were submitted to a final meeting of the group for comment.

The group as a whole is generally responsible for the book, though it cannot be assumed that its individual members agree with all that is written here. Complete responsibility for the chapters rests with the respective authors of them. The main message of the book is shared by the group, although differences of opinion remain. For example, Biblical scholars among us disagree on the precision with which the Bible may be said to have a direct message for daily work; and the sociological and psychological analysis will be sharpened at some points and restricted at others by different members of the group.

The variety of outlook and of experience within the group, coupled with its common concern for Christian vocation, has been rewarding. The gap between scholars and theologians on the one side and laymen on the other, as well as between the viewpoints of labor and management, is well known. At the beginning of our discussions, the distance between these groups was felt in full measure. It was clear to all, however, that a discussion of Christian work and vocation must be carried on only with the participation of representatives of all these groups. We have been shown again that patient work together brings its reward in understanding and in the stimulation of new lines of thought. May it be suggested that this experience could serve as a model for similar groups throughout the country concerned, as we have been, to explore the road toward a fresh understanding of Christian work and vocation.

Work and Vocation
A Christian Discussion

Introduction

JOHN OLIVER NELSON

---

1. Dilemmas and portents. 2. Blind alleys in modern work. 3. A gospel with faltering vocation. 4. Signposts to ways ahead. 5. Facing the larger questions.

BOREDOM on the industrial assembly line, ulcers or hypertension at the office, frantic "relaxation" on weekends, wistful spectatorship in retirement—are these true highlights of modern work? Millions of us, according to surveys, think so, and many a sociologist and psychiatrist can adduce statistics to say so.

Even granting that such an evaluation is largely caricature, it links up with what was said seriously about modern work by a corporation executive after World War II: "You can buy a man's time, you can buy a man's physical presence at a given place; you can even buy a measured number of skilled muscular motions per hour or day. But you cannot buy enthusiasm; you cannot buy initiative; you cannot buy loyalty; you cannot buy the devotion of hearts, minds, and souls. . . . It is ironic that Americans—the most advanced people technically, mechanically, and industrially —should have waited until a comparatively recent period to inquire into the most promising single source of productivity: namely, the human will to work."

Manifestly, something is wrong with work life for a great many Americans. Recently industry has begun to spend millions of dollars to follow out the concern of the industrialist just quoted, to discover why people do work, and what will make them more happy (and productive!) in their work. The goal of this comparatively new effort, which is broadly known as "Human Relations in Industry," has been synopsized by *Time* with characteristic brevity: it is simply "to make life more fun by making work more meaningful."

This lack of meaning in work, earnestly analyzed and dealt with by Human Relations, is no mere industrial phenomenon. For farmers and lawyers, schoolteachers and janitors and bakers, indeed all of us, are affected by the pace and mechanization of modern life. Our whole culture needs to discover how to make work "more meaningful." The purpose of such an effort is not just increased production with contentment among workers, but rediscovery of significance and integrity in existence itself.

1. DILEMMAS AND PORTENTS

To a good many people who have studied the stresses and strains of our work today, it has been clear that whatever their *religion* may do for those engaged in occupations, it has little or no relation to their jobs as they see them. A survey made by a national agency several years ago among several thousand young men failed to find a single instance among them all, in which religious faith dealt with any aspect of daily work.

So a first concern from which this study begins is *the gap which has grown up between faith and work*. One reason for it is a conscious adherence to the traditional slogan, "Don't try to mix religion and business!" One does often cramp the other. Yet more often the cleavage takes place because modern men and women have never thought of any real connection between the two. Religion does have a bearing, they may agree, as it tends to make a person honest or dependable or gifted with some sort of peace of mind: as it does this to people personally, it is "a good idea." Beyond that point, however, how could Christian faith or any other faith affect job life, or "re-create" an occupation?

Even in church, where sermons and study materials usually declare that faith deals with all of life, there is a subtle "hands-off" policy when Christian demands reach gainful daily occupations. This seems true as often in middle-class congregations as among store-front revival groups: for the former, religious considerations might well cramp secular job activity, and for the latter, religion itself may be an antidote or compensation for job life which is menial or otherwise unsatisfying. So the estrangement between work and faith continues—even as it arouses, increasingly, a certain uneasiness between both those concerned about work and those concerned about vital religion. As more and more people seek to explore this splitting up of daily life, their interest is a first reason for the discussion represented in this book.

Another starting point for this inquiry is within the Church itself, as *new interest among Christian laymen* is found in many places. Our generation is seeing a fresh rededication of lay people to the task of the Church, and to their role in its ministry. Prompted in the long perspective by an unprecedented program of youth conferences and student programs in this century, this lay interest is an adult demand that everyday Christians again become the Church. When laymen deal with the question as to what their task actually is, as nonclergy, they inevitably find high on their agenda the topic, Daily Work. How can laymen be Christian, they ask, so long as they cannot apply their faith to the occupational activity which dominates their lives? Thus meeting halfway the restlessness or boredom of many workers, laymen from their side, within the Church, ask how they may reconsider their jobs to make them specific service of God.

A third incentive to exploring this area, paradoxically, is *the growing problem of nonwork, or leisure.* Confronted with shorter work days and longer vacations, larger pensions and earlier retirements, we are finding that our contemporary definition of "life-work" must include a great deal of spare time. Can retirement be given any exciting purpose? Can our work-free hours and hobbies and relaxations be somehow bound up with our gainful tasks to make some sort of unified picture? No set of answers about modern work and its meaning can be complete without attention to leisure. There has traditionally been difficulty in explaining drudgery spiritually; nowadays there is an even more urgent need to account spiritually for spare time.

Another circumstance prompting this study is our seeing more clearly *the implication of our daily work in the whole work and progress of the world*. The isolated farmer a few decades ago had no idea how his crop might affect eating habits in the city or across the continent, whereas now his television screen and his fast means of travel link him up closely with the whole larger economy of peoples. A number of the first A-bomb scientists were shocked at the news from Hiroshima, that this was the unexpected result of their quiet, abstract laboratory researches. An armament worker recently spoke of his frustration at finding his current output not munitions for the United Nations armies, but shells and bombs for a Latin American dictator—on which he was decidedly reluctant to work.

His uneasiness was typical of the attitude of millions today whose whole life is spent providing the means of violence and death. Even as they take their pay with a shrug, and are not quite articulate about their misgivings, the climate of achievement in which they work day after day, year after year, is a nettling and unsatisfied one. There is no petty job morality here, but a new ethical climate of internationalism in our day which has set thousands to wondering and often to inquiring about the end results of their daily endeavor. To the extent that our economy does build upon war and expectation of war, can workers be completely fulfilled and committed in their tasks? Such questions call for some word of idealism and Christian interpretation. Ambiguous final outcomes of work make people newly eager for warrant or warning from spiritual sources.

Alongside these four background causes for our inquiry into the meaning of work and vocation, there must be placed *the specific study program already initiated by the Church* in various of its branches and agencies. Work being naturally an international concern, as well as an interdenominational one, lends itself to ecumenical study. Thus men and women at the several great Church gatherings of our generation, looking at the whole balance of Christian teaching and life, have pointed to work and vocation as an area for new discovery and discussion. Their interest has of course been kindled by the factors we have just mentioned, as well as by an intense commitment to the Lordship of Christ over every aspect of human experience and existence. It now becomes an important task for the Church to map out and reclaim in our age an ancient Christian province, as well as to discover new trade routes and new continents for the Gospel, in the whole broad sphere of modern work life.

2. BLIND ALLEYS IN MODERN WORK

In the busy, money-making activity of our society, is there really a "problem of work"? All the chapters which follow here may help answer that question. Without burning over the ground which will be dealt with later, we shall do well to glance rapidly at the general picture, realizing from the outset how pervasive and acute are some of the complexities of our inquiry.

Job problems begin, for millions, with the process of *choosing the job itself*. Some 70 per cent of all Americans have already chosen their occupation by the age of fifteen. Most of the choices are made on the basis of "the first chance I got," or a casual response to a want ad in the paper, a following-out of family destiny, or some equally predetermined or capricious cause. Whether or not most of these young people do have any real option in their job choice, it is a fact that a large proportion of them believe they did not. Many a high school student yearns for the open-frontier days of Horatio Alger or the pioneers—days which may never have existed—when everybody was free to choose the lifework he wanted, and for which his talents fitted him. Now, by contrast, he finds circumstances "stacked." Even the science of vocational guidance, sometimes woodenly matching tested "abilities" with listed openings, contributes to this fatalism and inevitability. Thus in the entire process of selecting a lifework, with the job market rigid for most young people, and training opportunity circumscribed by family background, there is an initial handicap of morale for many workers.

A result is that rightly or mistakenly, millions of men and women work along year after year making the steady protest that this is not the right occupation for them, not the "break" or the ideal work situation to bring out their real abilities. Voca-

tional guidance has wrought wonders, and saved many a career
from tragedy, but it has not yet succeeded in conquering the
sense which most young workers have, that the choice of their
occupation was haphazard or mechanical, not freely determined.

Beyond this is the fact that *much modern work is boring and
deadening* for anyone with creativeness or imagination. This is
by no means a distinctively modern situation. Past centuries did
hold more drudgery and downright hard toil than we even dream
of today. But a good deal of our work today is not difficult—it is
only deadly. The unrelenting assembly line, demanding one tiny
gesture of each worker; the sales counter, with identical words
for each customer; the deafening machine, in which the tender
is really a replaceable part; the endless filing of papers in
hundreds of identical drawers; washing endless windows, serving
endless frankfurters at a stand, ironing endless sheets at a mangle,
packing endless sardines in identical cans—can such work ever
become "creative"? It has been claimed that such jobs are far
more intolerable to a survey taker—who probably has a Ph.D.
degree—than to the more simple-minded worker himself. This
is doubtless so. But granted that in a machine age such jobs
must apparently be done, and granted that certain persons find
no great revulsion in doing them, the fact remains that work of
this sort is stultifying and somehow subhuman. Even if he does,
we ask, *should* a human being enjoy such machinelike repetitive
toil?

Another problem, beyond monotony, is that *modern work may
be unattractive or even revolting*. The hog killer at the stock-
yards, the garbage collector, the coroner making autopsies all
day, the janitor cleaning latrines all night—can we ask these to
relish their work? We shall have to go far for a view of vocation
which can cover these workers as well as the craftsman and the
philosopher.

To the difficulties represented in job choice, in monotony,
and in distastefulness, add a fourth: *work nowadays tends to
depersonalize people*. In plants, on ships or farms, in offices and
stores, millions in our world are working for an employer they
have never seen, and who has never seen them. They are known

to their superiors only as a number. They may be spending their days on a product, large or small, about the use for which they may have no inkling—and about which no one finds it important to tell them. They have never seen the people who provide the raw materials they use, or the machines they operate; nor do they know anyone personally who will use the end product of their work. Thus their work life may be spent in an almost completely impersonal process.

To be sure, each worker does have friends among fellow workers. Often indeed he is a member of a team which enjoys real social relationships, inside and outside the plant. But the large outlines of his work are a maze of impersonality. Especially before the coming of Human Relations in Industry, employers have assumed that workers need know nothing about their activity except what motions it entails and what paycheck it draws.

Objection is due at this point, that we speak too exclusively of industry, whereas the great majority of American workers are in other sorts of jobs. This is true. But as we have already suggested, mechanization and the whole psychology of industrial work have spread out into all our occupational life. Huge machine-operated farms, mass universities, robotlike military programs, skyscraper offices, thousand-bed hospitals—all occupations share to a degree the depersonalized atmosphere of big industry. The industrial worker, with his many satisfactions as well as with the problems we have noted, is a symbol of work in our time. He typifies "work" to the same extent that technical process distinguishes our contemporary culture itself.

Problem five is that *such work often destroys retirement and leisure.* We are familiar with the poignant situation of the business executive who dreads retirement because all he knows is business, and life will lose its meaning completely when he can no longer report daily at the office. This difficulty arises from the fact that he has let his job, demanding as it is, dominate his life so completely that there has been no room for a hobby or avocation. Here is a man who has never known how to live outside his effort to make a living. Any real feeling for the arts, or for community and church, or for reading, or for people, has been withered by the claims of daily work. Futility in spare time is merely compounded as futility in old age.

Certain large national business organizations, facing this poverty of worker interests, have begun to require that every worker have a hobby, with instruction and encouragement provided before retirement, as a condition for being annuitized in later years. It has been revealing to discover, we are told, how few employees do already have some interest outside their occupation, in which they can find satisfaction. Television, spectator sports, and other minimum-participation ways of spending our leisure seem to be encouraged by the pressures of modern work.

A final cause for reappraisal of modern work life is the evident limit to which the science of Human Relations in Industry can go: *the deepest questions of workers are questions about life itself.* They involve factors far out beyond factory walls, and beyond mere pleasing relations with colleagues and superiors. As the employer takes laboring men into his confidence about plans and schedules, or scans their work conditions to improve them, output does rise and intraplant understanding flourishes. The worker feels better and works better.

But what if a worker should come one day to the personnel department with the question which is really his most basic query: "Why work at all? Why human existence, and human relations? Why live?" If he did, his difficulty would arouse polite embarrassment or even alarm. At this level, industry has no answers. The personnel adviser, trained in psychology, might most likely echo Pilate's comment, "What is truth?" and advise a psychiatric interview or a change of duties. Or he might refer the worker vaguely to "religion" for a reply to his question.

The fact is, once such a process as Human Relations gets started, interpreting to workers what they do, and why "love their neighbor" in industry, there has begun an interpretation of life and reality which cannot logically stop short of the really big questions about destiny and reality. Now that modern industry has begun to "explain," rather than leaving its employees unenlightened in mechanical servitude, it cannot in integrity refrain from deciding (even for itself) some of the paramount issues about the kind of God we worship and the kind of universe we inhabit as workers and human beings.

3. A GOSPEL WITH FALTERING VOCATION

Certainly modern industrial life, at which we have briefly glanced, has shaped the Church more than the Church has been able to shape the world of work. Occupational life has in this century been self-sufficient enough to relegate religion to the margins of personal and emotional life, denying it the center. As a result, Christianity, or any other form of faith, has found itself domesticated in the home, in private morality, and in Sunday services, but firmly fenced off from daily work.

This is partly because job life was unwilling to bear the judgment or satisfy the standards of Christian ethical demands: "If we cannot be secular in our occupation, where on earth *can* we be secular? This isn't Church; it's business." But the other aspect of how industrial life has molded the Church is that it has made a Sunday faith seem quite adequate to satisfy workers' needs. Studies have shown that for a repetitive assembly-line worker, authoritarian religion fits the pattern all too well: so long as it provides an unquestioned system, assures us of salvation, and periodically releases our emotions, it will do. As regulation and pattern in job life make the worker uninterested and unwilling to think for himself, the Church takes over with its own regulation and pattern, to which are added only a touch of mysticism and sentimentality. Too often Christianity has accepted this role. It has again and again accommodated itself to the demands of secular job life, impoverishing both sides of the transaction.

Looking at specific ways in which job life has thus vitiated religious life, consider the fact that *"a call of God" has in our day become for most Christians "a call to the ministry."* True to his absorption with secular work, the average layman reasons that businessmen and others would surely not be "called" by God, for they are completely preoccupied, too busy with other things. So when a Christian does feel that the Holy Spirit has laid hold upon his life, most church members assume that he or she will "leave the world" to prepare for service as a missionary or otherwise take up an employed Church task. Even the clergyman, himself sometimes insecure about his standing among other workers, often confirms by his precept and example the idea that he has been "called" in a way necessarily strange to any layman—thereby becoming directly responsible to God (or alas, even *for* God) in all he does.

Such narrowing of the ranks of the "called," to include only those ordained or especially set apart in church work, rejects the whole central idea of divine calling found in the New Testament, which was lived out in the first Christian century and in the Reformation. It results in the Church's being no longer a chosen people, a fellowship under covenant with God—but instead an institution made up of clergymen with which laymen may "communicate." By such a caricature of Christian vocation the Priesthood of All Believers and the real relation of Christianity and work have fallen away. Once, men knew that every Christian is summoned to his task and his destiny by Almighty God. Now the busy layman, suspecting no call of God in his own life, does perform certain minimal Sunday duties himself, but he pays a clergyman to handle the religious side of life on a professional, expert, specialized basis!

Together with this loss of the sense of vocation, *the Church has lost much of its power to communicate the Gospel through words and symbols,* because laymen have ceased to be the Church. Baptism has often failed of its meaning as a covenanted occasion in which parents and the whole fellowship take vows for a child—because the minister is the only one present who knows what this covenant means. The "Lord's Table" becomes for many thousands not a spread board around which believers gather, but a sacred high place from which a clergyman comes down to offer elements which he has now made holy by his spoken formula. To say this is not to deny that millions find their spiritual life sustained and deepened in these sacraments. Yet much has been lost.

Similarly "Sanctification"—the New Testament process by which every aspect of a life is gradually yielded to the Holy

Spirit—has lost value for many of us. It applies to laymen in only a limited degree, because we now assume that only the minister does face the demand of "full-time Christian service." Laymen are therefore "sanctified," for many Church people, only to the extent of part-time Christian service. Indeed, the common use of the phrase "full-time Christian service" to denote merely church vocations is a token of how far from the New Testament we have wandered. Such usage lets the layman off too easy. For the New Testament claim is that *every* Christian believer is summoned to full-time Christian work, while a few are called to church vocations. Happy is the layman who does find his occupation a veritable ministry to God: every Christian should share his dedication.

Further inroads have been made by job life in our interpretation of the Incarnation itself. In its historic, exciting reality, this is the claim that God is made real among men in the ordinary "carnal" (*carne*) aspects of life, not just in holy, set-apart acts and situations. Thus the Incarnation means that the Almighty lays hold upon all experience and makes it holy, showing forth glory in a manger stable, or in the life of a taxgatherer or a fisherman, through the life of one who was a carpenter. The Incarnation lays claim to every occupation. Accordingly, we deny its truth to the degree we limit and confine it to the church building, or to the ministry, or to sacraments mechanically considered, or even to the quaint archaisms of ancient liturgy and antique customs and colors. The Incarnation means Christianity in a workaday, practical life among laymen doing ordinary things as redeemed persons.

A further instance of how dear it has cost the Church to be separated from job life is that *many laymen have withdrawn from the Church into secular fellowships* where their daily work does matter. Businessmen have resorted to service clubs ("Rotary is my religion now"), and women's clubs have replaced many a missions group and ladies' aid. Such new secular groupings have begun to flourish during the very decades in which midweek prayer meeting, class meeting, or adult Sunday School class have tended to wither away. Now the service clubs, usually with quotas of members from each occupational field, are the nearest thing to a "guild" (aside from unions themselves) in our modern communities: here professional skills are honored, and a man's daily occupation is built into his fellowship with the whole company of his friends.

A crowning result of the alienation of daily job life from religion is that *modern man has set off in anxious pursuit of material and physical substitutes for spiritual realities.* The emotion, or devotion, once shown forth in worship is now poured out at a sports event or before a television screen—partly because there is no place for it any more in the house of God. Specifically, much of our world-renowned American preoccupation with sex and "thrills" is a result of this unsatisfied hunger for genuine, deep emotional experiences. The excitement of the sacraments, the *Sursum corde* (Lift up your hearts!) of corporate worship, the lively concern for the minister's message from the Word, and particularly the folksy town-meeting aspects of church life—all these have tended to fade, while the secular substitutes found for them have not been adequate. Often a laborer's restlessness, his decision to go out on strike, his clamoring for a larger paycheck—like the vexed social climbing or violent recreation of the subexecutive—are just expressions of emotional and spiritual undernourishment. Like the child denied normal affection and response from his family, who develops inordinate needs and insistences, unaware of what he really needs, so modern man frequently reacts to his religious starvation by a frantic pursuit of more and more excitement, or liquor, or sex, or amusement, or new cars, or the thousand other things from which his equally "sensate" fellow citizens may make a profit.

Can such emotion and eagerness ever again be linked up with the agelong, satisfying life of the Church? If the Church were to become again laymen, expressing their concerns in shared fellowship, bringing their work lives week after week into the Divine presence, both Church life and job life would reclaim a unity and glory which they largely lack today.

4. SIGNPOSTS TO WAYS AHEAD

Like the brief sketches given, a swift synopsis of where-we-might-go-from-here may well precede the main discussion of this volume. The whole book is not intended as a manual for action, or a guide to particular methods, but as a broad approach to the whole meaning of work and vocation. Thus what is said here—and again more fully in the final chapter—is not merely to suggest imitation or elaboration, but to provide a practical background for the reader who wishes to see the full picture, and to know some of the ways Christians have dealt with it.

Certainly one practical reaction to the sort of discussion this book provides is for Christians to get together for further exploration and decision in this area. For example, the great occasion at which this concern came to focus first in our generation was at Amsterdam, Holland, in 1948, when the newly formed World Council of Churches considered the theme of work and vocation, and asked that the member communions study it. Another large assembly, the Y.M.C.A. Centennial for the United States, in 1951, at Cleveland, took up the same theme with new vigor. The next year at Buffalo there was convened a memorable conference on "The Christian and His Daily Work" under leadership from the National Council of Churches, with several hundred laymen and a minority of ministers giving three days to the topic, and bringing out four meaty booklets dealing with it. As these three assemblies have shown, much is to be done by an assembly or conference at which work and vocation are taken seriously.

Probably no other group of laymen has been so numerous as the famous *Kirchentag* in Germany, an annual national assembly in which 500,000 have taken part at one time. It has symbolized the growing importance of lay Christianity in Western Europe.

A second means of enlisting lay interest in this field has been the gathering of study groups representing just one occupation. Pioneering in this technique have been the Evangelical Academies in Germany, at which several score or several hundred Christians in one occupational field have come together with leadership lay and clerical, for several days of discussion. They join in worship, realistic sharing of specific obstacles and problems of that particular vocation, and discussion of ways by which their jobs can be reclaimed as Christian ministries. Recently at Parishfield (Brighton, Michigan) a similar plan has been set forward, involving several vocational groups of some twenty members each, who gather for a study program three times a year for three years.

A third way forward is illustrated by national or international movements of Christians. Two of the most notable of these have been put forward by Roman Catholics, to whom lay vocational claims of this sort are a comparatively new interest. One is The Christophers, led by a dynamic priest, James Keller of New York, and numbering over 600,000 Catholics and others among its members. Christophers are especially concerned to "lift up Christ" in vocational life, especially in certain strategic fields, such as education, films, radio, and politics. A deeper movement, more widely felt, is the Jocists (Jeunesse Ouvrière Chrêtienne) in Europe and Canada. Originally a Belgian and French group, it now numbers among its members hundreds of thousands of young Roman Catholic workers in various countries. Jocists, clerically led like the Christophers, agree to a strict discipline in relation to their jobs, which involves regular worship, giving, rules of life, etc. Here are groups of Christian laymen who mean business, and who have reclaimed Roman Catholicism in whole areas of lay life.

Non-Roman national or international movements in this field have made already a real impact within the Church, even though they are just now gaining their main strength. International Christian Leadership (ICL), a movement begun in Seattle in 1935 to inspire laymen to take a more active part in political and community concerns, has spread to various countries and gathered some thousands of members. In America, the Laymen's Movement for a Christian World has led many a businessman to deeper commitment in interpreting his work as service of God; at its retreat center, Wainwright House, in Rye, New York, it has sponsored a notable series of colloquies on this theme. In a somewhat different way, Moral Re-Armament, an international Christian movement which is the continuation of Buchmanism and the Oxford Group, has led many thousands all over the world to dedicate their jobs to a renewed personal evangelism, with centers in Switzerland, Michigan, and Los Angeles.

Vocational guilds are a fourth creative activity in this field—with greatest progress here again shown among Roman Catholic groups. The Catholic Actors' Guild, Catholic Court Attachés, Guild, Catholic Newsmen's Guild, the Association of Catholic Trade Unionists (ACTU), and others, are alert to the cause of their Church in their various occupations. Non-Roman Christians, not being in the minority, have had less reason to band together in such guilds. A Guild of Christian Scholars (Protestant Episcopal) is a nation-wide group of teachers in America who are related to a single communion.

In passing, we may point out that this Christian guild plan may with profit be taken much further by Protestants and others. In a congregation or area where several physicians, or engineers, or salesmen, or labor leaders, etc. are like-minded, an informal guild organization can be abundantly useful to all its members. In England, the Christian Frontier, largely Anglican in leadership, has been a movement providing solidarity among several such groups, notably lawyers, doctors, and teachers.

Setting up study centers for vocational Christianity is a fifth way forward. In Europe since World War II, such centers for interpretation of lay life have sprung up with amazing unanimity of concern. At Driebergen in Holland the Kerk en Wereld movement centers in a new campus and program, seeking to enable laymen of the Reformed (State) Church to assume their proper role as Christians. Under the guidance of the World Council of Churches, the Ecumenical Institute at Bossey, in Switzerland, offers a similar series of short-term courses for laymen in various occupational fields, particularly the professions. At an older center in Sweden, Sigtuna, "a watchtower and a school," a quiet continuing program seeks to affect lay life in every diocese through the countryside. In Scotland, since 1938, the Iona Community has made a fresh witness to the meaning of the Incarnation in lay life and in the ministry. Kirkridge in Pennsylvania, and Pendle Hill near Philadelphia, are retreat-and-study centers where lay groups have for some years gone to study out the interdependence of their faith and their jobs.

Such examples indicate the variety of approaches which are being made to link faith and job life together again—but they also show how small thus far all such effort has been. In the reading list at the end of the book a number of further extensions are suggested. Possibly one result of sharing this discussion will be that laymen and their ministers may set forth larger and more earnest emphases in this field.

5. FACING THE LARGER QUESTIONS

In the chapters which follow, recurring problems and emphases will present themselves for discussion from the various angles taken by the different writers. The main queries with which all are concerned are principally these:

What is work? In the Bible, in Christian history and interpretation, in the mind of today's industrial employee or executive, the changing definition and importance of work is a key concern.

What is vocation? As this often neglected, often misused or misunderstood idea takes shape in the experience of high religion, it deals with the broadest and deepest interpretation of human existence.

Can our daily work link up with God's calling for each of us? This question, which never occurs to most of our contemporaries, and seldom to most contemporary Christians, has crucial bearing here. Such conjoining of the two as was apparently possible in Old Testament times, in Early Church monasticism, and again in the fresh days of the Protestant Reformation, may among millions of workers be impossible forever in a machine age. Whether or not it is, demands our most earnest attention.

What are the marks or notes of *my* vocation? If our discussion does not bring each reader into confrontation with his or her own daily work in new ways, it will have fallen short of its goal. For as we consider the vast forces at work about us, and the tired institutionalism with which much Christianity faces these, one decision we may make is that to take this whole subject seriously is to begin personally, individually to reclaim the truth. By such specific dedication the Church may be renewed, work life in our time repossessed for the claims of the Incarnation, and our own lives given vivid and unsuspected power. The whole theme under consideration is one of the urgent concerns of our civilization and our faith in God.

I

Work and Vocation
in Scripture

PAUL S. MINEAR

---

1. Four meanings of work. 2. The heart of the worker. 3. God as builder. 4. Summons to a whole people. 5. Tasks and talents. 6. Vocational guidance. 7. Son of man, servant of God. 8. The New Testament adventure in vocation. 9. Diverse gifts, one spirit. 10. The criteria of a calling. 11. Freedom in occupations. 12. Working with God.

What has a man from all the toil and strain with which he toils beneath the sun? For all his days are full of pain, and his work is a vexation; even in the night his mind does not rest. Ecclesiastes 2:22, 23.*

THIS wise man of the Bible has voiced a perennial complaint. To be sure, not all men are vexed by their work. Some find in it the source of deep and quiet joy. Yet most of us, as we come from office or shop, are vulnerable to the mood of Ecclesiastes. We may suppress sternly any inner resentments against our lot. We may sublimate our frustration into harmless hobbies or personal hostilities, into gay follies or feverish activities. Yet the awareness of futility keeps gnawing away at our minds. We cannot avoid a taste of bitterness whenever we measure our labor by the cost in effort and the return in joy. This bitterness springs from a deep instinct, from an inborn expectation that toil should yield more satisfying results. This instinct, also, is voiced by the Biblical poet: "There

* Scriptural quotations in this chapter are from *The Holy Bible*, Revised Standard Version. Copyright, 1952, by the Division of Christian Education of the National Council of the Churches of Christ in the U. S. A.

is nothing better for a man than that he should eat and drink, and find enjoyment in his toil" (v. 24). Is not this, after all, why we work? Should not work lead directly to this goal? Yet frequently it doesn't. And why not? As an answer we are inclined to blame ourselves, our Fate, our bosses, our competitors, or simply "the System" that so greedily devours the labor that is spent on it. How lucky are those whose foresight, industry, or "stars" unite to produce genuine enjoyment in toil! How lucky, and also how rare!

We may agree with Ecclesiastes in the bitterness of futile work and on the blessedness of fruitful labor, but we find it less easy to share his explanation of fertility or futility: "This also, I saw, is from the hand of God; for apart from him who can eat or who can have enjoyment?" (v. 24). Here we touch upon one of the strangest aspects of the Bible. We today find it difficult or stupid to discern God's hand at work within the daily round, but the men of the Bible seem to find everywhere traces of God's immediate activity. For them the workaday world is the place where both God and men are active, sometimes at cross purposes and sometimes in co-operation. The Bible has, in fact, far more to say about daily chores than most of its readers realize. Indeed, we may think of it as an album of casual photographs of laborers. Our first glimpse of man is as a farmer, cultivating and conserving the ground (Gen. 2:15). Every glimpse of God shows Him as a mighty worker who brings new things into existence and untiringly oversees all the enterprises in His vast domain. In accomplishing His greatest work, God sends a carpenter to construct a city into which men will bring the fruits of all their labors. There are vivid pictures, as well, of God's adversary, who plants weeds in the same field and erects towers in the same city. But at the end the works of God's servants will "follow them," and supreme among them all is the perfected work of God's Son. A book by workers, about workers, for workers—that is the Bible.

All this we may quickly recognize. Yet for most of us there is a chasm between the Biblical record and our own present occupations in the modern world. We may, to be sure, admit that this chasm exists, and that no bridge has yet been found across which traffic may easily move. The Bible may contain messages which God addresses to us at our daily business, but seldom do we hear His voice above the whir of modern machines.

It is not surprising that this should be so. After all, it is eighteen centuries since the latest of the books was written. No one need remind us how radically all conditions have changed since then. Few worlds seem more remote from ours than the world of Isaiah or of Peter. In few areas is this remoteness more conspicuous than in the type of economy, the forms of commercial organization, the conditions and the tools of work. It is unlikely, to say the least, that Deuteronomy will speak directly about his problems to the welder in the auto assembly line, or that the prophet John will be of help in the problems faced by an insurance executive. The Biblical writers undoubtedly retain a foreign accent. What is worse, they appear to be addressing an entirely alien audience. They do not provide explicit directions of the sort one expects from a vocational counselor. It is necessary, therefore, for us to be clear on this point. The Bible does not furnish a doctrine of work and vocation that can be easily applied to the tangled skein of modern occupations with immediately beneficial results. We must not expect to find in its pages an objective evaluation of the crafts and trades in which men are now engaged.

Having agreed on this point, we must move on to the next. Granting that the Bible does not provide explicit guidance on the relative merit of various occupations, we must listen for its indirect teachings and its implicit attitudes, because an indirect illumination of a subject may often be more effective than a direct one. To expect from the Bible an objective doctrine of work implies that we are quite competent to raise the right questions and to place the answers in the right context, and thus to retain control of the procedure. Our culture knows how to keep its vocational questions within bounds, and how to provide its own answers to those questions. For new light we are therefore dependent on truths that will seem foreign, truths that demand reexamination of attitudes which we have hitherto taken for granted. These truths may suggest new dimensions in the meaning of work and new contexts in which to place the daily "struggle for survival." It is for such truths that we go to the Scriptures, listening for its prevailing attitudes toward the work of men's hands.

1. FOUR MEANINGS OF WORK

Our initial concern is with the exact reference of this troublesome four-letter word "work." Its meaning presents no problem until we begin to examine it; when we do, we quickly discover that it covers a very wide range of experience. Work is one of the simplest words in our vocabulary, but often it is the simple word that causes the greatest confusion in passing from the ancient to the modern world. It is used in both worlds, but its cargo of meaning shifts imperceptibly as we pass from one to the other. Let us first isolate four meanings in our *modern* usage. Perhaps most readers will thus far have been thinking of work as "what I do from nine to five, Monday through Friday." "It is that for which I am paid regularly," "It is the occupation by which the census classifies me." We normally distinguish work from sleep, from leisure, and from anything done before the age of sixteen and after the age of seventy. Our work is what we do regularly for pay; and most of us work because we must. This is the first of four major circles of meaning: what a man or woman is hired to do. We may call this the *immediate* meaning.

No work, of course, is a purely private affair. Each worker works for others, and others work for him. Each act of labor is geared into wider processes, each job a tiny wheel meshed into other wheels within an intricate mechanism. In this context we sometimes use the term "work" to indicate a particular type of employment in which many are simultaneously engaged. A given individual finds work within a given class of workers. The labor force may be divided horizontally into various crafts, trades, or occupations, or vertically along the lines formed by separate industries, such as steel, mining, and agriculture. The work of carpenters is different from that of plumbers; agricultural work is not the same as engineering. The "problem of work" in one case will not be the same as in the other. This, then, is a second circle of meaning: work is *what a particular craft or industry contributes to the functioning of society as a whole.* This is the *collective* meaning of the term.

A third circle appears when we reflect on the different types of economy represented by various societies. In an industrial society, work has features very different from those dominant in an agrarian society. The conditions of work on a mechanized New Jersey farm may be closer to those of the auto factory in Detroit than to those on the farms of India. Each economy, by its processes of production and distribution, conditions the character of work in all areas of its system. Furthermore, economic history shows how each generation has its own typical conditions of employment, its own points of tension, its own rationalization of the labor market. The problem of work in America is not the same today as it was in 1900, because the entire economy is radically different. By the term "work" the economist may accordingly indicate the functioning of the total labor force available in a given economy, in accordance with the demands of that economy. He is concerned with the total impact of work on the economy and of the economy on work.

It should be quite obvious that these three circles of meaning overlap. A salesgirl in a department store sells a pair of shoes. This sale is part of the daily job for which she is paid. But she is part of the staff of the store, a smaller part of the union of store clerks, yet a smaller part of the clerical workers of the country, and a still smaller part of the labor force of the entire society. Her sale affects countless workers and her work is conditioned by an infinite number of factors that reach far beyond her control. The distinctions that we have drawn, however, may help us to understand the various meanings of the term; they may also suggest the complexities in dealing with the significance of a single job to the various workers involved.

It should be noted that these three circles of work do not exhaust the use of the term. Some people work harder at their sports and hobbies than in their office. Every person expends energy in some work for which he is not paid (e.g., the housewife). There is a sense in which every person works, regardless of age or wealth or economic position. Even to read these lines is one form of work. This suggests a level in the meaning of work that is deeper than a given type of employment or a given function in the labor force of a country. Work is a word that may include any expenditure of energy toward ends which the worker considers necessary or desirable. On this level all people of all ages meet in a shared experience of what work means. This is perhaps the most inclusive sense of the term.

From the earliest period of history until the latest, men have been workers. For them all, work has been an important ingredient in their existence as men. From time's beginning, work has been a source of deepest discouragements and highest dreams. It has conditioned all human relationships, has molded the soul of the worker, has shaped the pattern of community. This, then, is the fourth circle: work is *that universal, agelong activity of man by which he seeks to sustain, to vindicate, to realize that which as man he seeks in life.*

Having glanced at the varying meanings of the term in contemporary usage, we should now assess the basic connotations in Biblical usage. It should not surprise us to find that in the Bible the term is equally flexible, equally inclusive, and equally difficult to limit to one specific form of energy. We find references to the employment of a carpenter building a single house (the most immediate sense), and these very references may embrace the significance of all labor in the most inclusive sense. Contrari-wise, we will often note that general references to work often leave us uncertain as to whether they apply at all to ordinary menial labor. This difficulty we may illustrate by focusing attention on a single quotation:

> *Work* out your own salvation with fear and trembling; for God is at *work* in you, both to will and to *work* for his good pleasure. Phil. 2:12, 13.

Three times the accent falls on this word. Man is the one who works, and in whose work God is mysteriously present. The purpose of work, its manner, and its results are all included in the one command: But to what form of activity does the word refer? To weekday employment for pay? Most readers will answer in the negative. Certainly that meaning is not the only one, and probably not the primary one. Paul does not explicitly mention the "secular" jobs of individual Philippians. But are those jobs excluded from his thought? This passage does not permit a clear and certain answer. He had particular workers in mind, people engaged in simple mundane tasks. But was their daily employment a channel by which they could work out their salvation? If we include material from other letters, we have good evidence that Paul, as a matter of fact, did include ordinary menial occupations. Slaves, for example, had their opportunity to work out their salvation by obeying their masters "in the Lord." Each of their tasks could become a means of "fearing the Lord" and "serving the Lord" (Col. 3:22, 23). In any case, it is clear that the apostle used the term "work" in a much broader sense than is our custom. Of the circles of meaning which we have outlined, he was thinking in terms of the first and the fourth—the most immediate and the most inclusive. He paid little attention to the more collective, the more technical, the more analytic meanings of the term.

In this respect Paul's usage is quite characteristic of the Bible as a whole. The Bible does not discuss work as "the total labor force in the economy as a whole." It does not compare the conditions of work in one economy with those in another. Problems stemming from basic cultural changes are not, to be sure, totally absent. Especially during the Old Testament period, grave dislocations were caused by transitions from nomadic to agricultural, and from agricultural to urban economies. These changes created deep rifts in the fabric of society, and spokesmen arose to defend the old or the new, and often left their prejudices imbedded in the Scripture. Even in the Old Testament, however, there is no objective analysis of the structures of economic life. Nowhere do we find either complete approval or complete rejection of a given economy as such. Writers did not identify the problem of work with the problems produced by a particular system of economic organization.

On occasion, Biblical writers use the collective meaning of the term "work." It is recognized that slaves encounter conditions of work that give them common interests, in conflict with the interests of their masters. Prophets and sages were keenly aware of injustice shown to certain trades and classes of workers, and of unfair advantages claimed by favored groups in society. Normally, however, there was little interest in justifying or repudiating the several occupations or industries as such. Writers concentrated on the personal responsibilities of workers (including employers) within various crafts or at different levels of economic power. They attacked the oppressors and defended the oppressed, but seldom did they advance a program for the reorganization of classes. Rarely do we find any analysis of defects in the structure of power, or any effort to rate various occupations in a scale according to their desirability for individual employment.

In both Testaments, the primary significance of work was found in the immediate and the inclusive "circles." Each work situation confronted the worker with strategic opportunities for good or ill, opportunities that were actualized only in each successive moment. At the same time, however, each day's job was viewed as a universal element in human experience, a link between one worker and all other workers in all epochs. The Bible constantly stressed one of these areas because it stressed the other. The significance of any job stemmed from its bearing upon God's overarching purposes, Israel's enduring covenants, man's perennial rebellions, and his ultimate destiny.

Because the Bible treats the term "work" in this fashion, we do not find the kind of objective historical analysis with which the sciences of sociology and economics have made us familiar. These sciences usually concentrate on the more collective, technical, and historical meanings. Here is one point, therefore, at which the modern reader needs to make certain mental adjustments. He should not expect to find in the Bible specifications for improving the work conditions for the various occupations and classes in a streamlined industrial system. He should be patient enough to hear first what the Bible has to say about the immediate job and the universal meaning of work before he asks for light on the intermediate range of problems.

In spite of all contrasts, however, there remains common ground where Biblical thinking and modern thinking meet.

Both are interested in the task which a person does for pay. Both are concerned with all the labor of man, the significance of which is so closely woven into the ultimate meanings of life itself. Let us approach the Bible, then, with very simple questions, like those of Ecclesiastes: "What has a man from all the toil and strain with which he toils beneath the sun?" Let us begin with an idea of work so broad as to fit both worlds of thought: work is the deliberate expenditure of energy toward ends which men consider necessary or desirable. Let us not force the Bible to speak directly to all our occupational problems, but first of all let us listen to the context in which the Bible sets such problems.

2. THE HEART OF THE WORKER

Throughout the Bible it is the person who works to whom most attention is given, rather than the form or conditions of his work. A man works because of certain hopes and fears. By working, he surrenders some desires in order to fulfill others. By working, he gives voice to certain loyalties and obligations, taking his place in a community of burden-bearers. However repetitious his work may be, it remains an important projection of his inner being. As a person, he sees each job in terms of a whence and a whither; it is a step in a journey that has a beginning and an end. The meaning of work is contingent upon the laborer's purpose in life; the validity of the work rests first of all upon the validity of that purpose. Therefore, according to the Bible every work is dependent upon its hidden origins in the decisions of the workers.

> Unless the Lord builds the house,
> Those who build it labor in vain.
> Unless the Lord watches over the city,
> The watchman stays awake in vain. Ps. 127:1

Let us note some of the implications of these axioms. First of all we may observe that the Psalmist does not elaborate a general doctrine of work per se. He does not draw up a list of preferred occupations which God approves, separating them from types of work that are evil, futile, or profane. He does not discuss the merits of masonry as over against those of army life. He focuses attention upon the persons who work. Along with other Biblical writers, he emphasizes the agent more than the act, the motive of the laborer more than the mode of his labor.

Further, we may observe that what he states is, in effect, a general law, yet he states it in such a way that individual workers may recognize themselves as the men addressed, whether they are shepherds or merchants. The teaching is relevant to all types of work, and to every worker in his own employment. Even the most general Biblical maxims never lose this trait of singling out each man and dealing with his job as if ultimate issues were at stake in the way he does it. Thus his work is endowed with a significance that goes far beyond the visible results of that work.

This method of dealing with the problems of work seems at first to deflate the values of *what* a person is doing. It does not place a premium on the work of the carpenter as better than that of the garbage collector. Yet by placing the accent on the person who labors, the Psalmist gives to every kind of work a genuine, although derivative, significance. The tedious pacing of the sentinel is important not simply because of its social utility but because God is or is not present in that pacing. From this standpoint, no job can be scorned as a casual, trivial, transitory detail; it is the extension of a man's hand, and that hand is the tool of his heart. He invests his heart in the work of his hands. For his work to be "established" is the highest conceivable reward open to him (Ps. 90:17).

The Psalmist, we further note, addresses the mason and the sentinel in the midst of their work, not before it is begun or after it has been completed. This is entirely typical of the Bible. Its authors do not commonly indulge in an advance weighing of the various occupations that may be open to man in the future. They do not waste time in drawing the specifications of an ideal occupation. They do not feed self-pity or pride by comparing the actual occupation with an ideal one. They take it for granted that a person is now engaged in a given task. They call for a choice to be made among the immediate options open to the worker in the quality and motivation of this present job. The urgent question for the carpenter is not whether to build a house but whether in building it his energies will be properly related to God's purpose.

Because the Psalmist is not concerned with the choice of carpentry as a trade, but only with the choices made by the carpenter in his trade, the reader may conclude that this axiom has no bearing upon the problem of occupational decision. Even so, we would be entitled to draw two inferences. First of all, the Psalmist's attitude refuses to endorse the various dignities which society always assigns to preferred trades and the corresponding indignities which fall upon other trades. Sentinels are not encouraged to become diplomats. No priority is accorded to "white-collar" workers or to those who wield vast public influence. By implication the Bible encourages a great leveling of occupations, since the dignity of the worker does not depend on the prestige accorded to his profession. No one is saved merely by being in the right profession or damned merely by being in the wrong one. In the second place, this leveling of occupational walls is accompanied by an elevation of the potential significance of all jobs and occupations. From the worker's standpoint, every field or shop may become the place where he is recognized by God, where he is visited by God, where ultimate matters are at stake. God may choose to make the workbench the scene of creation, judgment, redemption. When this happens, the same workbench becomes the scene of decisions on the part of the worker in which the highest freedom and the highest responsibility are conjoined. The same job may thus offer a worker genuine slavery or genuine emancipation.

In drawing these inferences from a single verse in the Psalms, we are well aware that we have not yet "proved" our case. We are not, in fact, trying to prove any case. We are rather listening to typical Biblical teachings to hear what lies behind them, to understand how these teachers thought, and why they spoke about work as they did. Our observations need to be tested by many samplings, and by the climate of thought in the Bible as a whole.

Let us look at another intriguing and perplexing passage, a picture that Jesus paints of the coming of the Son of Man (Luke 17:26-36). Why, we may ask, is it so natural for Jesus to describe the final judgment in terms of the Judge of all men visiting two women who are grinding flour together and two men who are sleeping in the same bed? "One will be taken and the other left." Surely this has no direct bearing on the problem of work. Yet it may not be utterly fantastic, even here, to draw the same two inferences already noted. Negatively, we may observe that, since the same Judge visits men asleep who visits women at work, there appears to be no essential virtue in toil rather than in rest. Furthermore, there appears to be no ultimate significance in the act of grinding meal, since only one of the two women is accepted. And obviously Jesus could have spoken of men plowing in the field or of women gossiping at their leisure. In the earlier part of the parable (vv. 27, 28) Jesus indeed mentions the whole round of normal daily activity. This effectively lowers the significance of forms of work to a common level. Positively, however, we may also observe that the scene at the mill is as important as any other type of activity. The Judge appears not alone in the temple but in the kitchen as well. He comes not on holy days only. He visits people who are engaged in the simplest, most routine duties. That, in fact, is why his coming is always so surprising and unexpected. "No ear may hear his coming." No advance notice is given that he will appear at a given place or time, or in connection with a given form of human work. Yet every form of human work is potentially the place where the worker must give an account of himself to his Maker.

How, then, does the Bible view work? As an expression, an embodiment, of the worker's choices. Why is work significant? Because it is so closely tied up with the heart. The heart is really located where its treasures are. The work of the hands is a visible pointer to that location, a signpost, however, that God alone can read. God influences man's work by addressing his heart, but the road to his heart often lies through his work. In confronting the heart of the worker through his work God invests that work with awesome significance. In responding to God through his work, a person determines the destiny of his heart. Heart and work are inseparable. Inseparable, also, although not interchangeable, are the purposes of man and the purposes of God. We must look then more closely at this relationship by giving attention to how God works through the worker.

3. GOD AS BUILDER

The God of the Bible is pre-eminently a worker. In the idiom of the Psalm He is a builder of houses and a guardian of cities. He has done many marvelous things, is now doing them, and will soon complete them. From Him, through Him, and unto Him are all things. His activity embraces a wider universe than man's, yet He has chosen to seek the realization of His central purposes through this creature of dust. He intended that man should exercise dominion over other creatures. Through sin this dominion has been seriously perverted and curtailed. Yet God seeks its restoration. This will come about when in all of man's free activities God's sovereign purposes are realized. Until that day, man's labor tells a sorry story of defeat and destruction. Yet even the most terrible works of destruction shout a marvelous praise of the one true God. Even the collapse of houses points to His glorious power, though He intends the construction by human hands of houses that will weather every storm. His work thus precedes, interpenetrates, and either destroys or confirms the work of men's hands.

We must underscore this axiomatic outlook of the Bible. God is at work everywhere, and His work touches the work of man at innumerable points. He gives to the craftsman his artistry and cunning (Exod. 35:35). If the artisan achieves success he cannot say that it is solely due to his own skill, wisdom or power (Deut. 8:17, 18). God brings "forth food from the earth" (Ps. 104:14). All natural and human resources are from Him, not simply in terms of some long-ago act of creation but also in terms of continuous creation, sustenance, and purposeful guidance.

Since God is a master builder who insists on having a hand in the construction of every house, the human mason must answer the question: Is God building this house or not? Work that poses such a question may well produce fear and trembling. This fear of a Lord who is now working is the beginning of wisdom for the man who works. This fear is enhanced by man's inability to know with certainty which houses God may be building. How may he know what is true in the case of a given house? The materials and methods do not of themselves tell the story. The conscious motives and moods of the carpenter may deceive him. Neither the type of house nor the use for which it is intended guarantees survival. The prestige and craftsmanship of the builder are insufficient warrant. The worker's observance of religious rules and his participation in temple ceremonies fail to answer the central question. There are "gods many" and "lords many," any one of whom the worker may be serving in his labor. Is he serving the one true God? If so, the whole structure survives; if not, the most imposing building will become rubble (I Cor. 3:12-15).

All of this makes it clear that the decisive axis in Biblical attitudes toward work is the link between man's labor and the whole work of God, the Creator and Redeemer. Work derives its importance from the activity therein of both divine and human workers, with God taking the initiative and man giving his response.

Again we anticipate a reader's protest. "This interpretation places too much weight upon a single couplet in a single Psalm. When the Psalmist mentioned the carpenter and the sentinel, he was simply indulging in poetic metaphor. He didn't really intend to include man's menial employment; he was thinking only of man's mental and spiritual life. As a mystic he was absorbed in the moods of the heart, or as a priest he was concerned only with religious activities." Were we permitted to accept this protest, it would solve many problems and ease our conscience as well. But this easy escape is impossible. The Psalmist's metaphor is a metaphor, but it is more than that. He intended to include the digging and the pounding of the house builder, the trudging and listening of the sentinel. To be sure, he intended to include much more than these. But why? To the Psalmist the external, visible labor of the carpenter is only a fragment of his true work. The Psalmist looks beyond the motions of the hands to the complex origins and the complex destinies of each act. Just as the whole of life is embodied in a man's building of a house, so the whole meaning of his life is somehow echoed in the single word "work." Are its connotations elusive and ambiguous? Yes, but we cannot get along without that very ambiguity. By its nature, work incarnates and is incarnated in the worker. To isolate carpentry from the carpenter would be to make both meaningless. The Psalmist covers a wider universe in his references to house building than do we; but his conception may be the more adequate. At any rate, his attitude is fully supported by many other Biblical thinkers (Deut. 2:7, 7:12-8:20, 11:1-32; Neh. 2:17-6:16; Pss. 1, 90, 104, 144, 146; Isa. 29:13-16; Mt. 7:24-27, 12:30; John 15:1-10; I Cor. 3:5-15, 12:4-11, 15:58; Phil. 2:12, 13; Heb. 3:1-6; Rev. 14:13).

We now must ask how it is that a man may know what God is doing, so that he may orient his labor accordingly. Such knowledge is channeled through the whole epic of God's dealings with men, His election of Israel, and the unique pilgrimage of that people. We cannot here review this whole epic, but we can suggest some of its implications for the vocation of God's people.

4. SUMMONS TO A WHOLE PEOPLE

As soon as we mention the term "vocation," we stumble again over one of the radical differences between the Bible and modern usage. These differences will, we trust, become clear in the course of our discussion. We may begin by speaking of vocation as a person's conception of the central purpose of his life. He adopts this purpose consciously and voluntarily, and seeks to realize it through whatever channels may be provided by successive situations. In modern usage, the term has been corrupted until it means little more than the profession or occupation that an individual adopts as a "lifework." Even here, however, it connotes a little more than that, for lifework implies some attitude toward life itself, and the conscious adoption of a given occupation presupposes some dominating purpose. But, to clarify the problem, let us say that the element of occupation is primary and the conceptions of life and purpose are secondary. Now the use of the term "vocation" with this as its primary meaning does not appear in English translations of the Bible. The nearest thing to it is the word "calling" with its many cognates. In the Bible, the primary connotation of calling is the purpose of the *one who calls*, although the one called may understand and accept that purpose. The resulting effect of the call on the occupation of the one called is only a secondary meaning, and at times is marginal or practically ignored. Because of this sharp divergence in the meanings of vocation and calling the question must be faced: should we surrender the search for Biblical attitudes toward vocation, and conclude that the Bible says virtually nothing about it?

Two considerations induce us to continue. In the first place, the modern, Western history of the term "vocation" stems from the Reformation, from the discovery of the relevance of the Bible to all the "secular" occupations of the Christian. If, since the Reformation, the term has lost many of its originally Biblical associations, there is no reason why we should not seek to reclaim for the word those earlier associations. In the second place, the term "calling" (and its cognates in the Bible) originally conveyed many implications for man's occupational duties which have become obscured. These implications need to be recovered. The separation of the two terms has impoverished both. We may enrich the meaning of the term "vocation" by recapturing its genuinely Christian origins; we may recover the meaning of the term "calling" by grasping its implications for the full range of secular occupations. The two terms are not identical. Yet each term needs meanings that legitimately belong to it and that can be supplied by the other. We are primarily concerned with Biblical attitudes toward man's *calling* but we will often use the term "vocation" in describing those attitudes. This will require that the reader be alert to recognize that the term "vocation" in following paragraphs does not carry its modern secular weight but its original Biblical content as *calling*.

We have already stressed the most distinctive aspect in Biblical views of vocation: the sole origin of genuine vocation is the God of Israel. He determines whom He calls and for what end He summons them. He has a purpose even for those who are unaware of it, but the recognition of what one's vocation is demands self-disclosure on God's part and voluntary obedience on man's. Let us repeat that the Bible does not apply the term "vocation" directly to various trades and professions. It does not speak of the choice of farming or weaving as the choice of a vocation. The Biblical term is both narrower and wider. On the one hand, it is sometimes used to refer to a special mission on which God sends a person, a mission that can be rather speedily accomplished. On the other hand, it may be used to indicate the total, inclusive purpose of a man's life, that destiny for which and to which he is summoned. In either case, the significance of work derives from the significance of vocation. And whether one speaks of work or vocation, God's purpose remains the pivotal fact. Before there can be a calling there must be a person who calls; when he calls, there is always an intention, an objective.

According to the Bible, God has disclosed this reason primarily in the creation and guidance of a community destined to be His very own people. His covenant with them gives to them a corporate vocation that sets them apart from all other groups. This consciousness of having a special vocation based upon God's promise emerged at least as early as the Mosaic period. Early histories (the J document) told how God had chosen Abraham to be the father of a great family with this assurance: "In you all the families of the earth will be blessed" (Gen. 12:3 mg.). Amos was convinced that although Jahveh had a plan for all the nations, His special concern for Israel made the Israelites uniquely accountable to Him: "You only have I known of all the families of the earth; therefore I will punish you for all your iniquities" (3:2). The covenant with God required Israel's exclusive loyalty and wholehearted love (Deut. 6:5; 7:6). As Second Isaiah realized, this unique vocation could not be destroyed even when all political institutions had crumbled away. Israel remained God's servant, summoned to show forth God's glory, to bring forth justice, to bear His light and salvation to all nations, and to shout aloud to the ends of the earth: "Turn to me and be saved. . . . For I am God, and there is no other" (Isa. 45:22; 42:4; 49:3-6).

This establishment of God's covenant with Israel made the corporate vocation the primary basis for each person's vocation. Wherever an individual was given a specific mission, he was in one way or another carrying forward the mission of the whole community. Wherever the community was assigned a task, implicit in it was a vocation for every person within the community. Since the people's task was unique, each genuine member of the community shared that uniqueness. The one calling of the whole people encompassed all the crafts and trades necessary to its fulfillment, an immense range of specialized and nonspecialized occupations. (These assertions are inferences drawn from such passages as Deut. 4-8, with its account of the Mosaic covenant, Neh. 3-7, with its suggestive narrative of the building of the wall, Amos 5, 6, with his assurance of corporate responsibility for unjust economic practices, Isaiah 53, with his proclamation of corporate redemption through the vocation of the Servant.)

One effect of this was to give to workers in all trades a genuine equality before God and a genuine importance in the life of the community. Since God had endowed the community with the highest vocation conceivable, He intended workers in all employments to participate in that far-reaching mission. Equality was thus posited not on the basis of an immediate appeal to inherited rights or social utility but by reference to the horizons of God's call, by reference to the total mission of God's people. Where king and goatherd shared the same vocation, no ultimate distinction could be drawn between their separate professions. Only by resisting God's intention could the adoption of special careers become the basis for invidious distinctions, self-assertive ambitions, and priorities in preferment. The covenant tended to eliminate such tensions as spring from the assumption that superiority inheres in certain careers as such. No menial work was in itself beneath the dignity of prophet, priest, or king. In fact, God chose an obscure shepherd boy as king and an unheralded carpenter as Messiah. Over and over again, He assured His people that He dwells with those of humble estate, and that He metes out drastic severity to the nobility and tender grace to the leper and harlot, the alien and the beggar. It was in line with this accent on the one vocation of Israel that employers were ordered to deal justly with their employees, that the secure were commanded to befriend the hapless, and that acquisitiveness re-

mained from the beginning a major sin against both God and
the community.

Nothing that has been said should induce us to suppose, in a
romantic or sentimental fashion, that Israel actually fulfilled
God's commands and calling. Biblical writers everywhere stress
her failure and her sins of inequality and injustice. She was being
judged, however, more severely than were other peoples precisely because the Lord of all the earth had called her to a unique
mission. Here we are concerned not so much to measure actual
practice as to trace the implications of her distinctive calling.

We now turn to the unifying power of this true vocation. In
the Bible, the vocation of an individual is not restricted to one
segment of his existence, but embraces everything that he is and
does. His vocational tasks include hours spent in leisure as well
as hours spent in remunerative employment. They involve both
his physical labor and his worship. In fact, in both Testaments
the same words are often used to refer to both. Consider all the
connotations of the terms "servant" and "service." Consider the
ambivalence of the terms "minister," "steward," "shepherd,"
"witness." In the Bible, to hear is to obey, and vice versa; to speak
is to act, and vice versa. This engagement in vocation of the
whole range of a person's capacities, skills, and purposes breaks
down the segmentation of the worker's life and tends to eliminate
many of the psychological conflicts produced by such fragmentation. It undercuts, for example, the incessant competition between
"secular" work and "sacred" worship, between activities that
appear to be productive of good and those which appear to be
sheer waste. To be sure, conflicts remain. A man must still
distinguish between the things he is now doing and what he
should be doing. His heart and his eye are divided in the service
of several masters. He neither fully understands nor fully follows
the one true vocation. Yet that calling leads in the direction of
wholeness. The nearer he comes to it, the more his energies are
released to accomplish the genuine work assigned to him. The
more his life is integrated by his vocation, the more it will be
integrated into the life of the community. His own mission can

never be accomplished in isolation from the realized destiny of
Israel as God's elect. Even in the Old Testament period there
was only one Lord, one hope, one calling.

5. TASKS AND TALENTS

We have been thinking of ways in which the Bible linked every
man's vocation to that of God's people; we must now consider the
special callings of particular individuals. The Bible is replete
with stories of those whom God summoned for particular errands:
Abraham, Joseph, Moses, Joshua, the prophets, priests and kings,
the Messiah and his apostles. He anointed them to a given office,
assigned to them a unique task. There is special reason for con-
sidering the prophets, priests, and kings, because they, of all the
groups in the Bible, provide the closest analogy to the modern
use of the term "vocation." The Old Testament tells of prophetic
guilds, priestly families, and royal dynasties, occupations roughly
corresponding to modern religious and political professions. The
attitudes toward these special vocations are therefore of peculiar
interest to us.

In the first place, it must be indicated that the priority of
Israel's vocation was never abrogated, since these men were commissioned to plant and to pluck up, to build and to tear down.
Each leader was at once a servant and a representative of the
community. His work had no significance in itself apart from the
fulfillment of God's covenant with the entire people.

Second, it is noteworthy that the selection of men for special
roles did not diminish the prestige of humbler forms of service.
The prestige of the upper classes was not gained by robbing the
lower classes. The prophet, to be sure, might be summoned away
from his flocks or his vineyard, but he might also fulfill his special
mission without changing his form of livelihood. He could remain
God's servant in the field as fully as in the temple. His status
before God did not essentially change with each new assignment.
Never did the service of God become, in the Bible, a single profession distinct from the other professions necessary to a communal existence. Prophecy, for example, did not become the top
rung of a professional ladder, and prophets were constantly

warned against assuming that the office conferred any special immunities or privileges.

A third feature of the special calling is this: its character *as calling* was protected by the fact that a person did not seek it but, in fact, resisted it. "You did not choose me, but I chose you" (John 15:16). One recurrent reason for the dread of being called was the hardships implicit in the call itself. A prophet was wrenched loose from many familiar and cherished ties, forced out of that solidarity which is so essential to contentment. His errand would make him a social deviate if not a fool. Once seized by God's importunate will, his life would never again be immune to sudden dislocation. Yet the very intensity of this new relation to kin and to God was designed to make the prophet a more effective servant of both kin and God. Although Israel might flog the prophet, his stripes were designed to heal her wounds. If either the prophet or Israel had been the source of the call, the vocation would have been much easier and much less redemptive than this. But since God was the caller, though both people and prophet resisted His voice, the vocation remained the only clue to true redemption.

A fourth feature of genuine vocation must be mentioned. The capacity to accomplish God's assignment was never the proud possession of the servant but was always the gift of the Lord. The evidence for this may be found in the double reactions of men to the summons. On the one hand is the confession of weakness and unworthiness: "Lord, I am a child." "Depart from me for I am a sinful man." On the other hand is the discovery that the call itself brings with it the necessary resources of wit and courage. God never summoned men to vocation without at the same time issuing whatever might be needed to accomplish it. The relation between human abilities and divine gifts constituted part of the intrinsic mystery of God's work. To artisans and workers God had given their skill and artistry (Exod. 35:35), the power and resources with which they work (Deut. 8:17, 18), and such lasting fruits as accrue from their labor (II Cor. 9:10). These gifts embraced what moderns would call inherited capacities and environmental opportunities, and even more than these.

To priests and rulers had been assigned important functions in the community. In Israel, as in all societies, these functions gave rise to ecclesiastical and political dynasties, the profession becoming identified with the family. In this case, where the assignment of tasks had a longer term than a single lifetime, the "gifts" and capacities came to be viewed as inhering in the family line and in the inherited office. Israel was not immune to the rise of religious and political castes. Yet God retained His freedom and His control. He could, and on occasion did, withdraw the gifts and capacities; He could, and on occasion did, dethrone both royal and priestly families. By His Word, through the prophet or Messiah, He overruled the pretensions to power which they claimed by virtue of their office.

The call of the prophet held priority over the call of priest or king; accordingly the gift to Moses or Amos carried authority over the gift to Aaron or David. In the new Israel, the call of apostles and the gifts of apostleship were accorded a similar priority. But the more significant the office, the more was its execution dependent upon the immediate gifts of the Spirit. The authority of the apostle came from heaven and not from men. It was not vested in an institution or regularized in a profession. Talents and gifts were thought of primarily not as hereditary abilities, developed skills, social eminence, or economic power but as a measure of grace released in and through the activity as an apostle. Because men have ignored this fact, the parable of the talents (Mt. 25:14-30) has introduced great confusion in modern discussions of vocation. In the original context the talents were not inherited traits but special assignments and resources given by master to servants at the time of his departure. Throughout the period for their use, the servant's talents remained the possession of the master "loaned" for a time to his workers.

Fifth, all individuals who were sent on special missions came under the law of greatness, a law that was implicit throughout the Old Testament and explicit throughout the New. The last shall be first, the most humble the most exalted, the servant of all the greatest of all. The order of special callings was the order of the towel (John 13:4). No calling was self-contained or self-gratifying; it always led to ends beyond itself in the service of Israel in the service of God. God's servant thus always remained on mission, always in a minority, always engaged in self-emptying and self-humbling condescension. Those who turned this vocation into a professional excuse for claiming special privileges were bound, sooner or later, to lose their vocation and to forfeit their destiny (Acts 8:18-24). God would not tolerate those who turned things upside down.

6. VOCATIONAL GUIDANCE

One final mark of Israel's special vocations demands more extensive treatment. A perennial objective of these vocations was to provide what may legitimately be termed vocational guidance for Israel. Let us recall what has been said about vocation. It is, in the first place, wholly dependent on the will of the God of Israel; in the second place, it is an authentic basis for life only when it is fully oriented around God's purposes. It therefore is imperative for Israel and for each Israelite to know clearly and surely the bent of God's design. And how shall they know this unless they receive guidance? This is the function of the prophets and apostles, a function that takes a threefold form: (1) the reminder of what God has done in the past in each successive stage of Israel's pilgrimage; (2) the vision of what God is about to do in fulfilling His covenants and in disclosing His judgments; (3) the proclamation of what God is even now doing in the tangled events of the day, His mighty works and man's appropriate responses. Let us look at each of these.

The reminder of things past, as an instrument of vocational guidance, frequently took the form of narratives of what God had done in establishing and continuing the covenants, and what Israel had done in honoring or dishonoring them. In the New Testament this reminder most frequently focused upon the covenant that God had sealed with men in the death of the Messiah. In the Old, it focused most often upon the covenant sealed with Israel in the Exodus from Egypt. Both covenants had perennial relevance to every job of every servant, and it was the special vocation of God's authorized spokesmen to make that relevance sufficiently clear to serve as a basis for action. In both covenants the accent fell upon God's recent acts of redemption, but in both there was also a place for recalling the ultimate origins of things. The Genesis narratives were more influential in New Testament times than earlier, and we should be careful not to exaggerate their significance. Yet they reflect profound thinking about the place of man's work in God's design, and we should not overlook the rich if elusive connotations in Adam's story, because as the first of all men, Adam represents both himself and the race. When we listen to the stories as a reflection of the narrator's conception of the primal factors in human experience, we may discover overtones that have some bearing on our subject.

In the beginning God worked and then rested. Both work and rest were good, producing results which, according to His sovereign purpose, promised a high destiny for man. The created world is not looked upon as a lower order of being but as itself the instrument of God's goodness. God's chief work, it may be noted, was performed during the week rather than on the Sabbath, a fact that in itself indicates the significance of the working week. Adam, made in the image of God, was a worker whom God set in Eden "to till it and keep it" (2:15). He was created to "fill the earth and subdue it; and have dominion" over all living things (1:28). Like his Creator he was meant to work six days and rest the seventh, both work and rest being good. The primary fact in Adam's existence from the first was his relation to God, a relation that alone gave meaning to his life in the world.

Adam's sin seriously dislocated that relationship; the result was a corresponding dislocation in his whole existence. The conditions and results of Adam's work after this rebellion were very different from those which prevailed before it.

Cursed is the ground because of you; in toil you shall eat of it all the days of your life; thorns and thistles it shall bring forth to you; and you shall eat the plants of the field. In the sweat of your face you shall eat bread till you return to the ground, for out of it you were taken; you are dust, and to dust you shall return. 3:17-19.

Through his sin, man's work became both frustrating and toilsome. The conditions in which he worked became more difficult and unpleasant. The way *back* to Eden was securely barred, so that Adam could never regain Paradise merely by changing the organization or methods of his work. The world became for him an arena of self-seeking rivalry among men who were unable by themselves to accomplish a return of peace or to avoid the destiny of dust (Gen. 4).

Nevertheless, the cursing of the ground, with all of its accompaniments, did not terminate God's interest in Adam. In frustrating man's labor and in issuing the sentence God was dealing with sinful man with an eye to his redemption. Implicit, therefore, in the realm of death was the promise of life. God remained sovereign over His creation. Hidden behind the things which He created, He was yet present and active in them, seeking to bless man by calling him back to the "fear of the Lord." Man's toilsome effort to win his bread from a seemingly hostile earth became now a reminder of the gulf between Creator and creature, between Paradise and present toil, and at the same time a reminder of the presence in the daily situation of a God who can both thwart and fulfil man's work. In his work, however burdensome, man had to deal with a God who alike in His creating, judging, and redeeming work remained faithful to His covenants. So the Genesis narrator, in sketching the beginnings of man's life, indicated what he considered to be perennial constituents in man's labor. In his drudgery and social strife man longs for the peace, comfort, and security of the Garden, but his longing does not produce the desired return. To be sure, the form of social economy changes from generation to generation, and each change affects the conditions of labor. One form may be preferable to another and efforts at reform need not be wholly futile. Some segments of the Bible favored nomadic culture as superior to agricultural; some were disposed to prefer agricultural modes of organization to the more urban and commercial modes. But none of these changes, none of the relative advantages of one over the other, could ever be as decisive as the change that occurred in Adam's sin, or as decisive as the change when Adam's dominion

over the earth will be re-established and perfected. Only a future
Day, in which sin is overcome by a redemptive act of God and
perfect obedience of man, will disclose a creation restored to its
intended harmony.

Toward this coming consummation God's work has from the
beginning been oriented. His word always conveys a threat of
evil and a promise of good. By his fears and hopes man's toil
is also oriented toward a desired goal. God has called man to
choose life. Prompted by the desire to choose and control his own
destiny man has actually willed his own death. Therefore any
prophet or apostle, who would recall Israel to its true destiny,
must provide fresh vocational guidance grounded in a new disclosure of God's promise for the future. This entailed the proclamation of coming judgment on the rebels. Because the people
had repudiated its true vocation, the wages of its labor would be
death. Its work could not be established. Harvests would fail to
satisfy the harvesters (Deut. 28:38-40; Mic. 6:15). Only repentance
and return to right vocation would enable God to transform their
sorrow into joy. To persuade them to turn, God's spokesmen
reiterated in a multitude of ways the promise of Paradise Re-
gained. What made the transition so difficult, however, was the
price in terms of hopes. Since the false vocation was usually rooted
in earthly hopes, the act of repentance required the jettisoning
of those hopes, a sacrifice that often seemed too great. False
prophets were always on hand to offer a salvation that simply
buttressed ambitions, in contrast to the narrow way that, as the
true prophets saw, alone leads to life. Only a tiny minority were
willing to rest their hope in God alone, and to orient all their
work toward His promise.

A third assignment of the prophet was the disclosure of the
vocational significance of the historical situations in which his
hearers stood. In addition to a backward and a forward look,
men needed to grasp what God was even then doing among them.
The prophet must make articulate what God was saying through
contemporary happenings. Hidden within and behind the daily
routines were clues to the divine purpose. The terms of God's
calling were spelled out by the concrete possibilities presented by

the particular jobs on which men were engaged and by the station
in life to which God had assigned them. Every person was either
a parent or a child, an employer or employee, a seller or a buyer.
Each relation of equal to equal, or of superior to inferior, became through the prophet's word a potential channel for serving
God. A man's superiors and underlings in the scale of economic
power became mediators of God's government. So, too, did the
stuff and tools with which men worked. Here where God had put
him was where he had sinned, and where he was summoned to
repentance and new tasks. Here where he had bound himself by
self-pity and self-deceptions was he offered freedom and new
health. If he rightly heard God's command here, he could enter
again on his one true vocation. But to do so he must listen to
what God was saying through his neighbor. To the husband God
spoke through the wife, and vice versa; to the employer through
the employee, and vice versa; to the seller through the buyer, and
vice versa. No human relationship was of such a nature that God
could not speak through it to man concerning his calling. No
menial form of employment and no pagan environment could
surround man with a profane realm where God's will did not
operate, and where man's obligation to his God could not be
honored. Man lived no longer in the Garden, but he still had
to reckon with the God of the Garden, who reiterated in every
situation His command and promise. It was in his workaday
world, with its stultifying efforts and its electrifying emergencies,
that man could encounter the hand of God. But it required a
messenger from God, appearing in that world as a worker, to
disclose to other workers the true dimensions of their common
vocation as the people whom God had chosen for His own inheritance. Such a messenger was Jesus the Messiah.

7. SON OF MAN, SERVANT OF GOD

Each lawgiver and prophet in Israel's history had, as we have
noted, been commissioned to provide vocational guidance. (Let
the reader remember that this term "vocational" refers to *calling*
in the Biblical sense and not to *occupations* in the modern secular
sense.) These guides together formed a glorious succession of men

of faith, each fulfilling his mission in his own way and time. The same history, however, was a sad chronicle of failures, for Israel perennially refused to heed the Word. The climactic event in the long epic was the sending of the Messiah, who was perfectly faithful to his vocation. Coming in the form of man, he accomplished his work in the form of a servant. Those to whom he came rejected him, but God used every rejection to accomplish His gracious intention. Through him God created a new world and a new Israel. In him humanity was born anew, with a difficult mission but with sufficient power for it. As living Lord he carried forward his work of providing dependable vocational guidance for his people. In him was disclosed the meaning and purpose of all the earlier covenants. He revealed to his servants how God is working for good in every tangled alignment of affairs. In him will be consummated and established the works of men's hands. In him, therefore, the disciple arrived at whatever understanding of vocation God chose to grant, according to the measures of grace and faith.

This vocational guidance, let it be said at the outset, does not offer a premature solution to all of man's vocational dilemmas. The Messiah did not issue pontifical edicts concerning the forms of work in which men may or may not engage. He himself was a carpenter, but he did not encourage his disciples to follow that trade. Peter was a fisherman and Paul was probably a tentmaker, but these trades did not derive any new sanctity from that coincidence. The imitation of the Messiah or apostle did not take the form of choosing one occupation rather than another. Disciples did not wear at their work any distinctive costume, any visible sign of separateness from their workmates. In fact, none of the existing methods of employment derived special prestige or sanctity from the fact that leaders of the Church had been engaged in them. If work be defined purely in terms of remunerative employment, if the word "vocation" refers solely to the occupations of the business world, then we would be forced to say that the mission of Jesus had virtually nothing to do with work or vocation. He did not concern himself directly with the problem of how to reduce the boredom in work or how to avoid vocational maladjustments. Readers whose central interest lies here will naturally feel that Jesus' work as Messiah is too remote to have any relevance to their work as mechanic or waitress. The Bible ceases to have relevance not simply because the book is too ancient but because the ideas are too other-worldly. We hope that these readers will not be stopped by this apparent irrelevance. Let them remember what we said earlier in this chapter about direct and indirect illumination, about the problem of definitions. The Bible does not mean by vocation what is current coin in the modern world. Yet one thing is true in both ancient and modern worlds: the meaning of vocation stems from a person's awareness of the central purpose of his life. And in both worlds the importance of each particular job depends on its connection to a person's vocation. Let us explore further, then, the New Testament attitudes toward what determines an authentic vocation.

Before we can think clearly about the central purpose in life we must first think about what life actually is. The New Testament presents us with radically new conceptions of the nature of life itself. Jesus Christ is the Living Lord who reveals life, shares it, gives it, invites and empowers men to enter into it. He is Life. For a man to live is Christ (Phil. 1:19-26); his life "is hid with Christ in God" (Col. 3:3, 4; 2:6). Apart from Christ men have supposed that life begins with birth and ends with death. In Christ they learn that they have really been dead, though supposing themselves to be alive. They learn that true life begins in a new birth, and that this new birth comes by dying to themselves and to the world. True life begins with death and has no end, except in the consummation of the purpose for which they have been born anew. A man lives no longer to himself but "to the Lord" (Phil. 2:12, 13; Rom. 14:7-9). Having been bought with a price he is now the slave of a new master (I Cor. 3:23; 7:22). Baptism with the Holy Spirit marks the transition from one life to the other; this baptism is a voluntary sharing with Christ in his death to the law, the flesh, sin, the world, and the whole realm of bondage. The transition is described by many images and in many colors, but all underscore the radical and final character of the change from a living death to a dying life. The new life of the disciple is integrated at every point with the resurrection of the Messiah, the creation of a new community (the Church) which is the nucleus of a new humanity (the Second Adam). The life of this new humanity is *one*; it does not perish or fade away, but moves toward a single glorious destiny.

Intrinsic to this life is one all-inclusive purpose, and this purpose is best defined by the mission of the Messiah. The pattern of the Lord's work may be seen in the Gospels where the Kingdom of God is spelled out in human deeds. There his activities demonstrate the motivation of the Servant of God and the perfect Man. There God's will and work are integrated with His Servant's will and work. Therefore, the pattern of Jesus' ministry remains the pattern of the Church's ministry. This pattern is all the more compelling, since the Living Lord is continuing his messianic warfare. To live in a world where Jesus is Lord is to work in a world where this Lord is aggressively completing his avowed intention. Every function of the members of Christ's Body responds directly to the authority of the Head of that Body. "There are varieties of service but the same Lord" (I Cor. 12:5).

"As members of his Body we are made one with him in the fellowship of his life, death and resurrection, of his suffering and his glory. . . . The shape of his life is the shape of the Church's life. The mystery of his life is the mystery of the Church's life" (Lund Conference on Faith and Order).

God commissioned His Servant to proclaim the good news of God's Kingdom, and in this proclamation to relate what God is now doing to what He has done and what He is about to do in final judgment and mercy. As agent of the Kingdom's powers, the Servant is sent to heal the sick, to cast out demons, to cleanse lepers, and to raise the dead. He is sent to bear the burden of the world's sin and alienation, and to incarnate by humble identification with the lost the healing power of God's love. The Servant makes clear the terms of the new covenant with God, the Law that governs the Kingdom, the way that leads to life. This "way" is intended to permeate and to transfigure the attitudes and actions of men in the total orbit of their existence in a workaday world. These tasks lead the Servant into places of danger, into criminal courts where he will give his confession before councils and kings, or into sudden lynchings or secret liquidations where no opportunity is given for him to speak. Whatever the form of danger Christ's victory over Pilate will be manifested in his disciple's courage, in his compassion for enemies, and in his reliance on the Spirit for wisdom and strength. These aspects of the Servant's vocation may appear to be restricted to leaders who have been selected by the Church for major public roles, yet this appearance is deceptive. The life of the Church as a whole must be represented in the sacrifices of its leaders. Moreover, these leaders are often found outside the professional categories of ecclesiastical office. None of these services (e.g., the proclamation of the Gospel) can be reduced to a single form of labor; all of them, in fact, must take manifold forms, direct and indirect. The humblest disciple proclaims the Gospel wherever he is at work, proclaims it in his deeds and in his silences as well as in his speech.

There are other aspects of the Servant's vocation that more obviously pervade all areas in every servant's life. The Servant is an agent of reconciliation who is commissioned to replace estrangement with peace. This work is done wherever walls have been erected between personal enemies, between races, between classes, between nations. All alienations that permeate social and historical structures have their origin in the invisible realm where principalities and powers are engaged in unceasing warfare. The Servant has demonstrated his power over "the rulers of this darkness," and his disciples, by their service of reconciliation, participate in his victory. They do this, in part at least, by bringing all their political, economic, and family tensions within the realm of redemption, by fulfilling all their humble duties "in the Lord." Thus the Servant of the Lord transforms every evil day, every situation of work or rest, into an occasion for emancipation and renewal. This service of reconciliation involves suffering with and for others. The love that knits together the Body of Christ enables each member to carry

his own burden and the burdens of other members, each serving
and being served by the others. Together they give themselves
for the sake of the world, participating in the sufferings of Christ
and entering into his glory and joy. Daily each disciple is summoned to take up his cross with the promise that the yoke is
made easy through a strength that is not his own. In the Kingdom of the Son, costly humble service is the only nobility that
is recognized, for here the last are first and the humiliated are
exalted.

8. THE NEW TESTAMENT ADVENTURE IN VOCATION

Here we may catch a glimpse of the astounding implications
of this one vocation. The highest calling is open to the humblest
servant; it in fact demands that status. Furthermore, the most
inclusive purpose is bound up with the most specific and immediate tasks. The cup of cold water given in Christ's name is
an expression of ultimate hopes. Every job may and must be
done as a divine service to the glory of God (Eph. 6:1-9; Matt.
5-7; Rom. 12-14). Everything that a man does is an answer given
to God's calling. The mind that becomes controlled by the
mind of Christ produces "work of faith and labor of love and
steadfastness of hope in our Lord Jesus Christ" (I Thess. 1:3).
Vocation is thus determined inwardly at the point where God's
willing and working are united with man's will and work (Phil.
2:12). Such a vocation embraces both the menial labors of a
chattel slave and the supervisory labors of his owner (Col.
3:18-4:1; Eph. 6:1-9). This is clear evidence that to the apostle
the most lofty vocation could be realized within the lowest
forms of drudgery.

Because Jesus Christ is his Lord, the disciple's vocation is
determined outwardly at the point in daily activities where
God's call is channeled through the need of the neighbor. To
love God and to love this neighbor becomes one command and
one love. This was true for Jesus in his ministry; it becomes
true for the follower in his ministry. Because God is seeking to
fill all creation with His glory, His servant glorifies God through
loving the brethren. Because God seeks to conform all men to

the image of his Son, each servant participates in the work of uniting all things in Christ. Obedience to God and the redemption of the world become one activity. To be a slave of Christ is to become a slave of all (II Cor. 9:19). In such slavery Christ works in and through his disciple as the hope of glory, as the power that triumphs over every adversary. Therefore, the Christian cannot be content with the formulas "to work in order to live" or "to live in order to work" or "to love to work." More appropriate is the formula "to work in order to love," although even this love needs to be understood as a power that begins and ends in God.

Because his Lord is a King who will come again to complete his work of unifying, restoring, and redeeming the world, the disciple's vocation is determined in a forward direction at the point where God's promise elicits his hope. Just as Jesus had run his race "for the joy that was set before him," so too do his followers run their race, looking toward the pioneer and perfecter of their faith (Heb. 12:1-3). As King, Christ must reign until he has subdued all other powers. This work is now proceeding. His servants find themselves in the midst of this campaign. Christ intends through them to complete and to manifest his victory. He equips them with his weapons and armor. He determines the shifting strategies of the battle and assures them of victory within the struggle (Eph. 6). Each subsequent situation tests their confidence and patience, whether by deceptive adversities or by equally deceptive lulls in the battle. Each task on however obscure or limited a sector tests their faith in his faithfulness. Where his promise is met by their hope, there is the true vocation.

In a sense, then, the Christian's vocation is determined ever anew as he listens each day for the guiding commands of his Chief. Obedience, to be genuine, must be yielded in each successive situation. The freedom that springs from that obedience is a daily gift. Each of his responses to the Gospel—repentance, faith, love, hope—enhances that freedom. Each, in turn, offers him the opportunity to use his freedom. He is freed inwardly to accept himself as he is; he is freed outwardly to love his enemy;

he is freed from anxieties to seek first the Kingdom of God. The Lord who has freed him now guides his decisions in the use of his freedom, and opens the way through them to a more perfect freedom. This freedom is meant to pervade every mundane task, all the various labors of all Christians: husband and wife, employer and employee, king and subject. The place in which a person is called is the place for realizing this freedom. His immediate associations afford him ample opportunities to treat every person as one for whom Christ died, to redeem this particular day, and thus to give witness to the transforming power of the Gospel. Whatever commands the Lord may issue, he also issues strength to fulfill those commands. In whatever work the disciple may be engaged, he can with this help serve without bitterness, fight without hatred, pray without ceasing, give thanks without reservation, rejoice without fear, love without self-concern, hope without anxiety.

He who receives the new freedom recognizes it as the gift of the Holy Spirit. Possession of and possession by this Spirit thus becomes a distinguishing mark of Christian vocation. The Spirit is promised to all whom the Lord calls as the living link between the Father and the Son, between the members of the Body and their Head. Through the Spirit Christ takes captive every thought, making each believer and each congregation his temple. Through the Spirit God makes effective His calling of sons, the accomplishment of those ends for which He has called them. Through the Spirit every brother of Christ responds with gratitude, living and working by the Spirit. His presence is indicated whenever a person confesses Christ as Lord, whenever the Spirit utters within him the "Abba" of joyful prayer. Through the Spirit a person hears what God is saying through his brothers, and they are able to hear what God is saying through him. God writes His message on their hearts, each servant becoming a bearer of this message (II Cor. 3).

9. DIVERSE GIFTS, ONE SPIRIT

To all who receive the Holy Spirit is given a share in a single vocation. All participate in the highest benefits. These

benefits include: freedom, peace, joy, righteousness, faith, hope,
love. Each gift is simultaneously a task, because it draws a person
into the continuing work of the Spirit, aimed at the glorification
of all creation. Because all believers share alike in the greatest
gift and the most far-reaching task, none can boast of having
a vocation superior to the others (I Cor. 1:26-31; 12:31 f.). Because none was chosen because of previous merit (capacity,
industry, wisdom, piety or social status), none can boast over
those who remain unconverted. Their new existence constantly
reminds them that God has chosen men who are foolish, weak,
ignoble, and despised, "even things that are not" (I Cor. 1:26-31).
Christ has thus conferred on all an equality that is the substance
of both grace and duty; they are given the grace to become last
of all and servants of all.

Within this shared vocation, however, each individual receives his own unique call, his own unique gift and task. We may
mention the gifts of apostleship, prophecy, teaching, administration, healing, acts of mercy (I Cor. 12:4-11; Rom. 12:3-8). Every
servant receives some gift. Each gift is "spiritually discerned"
both by those who receive it and by others within the household
of faith (I Cor. 2:12-14). Each gift carries with it the requisite
authority, in some cases the duty of ruling and overruling the
brothers. Such authority, however, remains the authority of the
Spirit and is subject to controls by the Spirit. The God who
gave the gift may alter or revoke it.

We must now explore the connections between the shared
vocation and the various occupations held by members of the
Church. What impact did faith have upon one's economic position? The first answer is that faith brought a high degree of
freedom. Some apostles felt constrained to continue their previous
means of self-support (Paul); others surrendered their trade and
became dependent on the Church for their sustenance (Peter).
Each recognized the validity of the other's decision in this matter.
Within the New Testament period, none of the distinctive tasks
within the Church had become established as a separate profession, to be chosen by a young person looking for employment.

The call to leadership was normally channeled through the local congregation acting as temple of the Spirit. Acceptance of such a call might or might not alter the previous status or form of employment; whether it did or not, the one called was expected to utilize all of his energies and capacities in his service. Shifts in occupation depended upon the circumstances of the call itself, but in no case did a change in manner of employment place one automatically in a higher echelon of prestige. The basic equality of all ministries retarded the formation of new castes or classes. It is not surprising that a man like Celsus found it difficult to understand how this new community chose its leaders. He complained that even "wool-workers, cobblers and fullers, the most illiterate and vulgar of mankind," became venerated as teachers.

We should not neglect to mention the fact that the Church believed itself to be fulfilling its work through the vocation of each of its members. It was not difficult to see this in the case of the apostle, in whose suffering and joy the whole community suffered and rejoiced (II Cor. 1). Less obvious but no less important was the extension of this solidarity to the labors of every member. Early Christians did not so much speak of a person going to church, but more often thought of the church as being present with each person at his place of daily employment. To the degree that his work represented the Spirit's call and the Spirit's response, to that extent the Church was actively fulfilling its mission through him. In his chores were embodied its repentance and forgiveness, its struggle with temptation, its victory. In his inward thoughts and outward activities were manifested its faith, its prayers, its hopes. His faithfulness in love helped to knit the Body together. Thus early Christians located the frontier of God's war along the line of human associations and decisions encountered in their day-to-day living. They were called to give their witness to the emancipating power of the gospel in the freedom and joy within which they accomplished their routine jobs. Faith produced a quiet revolution in all their attitudes toward the ordinary work situation. It is this revolution which the Reformation partially re-enacted, and which may yet again in our own day break out with its pristine power.

10. THE CRITERIA OF A CALLING

From what has been said the reader may have gained the impression that early Christian perspectives on vocation were lofty, perhaps so lofty as to be idyllic and unreal. Such an impression would be quite false. There was much confusion in the early Church over the relative merits of various services. There was competition for places of prestige and power. There were leaders who claimed a monopoly control of the Spirit, as there were followers who saw no connection between religious beliefs and the daily struggle for bread. Each congregation needed continual vocational guidance, needed to hear what the Spirit might say to it concerning its mission, needed the wise counsel of astute leaders whose own ambitions had been transformed by the mind of Christ. These counselors often had to advise concerning the genuine marks of discipleship. By what tests did they measure the rightness of one's livelihood?

Men usually gauge their occupations in terms of the success or failure to which they lead. Success normally indicates that we have chosen the right one. It often determines whether we desire a given type of employment. Here it must be said that living by faith gives priority to other criteria. By the measures which the world applies, the Cross indicated the complete failure of Jesus' mission. Faith, however, sees in this apparent failure a tremendous victory. The believer is thereby inhibited from viewing the success of his own vocation merely by reference to its immediate, tangible and quantitative results. The number of earthly treasures is no index to heavenly glory (Mt. 6:18-21); on the contrary, the ambition for earthly success is the source of the most subtle and tragic bondage. From this bondage a person is delivered by the high calling in Christ.

One mark of this freedom is the surmounting of anxiety over his own food and shelter. "Be not anxious" is a command that can be obeyed only in freedom. Christ devalued the currency of self-preservation by transforming the meaning and measure both of "self" and of "preservation." Life is to be saved by being lost. Of both the losing and the saving, Christ's ministry was the clearest image. According to the Fourth Gospel, Jesus' own freedom from anxiety was made possible by his reliance on heavenly food. His meat was "to do the will" of the One who sent him; the same is true of each of his followers. Christ makes available to them a bread by which they can live. With this bread they know how to be content in famine or plenty, adversity or prosperity, death or life.

Another mark of emancipation is the readiness to remain a slave to human masters and to serve them in the Lord whether they are brutal or kind. Before meeting Christ Onesimus, for example, was eager to run away from his bondage, so intolerable was the yoke; after his conversion he was willing to return to that same bondage. Slavery to Christ had exerted a stronger compulsion than his own desire for an easier lot (cf. The Epistle to Philemon). If freedom is offered, a Christian slave may accept it (I Cor. 7:17-24); but if it is not offered, he will continue contentedly at his post. In either case he will refuse to measure Christ's love for him, or the success of his own servanthood in Christ's name, by the relative dignity of his human status. (For further discussion of slavery, cf. below, page 72 ff.)

Joy and peace accompany the Christian's vocation, but like obedience they are made perfect in suffering. The Lord chastens those whom he loves. He teaches those who love him to accept suffering as a discipline through which God is working for their good. Their suffering thus produces hope, a hope that may be contradicted by visible evidences but is never put to shame by them (Rom. 5:1-5; Jas. 1:2-5). "Faith is the assurance of things hoped for" (Heb. 11:1 f.). This faith in a Crucified Lord furnishes the assurance that no work that is done "in the Lord" is futile (I Cor. 15:58; Rev. 14:13).

The Christian is so free from bondage to earthly results that he is ready to trust God's ultimate judgment concerning success or failure. Not even the apostle can rely upon his own estimate of the fruitfulness of his labor. It is his obligation to obey; it is

God's faithfulness that determines the recompense. The validity of the vocation as a whole, then, depends on the faithfulness of God. That faithfulness has already been proved in the victory won by Christ over every adversary. At the return of Christ this proof will be published to all the world, and with it the "success" of the Church's vocation. To the New Testament disciples, that consummation was so near as to require expectant industry and so distant as to require patient endurance in the daily tasks.

The power of this expectancy to reverse the world's appraisal of vocational success was set forth very sharply in this advice of the apostle:

> The appointed time has grown very short; from now on, let those who have wives live as though they had none, and those who mourn as though they were not mourning, and those who rejoice as though they were not rejoicing, and those who buy as though they had no goods, and those who deal with the world as though they had no dealings with it. For the form of this world is passing away. I Cor. 7:29-31.

This teaching has provoked many problems, not the least of which is its applicability to Christians of the twentieth century. However we may view that problem, we should recognize these basic points: The teaching indicates that the vocation of the early Christian was oriented toward a different goal from that to which his work had been directed "before faith came." This goal was related in a double way to the previous temporal goals. On the one hand, the promise of God's coming reign relegated to a position of strictly temporary value the usual goals of the world's professions and occupations. (We may also infer that this demotion of worldly ambitions was not easy for all the Corinthian believers to accept.) On the other hand, the investing of all treasure in the coming age did not tear men away from the normal processes of buying and selling. Their hearts were now free but their hands were still expressing that freedom in ordinary enterprises. It was an error, then as well as now, to infer that disciples must withdraw from the world because of its transient form (I Cor. 5:9-10). It is clear that the teaching repudiates the various "futures" by which the world measures progress, and it repudiates the various vocations that are grounded in the world's hopes and resources. But it also clearly affirms the possibility of experiencing in present situations the saving grace of God, the possibility of working with God in saving men from destruction. It affirms that true vocation determines how men deal with the world in all of its activities, however transient.

Let us now try to sum up the New Testament understanding of vocation. Its source is God's calling of a man to be His son. This calling has already been received but it is yet to be realized fully through the response of the son. The son has responded, and yet knows that his obedience is nevertheless far from total. The perfect pattern of vocation becomes clear in the person of Jesus Christ, in whom both the divine calling and the human response meet. He is the image of the new Man. In him mankind is being restored to its authentic vocation. To each believer the Holy Spirit gives tasks appropriate to his calling and capacities needed for their accomplishment. All of his work is intended to become part of the continuing work of Christ, his efforts becoming expressions of the new life in Christ. Christ continues to guide the mission of his Body, in which Body there is a distinctive function for every member. There is one vocation for all, yet each has his own distinctive work to do. Wherever present labor does not advance his vocation, that labor is sinful and futile. It is done neither "in the Lord" nor "to the Lord." Such work, however, is to be viewed as one place (though, of course, not the only place) where Christ encounters him with a summons to repentance. This summons is supported by the constraint of love which enables the worker to integrate this activity into the one vocation. To the extent that his work springs from a will that is obedient, that work is redeemed. It is transferred from a realm of sin to a realm of grace, from the kingdom of frustration to the kingdom of joy. It becomes the right earthly means for fulfilling a heavenly calling. So long as his work fails to do this, it remains part of the realm of rebellion, a segment of the world that is passing away. This area is owned by other Masters to which the worker is enslaved, however free he may feel. This area is still to be claimed for Christ's kingdom. We may now ask precisely what happens when sovereignty over one's work is transferred to Christ.

11. FREEDOM IN OCCUPATIONS

Perhaps the most striking changes take place in the motivation of the worker. When Christ calls, he must be ready to leave everything behind in order to follow. This is true not only for the earliest disciple but for the latest, not only for the initial venture of faith but for every step of faith. "Let goods and kindred go, this mortal life also." Every follower of the Crucified must be willing to suffer the loss of all things, to count them as refuse in order to gain Christ and to be found in him (Phil. 3:8-15). At the same time, however, this readiness to surrender everything may take the form of remaining in the present occupational situation, buying and selling as before, although he now lives "as though he had no goods" (I Cor. 7:29-31). Christ may reassign him to his previous post, a tentmaker or a tenant farmer still, but serving through his former associations in market and field. What determines when the change in vocation should alter the means of employment? Not the form of the world, for it is passing away. Not a person's own desires for greater ease, wealth, or dignity, for these desires belong to the world. No, this decision will depend upon continuing vocational guidance provided by the Lord through his Body the Church. This guidance will be more closely akin to the type of vocational counseling found in the Bible than to modern secular advice on vocational problems, but for that very reason the Christian will rightly take the Church's guidance with greater seriousness, even though it may be less definite and specific. The individual remains free to interpret this guidance, but his freedom will be genuine only if he is completely willing either to stay in the old job or to give up any assured occupation.

Doubtless many problems have occurred to the reader in the foregoing summary. Two of these should now be mentioned. The first is the problem of the apparent irrelevance for us of the Biblical attitudes toward vocation. The connection between

Christ's calling and a given occupation remains indirect and elusive. Of this Paul's own occupation provides an example. Paul himself, on becoming an apostle, did not change his means of support; he continued to make tents (assuming that this was his actual trade). Yet he recognized that other apostles were fully justified in giving up their trades and in receiving support from the churches. Neither course received special sanction; either was legitimate. Faith gave no clear signal in the matter of the form of employment.

Paul himself, however, saw a definite link between his vocation and his occupation, and it is important that we discover it. What were the reasons why he chose to continue his weaving? In the first place, he wanted to make the gospel free of charge, fearing that if he accepted pay for preaching that pay might seem to be a reward for preaching. Thus the true motive would be corrupted and he would place "an obstacle in the way of the gospel of Christ" (I Cor. 9:12-18). In the second place, he was keenly conscious of the appropriateness of manual labor to the essence of the gospel. It symbolized the freedom-in-slavery of those who identify themselves fully with the conditions of the people to whom they are sent. In this respect Paul became weak in order to win the weak (I Cor. 9:19-27). He worked in order to share the blessings of the gospel with other workers. His exertion at the loom was part of that pommeling of his body by which he kept himself qualified for sharing in the gospel. A third motive was the desire not to become a burden to members of the church. They were his children for whom as a parent he should be responsible. His work was evidence of his eagerness "to be spent" for their sakes, a token of the fact that he sought "not what is yours but you" (II Cor. 12:13-15). His labor was evidence of his desire to be a blameless witness (I Thess. 2:9-12), to command the respect of outsiders (I Thess. 4:12), and to furnish an example for other Christians to emulate (II Thess. 3:8-13).

When we consider these motives it is hardly fair to say that his gospel was irrelevant to his occupation as a weaver. To be sure, he could have dispensed with such employment. He could have adopted another trade. Nevertheless, to him both the fact and the mode of that trade contributed to the fulfillment of his vocation as an apostle. They derived significance from that vocation. His vocation was not identified with his occupation, but neither were the two things completely separate.

The second problem is the apparent injustice, the apparent approval of injustice, implicit in the acceptance of chattel slavery as a valid expression of Christian vocation. "Every one should remain in the state in which he was called" (I Cor. 7:20). Should not a gospel of freedom demand a more radical reorganization of economic life? Does not the vocation of a Christian lie in attacking the cruelties of slavery, rather than in teaching each slave to be content and to serve his master "in the Lord"? It must be admitted that the New Testament teachings have been used to block economic change and to sanctify the privileges of the powerful. It is clear that Christian vocation is relevant to the life of a slave, but many people are troubled by the fact that this relevance appears to move in the direction of freezing existing economic conditions. There is too little space to deal adequately with this problem here, but several things may be said. First of all, we may note that New Testament teachers were not interested in discussing the relative merits of the existing class structure of society. They were called upon to provide guidance to particular slaves and masters on how they could orient their immediate tasks within the new vocation in Christ. It was in line with Onesimus' service of Christ that Paul persuaded him to return to his former master; in line with the same service Philemon was urged to treat the returning slave as a brother in Christ. Within this perspective, however, it was entirely possible for a slave to accept freedom and for a master to liberate his slave.

It should also be pointed out that both master and slave found the new vocation equally difficult and equally possible. If it was difficult for the slave out of humble love to accept the cruel treatment of unjust masters, it was also difficult for masters to renounce all their earthly treasures, and to treat their slaves "justly and fairly, knowing that you also have a Master in heaven" (Col. 4:1). Slave and master must alike make a total surrender of all wealth to Christ; God was not partial to separate degrees of economic power in His demand for self-denial. For both master and slave there was a link between vocation and occupation, and for both this link was located in the heart of the worker rather than in the external form of his work.

We should not forget that the Christian gospel provoked the most bitter resistance among the most conservative elements in ancient Roman society. It was not then viewed as a religious justification for preserving the status quo. Why not? It proclaimed the transiency of all the institutions (such as slavery) in which powerful men put their trust. It undermined the whole range of secular vocations, based as they were upon desires for wealth, prestige, and power. It assured the humblest serf a destiny as glorious as any that was open to the emperor. It produced among slaves, not a rebellious spirit, to be sure, but a source of peace and joy that delivered them from fear of their master. It thus set loose an outlook on life that forced a radical revaluation of the various ways of earning one's living.

It would be wrong to conclude that Christianity gave a blanket approval to every occupation in which a person might be engaged. Trades, for example, that relied upon idol worship soon felt the impact of the Christian mission (Acts 19:19-27). Here we naturally think of those who made and sold images. But where Paul's identification of idolatry with covetousness was adopted (Col. 3:5; Eph. 5:5), any trade which made acquisitiveness its basis would be viewed as idolatrous. In every generation many people have been offended by the forthright condemnation of wealthy and powerful landowners who exploited their employees (James 5:1-6). From the first it has been obvious that any employment that is inherently dishonest such as stealing is incompatible with Christian faith. It also goes without saying that New Testament standards of what constitutes stealing are much more rigorous than conventional standards. So, too, the Christian vocation excludes greed (I Cor. 5:9-13) in all its forms, including idleness, luxury, and mendicancy (II Thess. 3:6-12). It is difficult to equate such sins with specific occupations so as to produce a check list of trades which a Christian must automatically shun. On the other hand, it is clear that any occupation, however highly it may be respected, may become for a particular Christian a betrayal of his vocation if his work is driven by malice, pride, envy, or selfishness. We may conclude, then, that New Testament teaching does not draw the line between forbidden and approved occupations sharply enough to please many people who desire black-and-white distinctions. Yet it does draw the line between right and wrong motives in every occupation, and this line is too sharp to give any worker or employer the comfort of self-righteousness.

We have called attention to the fact that the new vocation in Christ encouraged a wider range in types of employment than is true of the various vocations encouraged by the world. This is a fact worth accenting. The person whose vocation is determined by his desire for self-realization, for steady increase in wealth, wisdom, or power, will resent many forms of employment because they thwart his desires. It is of the essence of worldly occupations that they are designed to enhance personal or group superiority, to reward achievement by promotion into the higher echelons of an economic or cultural class (Mk. 10:41-45). The inevitable frustration of these desires yields a large crop of self-pity, restlessness, and resentment. This picture, however, is transformed for the disciple of Christ, who finds that he can glorify God, love his neighbor, and walk according to the Spirit in work situations which earlier had made impossible the joys of self-realization and social preferment. Tasks that once seemed intolerable now provide ample opportunities for serving his Lord. Any honest work with one's hands (Titus 3:1) is dignified enough for any follower of him who "though he was rich, yet for your sake he became poor" (II Cor. 8:9; I Cor. 4:10-13; II Cor. 4:7-12). In fact the unity in Christ's Body terminates all distinctions of honor and status among industrial and professional castes (Col. 3:11; I Cor. 2:26-31). This is perhaps the basic reason why the New Testament gave so little advice on the selection of a particular trade or craft. It refused to label occupations in a scale ranging from illegitimate to dubious to acceptable to sacred.

This refusal has important implications when it is set over against the opposite tendency to solve the problem of careers by some fixed scale of relative dignity or utility. The latter, more casuistical, solution of the problem of vocational guidance is actually possible only in a free economy, and then only for the middle and upper classes whose wealth and education permit latitude of choice. Such a solution multiplies the resentments and despairs of men who do not inherit these options. It encourages moralistic hypocrisy among those who are able to enter the higher professions. It fosters the aristocracy of the higher cultural groups at the expense of fragmenting the community as a whole. Man in society suffers more than he realizes from this tendency to exalt one career at the expense of others, to glorify his own craft with a glamorous halo, to camouflage the dubious practices of his profession by pretentious claims to the social usefulness of that profession. The Gospel of the Jewish carpenter deflated the false superiorities of aristocratic careers by offering the highest vocation to workers in all trades, however menial. The acceptance of this Gospel introduced a person into a single vocation, shared with every other disciple. This vocation precipitated a revolution in attitudes toward all occupations. It did not normally require an immediate shift into another occupation, but it demanded the subordination of every motive of the worker to those motives intrinsic to the new vocation. This transformation of the worker's vocation was normally most apparent in new attitudes toward the daily job and toward those people with whom he was associated in that job. Let us now sample those attitudes.

12. WORKING WITH GOD

The work of the Suffering Servant made immediately clear what attitudes toward work are incompatible with the service of God. A worker must shun laziness and idleness, time-serving and time-frittering gossip. He must avoid becoming a financial burden to others, if that lies within his power (I Thess. 2:9; II Thess. 3:6-13). He must overcome the tendency to chafe at monotonous toil, to resent inadequate pay or difficult working conditions (Heb. 13:5; Phil. 2:14; I Pet. 2:18, 19). Toward his superiors a worker is enjoined to submissiveness and obedience, but not through fear. He must not grovel before them in order to secure special favors. He is "not to be refractory, nor to pilfer" (Titus 2:9, 10). He will accept unjust treatment without reviling, resistance, anger, envy, or jealousy. Such humility is made possible by his allegiance to the Lord and his new life in the Lord (I Pet. 2:18-23; Matt. 5:22-28; Col. 3:22-25). Toward his inferiors the Christian is obligated not to act in pride, condescension, or ridicule. He must not despise them, keep back their wages, or revel in exclusive luxury. He must treat them fairly, expressing love for them through the way in which he uses his superior power in their behalf (I Tim. 6:17-19; Col. 4:1; Jas. 5:1-6). The employer must remember that Christ is Master of both himself and his employee, and that Christ shows no partiality (Eph. 6:9). Rich and poor alike are warned against the love of Mammon. The rich must not become complacent or insensitive because of their wealth. Others must covet "no one's silver or gold or apparel" (Acts 20:33). The congregation may not show preference for the wealthy and mighty (Jas. 2:1-8). All must reckon with the transiency of wealth and possessions. In none may there be anxiety for earthly glories. All must subdue "the lust of the flesh and the lust of the eyes and the pride of life" (I John 2:16; II Tim. 6:10; Heb. 13:5; Matt. 6:19-24, 13:22; Jas. 3:14-4:10). Such high standards, seen against the corruption of the world, could easily lead to a life of monastic seclusion from the world. But Christian workers are counseled not to withdraw from the world's business in order to preserve their own purity. They must, to be sure, keep themselves "unstained" (Jas. 1:27), but this does not mean breaking off contact with robbers, idolaters, the greedy, and the immoral (I Cor. 5:10). In fact, a Christian has no right to judge those who are outside the Church. Nor need he fear that contact with the unclean will make him unclean. His food and his weekly schedule are not contaminated by their involvement in pagan life. Their cleanness is determined rather by the heart of the Christian participant, who knows that nothing is unclean of itself and that only that is sin which does not spring from faith (Rom. 14:23).

These sinful attitudes toward work which we have mentioned are so prevalent, so taken for granted in the business world, that it is very easy to take the gospel commands lightly. By contrast the New Testament takes them with a unique seriousness. In the Sermon on the Mount anger is declared to be as sinful as murder; lust is declared to be as sinful as adultery. Such attitudes are not merely condemned as wrong because they do not conform to a set of moral ideals; they are critically analyzed as the source of slavery, futility, and death. In adopting the desires of the world, a worker binds himself to the most fearful form of slavery. In adopting vocational goals set by the world, he is guaranteeing a harvest of futility. In following the crowd's craving for superiority, he is, in fact and not in theory alone, committing suicide. Conversely, when the new vocation in Christ produces new attitudes toward work, these attitudes are more than examples of private pieties. They are signs of the emergence of a new world, tokens of Christ's power to give life in the midst of death, symptoms of a permanent health, and proofs of a certain harvest. A new history lies behind the appearance of each attitude, and a new future opens before it.

The Christian worker, for example, avoids becoming a financial burden on others in order that he may help others in time of need (Acts 20:35; I Thess. 2:9; Jas. 1:27, 2:14-17). He is always ready for an emergency call that draws him beyond the bounds of his regular duties (Lk. 10:25-37). He is equally ready to labor inconspicuously at simple chores without any thought of special merit (Lk. 17:7-10). He views every associate, whether competitor or co-operator, whether Christian or pagan, as one for whom Christ died. He forgives debtors and enemies as fully as he has himself been forgiven. His hospitality exceeds all customary expectations, being extended to many who can never repay. Generosity to apprentice or employee far exceeds the narrow caution of legal requirements and contractual arrangements. He considers others better than himself, whether they are above or below him in the economic scale. His promises have an integrity that makes oaths entirely superfluous (Matt. 5:33-37). He remains cheerful at tasks where others would be morose and bitter. In prosperity or adversity he is thankful to God, trusting in God's power to produce good. He makes the most of the time, relating each day's routine to God's eternal purpose. He is more concerned for the needs of his neighbor than for his own rights and fortunes. Conscious of his own weakness before the tasks that confront him, he learns the sufficiency of Christ's strength. He lays up all his treasures in heaven and is confident of God's faithfulness as a warden. In whatever work he may be engaged, he "bears all things, believes all things, hopes all things, endures all things" (I Cor. 13:7).

If this is the New Testament picture of the way of the Cross, and if this picture is meant to describe the daily behavior of a person at his work, then one does not need to argue how radically distinctive this way really is. Nor does one need to expound the tremendous difficulties which such a picture poses for the individual worker. The distinctiveness and the difficulties alike spring from a vocation that is radically opposed to the world's notions of vocation and a vocation that is, at the same time, radically relevant to man's work in the world. The origin of this vocation is God's purpose in Christ to redeem everything that man does from the hopelessness and fruitlessness of a creation that "is in agony until now." This vocation is God's way of restoring integrity to man's fragmented and tortured existence, of restoring peace to an alienated society. The clash between this vocation and other vocations becomes most acute in man's soul at his place of employment. This place, therefore, becomes a most important pulpit for the proclamation of the gospel. This place is a most important arena where God's kingdom challenges Satan's. It is a most important stage for the demonstration of Christ's victory.

To be sure, it is the follower of Christ who knows best how acute are the temptations posed by the workshop or office. Like others he suffers from stultifying drudgery, from debilitating toil, from trivial time-serving, from the constant compromises and dishonesties that accompany business transactions. The law of love under which he lives makes him more aware than others of the ruthless competition that masks itself in "service," the impersonal industry that justifies its brutalities as efficiency, the militarized production line that turns plows into swords, allegedly for the sake of security. But where the temptation is greatest, there he listens anew for vocational guidance from his Lord. He will hear the gospel again as a proclamation of judgment and will recognize in this judgment the door to forgiveness and freedom. In and through his work he will accept "the chastisement of a son," groaning with creation as one who shares the futility of a world that is passing away. In the midst of this agony he will receive the assurance of his adoption as a son (Rom. 8:16-21). With this adoption comes the power to believe, to hope, to love, to rejoice. He will see, in the mill or office, God working "for good with those who love him" (Rom. 8:28), redeeming an evil time, and garnering the harvest of good works. This vision will be translated into new attitudes toward his work, into new acts of humble, obedient love. The fruit of the branch will be the fruit of the vine (John 15:4). Just as Jesus had seen his Father at work and had joined in that work, so, too, the disciple knows what the Son is doing and shares in his labor (John 15:15). The relation of Christ to God becomes the traceable image of the Christian's relation to Christ. This, in turn, determines the relation of Christians to one another, and gives them the one vocation of intercessory prayer and intercessory service in the world and for the world—the very world that is encountered in the daily grind.

II

Work and Vocation
in Christian History

ROBERT L. CALHOUN

1. Reviewing the Biblical roots—a. work as duty, redeemed; b. vocation as summons, election, and station. 2. Monastic work and Gregory the Great. 3. Crafts and the Thomist hierarchy of work. 4. Biblical freedom for laymen. 5. Christian vocation in fourteen centuries. 6. The genius of Luther: work as vocation. 7. Reformed success and decline.

Two main themes emerge from our review of Biblical teaching, to be examined further in the context of later Christian life. The primary theme, fundamental to both Jewish and Christian teaching, is the calling of men by the God of heaven and earth: the divine choosing of Israel and then of the Christian Church to be bound by a covenant with God, and so to become a people of especial obligation and promise; and the calling of each faithful member of the people so chosen to take his part in the common life of duty and hope. This is the Biblical understanding of *vocation*. Subordinate to it and essentially determined by it is a characteristic Biblical treatment of *work*, as a continuing activity of both God and man, that gets its significance from the sovereign being, purpose, and acts of God.

In the developing life of the Church, these two themes have always been present in some form, though not always with their relationship clearly indicated, and sometimes with restrictions and separations that have seriously affected the right understanding of both. The course of this development has been examined by a substantial and steadily increasing number of scholars since Max Weber's provocative essay was published in 1904-5, and its main lines have become widely familiar.[1] No more than a hurried sketch is possible here. For the sake of clarity, at the cost of rather serious oversimplification, we may summarize in four statements the development to be examined:

1. The Old Testament doctrine of *vocation*, present even in very early documents (e.g., Gen. 6:18; 12:1 ff.; Exod. 3:4-10; 12:1-51; etc.), reached its most mature, explicit, and strongly highlighted form in the late teaching of the Second Isaiah (chaps. 40-66), from which it was taken over and further developed in the New Testament, especially in the letters of Paul and the Letter to the Hebrews. At the same time, there grew up a striking and powerful conception of *work*, grounded in the Hebrew faith in the creating, ruling, and redeeming God—a faith always implicitly and sometimes explicitly tied in with the doctrine of vocation that covered the whole life of every member of the chosen covenanted people. This ground has been covered in the preceding chapter, and will be touched briefly in the present one, in line with the development that followed.

2. In the centuries between the New Testament age and the Protestant Reformation, the most distinctive and influential movement in the Church was monasticism. During these centuries the basic doctrine of *vocation* was kept alive under one name or another, and given special significance for the monastic life, long considered the most intense, heroic, exemplary form of Christian living. At the same time, thanks mainly to the influence of monastic discipline, the Church's theory and practice with respect to daily *work* became at once more systematic and more complex than it had ever been in Biblical times. The specific relevance of this theory and practice to *vocation*, however, was understood very unevenly by the leaders of Christian thought, and almost not at all, one may suppose, by the rank and file.

3. The sixteenth and seventeenth centuries brought a sudden re-emphasis and integration of both doctrines among the leaders and many followers of Protestantism. Luther and Calvin, hewing to lines already sketched out by Wyclif and Hus, rejected

vehemently the "double standard" of Christian life long encouraged by much monastic thought and practice, and frankly identified in various essential ways Christian *vocation* and daily *work*. In some respects, what they did was to revive the Biblical perspective of men like the Second Isaiah and Paul, in which devotion to God and service to neighbor were inseparably bound together in the concept of calling. In other respects, especially in revaluation of everyday life and the detailed application of the term "calling" to this latter, they boldly ventured beyond anything explicitly spelled out in the Biblical text. Their intent was nothing less than to reaffirm, with new fullness of detail, the penetration of every nook and corner of the Christian life by the summons and promise of God.

4. But the breakup of traditional ways of life, especially in Protestant lands, the spread of free thought and resistance to authority, the disruptive and exhausting wars of the seventeenth century, the beginnings of the industrial revolution, and the rise to power of a new middle class—merchants, manufacturers, bankers, and independent small landowners, impatient of control by either Church or State—brought a new kind of disintegration. Individualistic tendencies in Protestantism, legitimate and salutary but one-sided, were stressed at the expense of its great unifying principles: the universal Reign of God, and the corporate life of Christians in "one body and one Spirit." Moreover, in a time of growing human prowess, the Protestant identification of daily work with divine calling was inverted, so that calling came generally to mean simply human work, with God left out. There followed a growing isolation of daily work from the acts of worship that most people think of as religion, the dividing of the world for many into sacred and nonsacred (secular, godless) parts, and a widening triumph of secularity that has made the traditional appraisal of work as religious vocation sound naïve or hypocritical.

This is the course of development to be sketched in the current chapter. The resulting situation will be described more fully, in a different perspective, in the chapter that follows.

1. REVIEWING THE BIBLICAL ROOTS

We may begin with a quick glance back at the Biblical teachings examined in Chapter I, adding one or two notes on *calling* in the New Testament.

a. Work as Duty, Redeemed

As regards work, the most obvious characteristic of the teaching of the Old Testament is its realism about work and leisure, and its steady insistence that both get their meaning from the active presence of God. There is frank acceptance of work as man's duty, without either disparagement or sentimental glorification. There are some clear expressions of preference for leisure, in passages that voice the joy of the priest or the scholar in the opportunity to dwell upon the truth and beauty of God without the interruption of daily toil. On the other hand, there is little or no sign of a fastidious contempt for even rough manual labor that has so often been remarked (with some misunderstanding and exaggeration) in the literature of ancient Greece. The Hebrews of Old Testament times were, by and large, a practical, morally responsible, activistic people, not much given to lengthy contemplation, insistent on the rights and dignities of free men, and seldom tolerant of aristocratic claims to immunity from the common lot.

It is characteristic, moreover, that whatever is said about work and the men who engage in it stands in a moral and religious context full of vigor and dynamic power. The God of Hebrew faith is a working God, Creator and Ruler of the universe, whose heavens are the work of His fingers and whose living creatures receive their food at His hands. Man himself, in the oldest account, has been molded from moist earth by the divine Craftsman and imbued with the breath of life (Gen. 2:7), and God maintains direct supervision over man's performance of his assigned task. In the later accounts also (e.g., Gen. 1:26 ff.; Ps. 8, 90, 103-7, 139; Isa. 42:5-13, 43:1-13, 45:8-25), man has been created for responsible service, to live and work and pray as one who, alone among earthly creatures, is capable of hearing

God's voice and answering Him. The people of Israel, in particular, are drawn into a covenant relationship with God and with one another. Their whole lives, whether at work or at prayer, during the six days of labor or during the seventh day of rest, are lived in the constant presence and under the perpetual care and commandment of their Maker, Judge, and Redeemer. Work done and prayer offered gets its significance from the way in which it fulfills God's will and His law. When men build an arrogant tower, or grow rich in houses and land but disregard "the work of the Lord," they court disaster (Gen. 11:1-9; Isa. 5:8-12). When the skill of the craftsman is turned to the making of idols, it deserves and suffers ridicule (Isa. 44:9-20). But when the broken walls of Jerusalem are restored for the safety of the people and the glory of the Lord by faithful and fearless returning exiles, their leader can say: "This work was wrought of our God" (Neh. 6:16).

For Christian faith, new light came with the revelation of God in Jesus Christ. He himself, the Messiah, in whom the Word of God took visible, tangible form, was a man of the people. He was not, like John the Baptizer, an ascetic preacher of doom, having his dress, his words, and his manner of life shaped by the desert. "The Son of Man came eating and drinking." On the other hand, he was not a man of privilege, set apart in special piety or in financial and political comfort. One may suppose he was reared in a carpenter's shop and in the life of a workman's household. After his public ministry began, he found his friends among fishermen, taxgatherers, women of the streets, and simple householders, as well as among men of wealth and position. In his career there was no hint of alienation from everyday living.

His teaching, in word, act, and total life, was centered on the overwhelming reality and inescapable demands of the eternal and impending Kingdom of God. In this sense its focus was "other-worldly" and its significance revolutionary. But it bore trenchantly on every aspect of men's daily lives. His discourses were full of illustrations from the work of vinedressers, builders, farmers, woodworkers, shepherds, stewards, magistrates, harvest hands, and men of other common occupations. He saw no im-

propriety in comparing God's concern for a sinner with a housewife's anxiety over a lost coin, the quest of souls to the work of
fishermen or harvesters, the gospel to seed strewn over the
ground, or the Kingdom itself to baker's yeast, to a mustard seed
planted and growing, or to a net loaded with fishes. All this was
kept in perspective by condemnation of anxiety about worldly
goods—the stupidity of the rich fool, or of those who paid more
attention to signs of coming weather than to signs of coming
judgment; by praise of the faith of Mary rather than the worry
of Martha; by the radical unworldliness of the Sermon on the
Mount. Jesus was no teacher of prudential morality or of
worldly success. But he was one who understood, appreciated,
and honored all sorts of people, who found his own closest associates chiefly among toilers rather than among scholars and
aristocrats. As a man at home with all sorts of fellow men, he
met on their own ground, with the insight and transforming
power of love, despised publicans, Roman soldiers, a "Canaanite"
woman, a blind beggar, a ruler of the Synagogue, a member of
the Sanhedrin.

Apart from all specific references to worldly occupations,
moreover, Jesus' teaching and example were alive with devotion
to his own calling: disclosure of the love and power of God, in
service to needy men. This was the basis of his requirement
that his followers should imitate him in lives of service, seeking
always first the Reign of God. Instead of efforts to achieve
dominance through power, their rule must be to serve one another. Calculating effort to save one's own life will lose it; only
devoted giving of one's life can save it. This principle holds for
the Master as well as for his followers. He shows the way, as
Messiah crucified. And as the risen Lord he may well have
brought reassurance to his shattered disciples first in the familiar
work places of Galilee.[2]

The judgment of the Church was that he had in fact become
the pioneer of a new way of life, the founder and foundation
of a new community. By the very fact of his incarnation and his
earthly life, he had repudiated that scorn for the body and for
the ways of plain men that characterized many of the proffered

ways of salvation. He had taught and lived not seeking escape
from the conditions of everyday life, but manifesting obedient
and triumphant realization of the power of God in the midst
of the everyday world. All this Paul clearly recognized when
he spoke of the Church as the corporate living body of Christ,
actuated by his spirit, and wrote of himself and his associates
as "God's fellow-workers."

b. Vocation as Summons, Election, and Station

This Pauline understanding of individual and corporate
Christian life involved a powerful new emphasis and development of the ancient (and especially the Deutero-Isaian) doctrine
of vocation. In the Greek New Testament, the basic terms for
this doctrine were the words "to call" (*kalein*) and "calling"
(*klēsis*), by which several different words in the Old Testament
had been translated, and several different meanings were conveyed. Most of these have been made clear in the preceding
chapter. For our purpose, three meanings are most important:
two that are found often in both Testaments, and a third that
is unique, perhaps original with Paul, and not entirely clear.
First of these meanings is to *summon* (often by name), to con-
voke an assembly, to invite (as to a feast or a truce). The second
is to *choose*, to select and assign to an office, a task or a special
status. Israel and every true son of Abraham were "called" in
both these ways. In the New Testament, the second meaning is
often conveyed by another pair of words: "to choose" or "elect"
(*eklegein*), and "choosing" or "election" (*eklexis*). Election is
sometimes contrasted with calling (Matt. 22:14; cf. Luke 14:16,
24), sometimes distinguished from it but closely connected with
it (II Thess. 2:13-14; Rev. 17:14). Most often, especially in
Pauline thought, calling and election are substantially or wholly
identical, so that to be called is to be both chosen and summoned
(I Thess. 2:12; I Cor. 1:9; Rom. 8:29-30, 11:28-29; so too Heb.
9:15; I Pet. 1:10; II Pet. 1:3-4, 10; etc.). In this perspective there
comes to new expression, with new force, the old Hebrew conviction that human life gets its meaning in and through a "calling and election" by the sovereign word of God. For Christian

faith, that Word is disclosed with new power and wisdom in Jesus Christ—at once a promise and an imperative demand for devotion to God and love to fellow men. Hence the Church itself was appropriately called *ekklēsia*, an assembly of those convoked into a new community.

In one passage only (I Cor. 7:17-24), Paul used the word *klēsis* in another closely related way. "Let each man abide in that calling (*klēsis*) wherein he was called" (v. 20, A.S.V.). The context makes at least thus much clear: that "calling" is used here in the secondary sense of the outward state or station of life in which one has heard the divine summons and answered it. Whether one were a slave or a freeman, married or unmarried, circumcised or uncircumcised, it is well that he remain in that "calling," that outward state of life, which God has assigned to him and in which he has been called to the life of faith. The immediate motive for this advice is expressly stated: the "appointed time" until the end of the present age is short (v. 29) and there is no need for anxiety to change the state of one's earthly life. One deeper reason is also clear: each can serve God and fellow man as slave or as freeman, as Jew or as Gentile Christian. And since each man's and woman's station is itself allotted by the Lord (v. 17), it may itself be regarded as in that sense a divine "calling" or assignment to a task.

2. MONASTIC WORK AND GREGORY THE GREAT

Through the centuries that followed the apostolic age, the Biblical vision both matured and changed. There have been times when social and ecclesiastical developments have helped to obscure its meaning. In other times it has come clear once more, and taken on new depth and concreteness.

Among the early Fathers of the Church, especially while the speedy end of the present age was still confidently awaited, and indeed as long as the Church was treated as an "unfriendly alien" in the Roman world, comparatively little attention was paid to the details of the Christian's working life. Here and there, a Clement of Rome (A.D. 97) urged that Christians imitate God in his working,[3] or the unknown author of the *Letter to Diognetus*

insisted (v. vi, x.4-6) that Christians were devoted to the maintenance of wholesome life and peace in their citizenship. The
Roman Hermas used in his prophetic work the elaborate figure
of the building of the Church eternal, dwelling heavily upon the
imagery of stone masons' and builders' activities, with the Lord
himself as foundation, supervisor, and master builder;[4] spoke
of toil as a gift of God, from which the Christian must give freely;[5]
and at the same time took pains to define carefully the perils of
preoccupation with worldly affairs.[6] Clement of Alexandria (c.
200) could urge his pagan neighbors not to desert their proper
occupations but to find God in the midst of them, as their Christian fellow citizens already were doing.[6a] But these were excep-
tions, I should judge, rather than typical voices.

At the same time, even while Christians were compelled by
hostile public opinion to think of themselves very literally as
"pilgrims and strangers" in pagan society, in and for which
they were not encouraged to assume large-scale responsibilities,
the Church emphatically rejected the teachings of Gnostics and
Marcionites who urged total condemnation of the present world
and escape from it into ascetic seclusion. "Other-worldly" in
principle, looking not only to this "age" but also beyond it, the
Church surely was; full salvation was not to be had here and
now. But world-rejecting the orthodox Church was not, since
God made the world, reigns over it, and loves it with infinite
love.

When the favor of Constantine made Christianity respectable
and safe, the temper of the more radical Christians changed
again. The new monastic movement,[7] beginning to achieve
momentum and prestige at about that time, urged the need for
devoted Christians to withdraw from the complexities and cor-
ruptions of the world and to seek freedom and purity of life in
isolation, intent on the greater glories of the life to come. Some
of those who followed this line, especially some of the hermits
or solitaries as distinct from the members of monastic communities, despised bodily work and sought perfection in a life of
unsullied prayer and rigorous self-castigation. But Antony himself, the prince of hermits and ascetics, worked with his hands

voluntarily,[8] and kept his body fit, though severely disciplined. Still more explicitly the wiser leaders and counselors of monastic settlements, of whom Augustine and Benedict were typical, turned resolutely away from the vagaries of their extremist fellow ascetics, and sought to make of the monastic life a way of superior normality and health. The very word "ascetic" (*askētēs*, from *askein*, "to work") meant craftsman before it came to mean athlete or monk, and the implied stress on disciplined skill was apparently the original basis for its use in the latter sense.

The trail breaker on this road of communal asceticism was Pachomius, an ex-soldier (d. 346), who founded in upper Egypt a monastic community organized like a military regiment, and drafted a *Rule* that provided for adequate food and sleep, required that every monk work at a skilled trade, with three years' apprenticeship for candidates and humane but firm discipline for members of the growing order. At Pachomius' death, nine monasteries and two nunneries were living by his *Rule*. In Asia Minor the outstanding leader was Basil, the great archbishop of Caesarea from 370 until his premature death in 379. He himself, a graduate of the Platonic Academy in Athens, would have preferred a studious contemplative life, admired the austerities of ascetics in many lands and seems to have neglected his own bodily health with unhappy results.[9] But in a troubled, dangerous time under a heretical emperor, he took on himself a heartbreaking practical burden as primate of the straggling, desolate Cappadocian *hinterland* deep inside eastern Asia Minor. He built a suburban monastery with hospital, guest house, and shops for vocational training that became a new center of life for Caesarea;[10] preached to workingmen on the six days of creation;[11] and formulated *Rules* that became the standard for Greek monasticism, laying down as the basic principle "the law of love" that can be fulfilled only in service to neighbors,[12] forbidding excessive and erratic individual austerity, and requiring systematic, trained, devoted work "to exhibit love for our neighbor."[13] "Zealous work is as necessary as daily bread."[14]

In the West, Augustine (d. 430) wrote to similar purpose in

a treatise *On the Work of Monks,* which one critic[15] regards as "perhaps the most significant document in the history of economic theory since the end of the fourth century." Like Basil,[16] Augustine insists that the basic demands apply not only in the monastery but to every Christian and to all work. No view less ample, indeed, would have been consistent with his tremendous vision of human history in the eternal providence of God.

To the mind of Augustine, looking out on a Western Roman world in immediate danger of collapse, the life of the Christian community seemed a clear indication of the working of God in history from the beginning. His perspective differed both from the excitement of the earliest Christians expecting a speedy end of the age, and from the efforts of the third- and fourth-century Church to enter more fully into the secular life of the empire. Like the early Christians, he saw the secular world moving toward final ruin, with no single resting place and no secure protection to be found in any earthly achievement. But like the more humane Christian authors of the intervening years, he saw throughout history itself the creative and redemptive activity of God, that could give to faithful human effort a true perspective and a glorious meaning.

Human life can find fulfillment only in a society;[17] and the character of a society is determined by what it most loves.[18] Wherever men are banded together in quest of pleasure, profit, or power for its own sake and for the sake of self-aggrandizement, there the toxins of destruction are always at work. The egoistic, power-mad empires of the ancient Assyrians and of the later Romans stand as the supreme instances of a way of life that is cursed with death.[19] Everywhere the "earth-bound city" (*civitas terrena*) is, even in its most splendid achievements, a devil's snare. Work, social life, and government when devoted to the service of truth, justice, and peace, display the marks of divine ordering and become instruments of human welfare.[20] But when these secular activities and institutions become self-centered, turned away from justice and truth and the will of God, they are doomed, and carry down with them in ruin all those who have made creaturely goods their chief end.[21] But side by side with the earthy city from the beginning of history and on toward its approaching end, "the commonwealth of God" (*civitas dei*) has lived and grown with miraculous tenacity.[22] Its members are the faithful servants whose love is first of all for God, and who find their security not in self-seeking, aggression, and earthly power, but in truth and right (XIX.iv, x-xiii). The Catholic Church does not contain all of God's servants, nor are all its members true citizens of the city of God.[23] But the Church in its purest and most authentic expressions is the best earthly embodiment of God's will, and of the human love that is turned toward the one true ground of human well-being.[24] Without the power of great wealth or of military force, the Church of the faithful will outlast kings and empires, growing toward a glorious transformation and fulfillment as they decline and fall.[25] This is the meaning of history, and the promise of salvation beyond history.

Within fifty years after Augustine died in 430, the Roman dynasty in the West had fallen, and power thenceforth was in the hands of Teutonic chieftains who knew nothing of the elaborate engineering and political skills of the conquered world. Within another hundred years, the intricate social and political fabric of Western Roman civilization had crumbled, leaving the Byzantine world—the Eastern empire—to stand alone for another thousand years. But meanwhile Western monasticism under the inspired leadership of Benedict of Nursia was becoming, without intending to do so, a new center for a new civilization. Benedict's *Rule* for monastic life (c.529) followed Basil in rejecting once for all the undisciplined individualism and wild asceticism of the earlier solitaries. Life in organized communities was made the basic pattern of monastic development. The ascetic craving for simplicity in food, dress, and shelter, and for freedom from the corrupting entanglements of the secular world, was continued and nurtured as a true pattern of Christian life.[26] But the monasteries were to become places of normality and health, with enough sleep, enough plain food, and enough hard work to keep their inhabitants sound in body and mind.[27]

Chapter 48 of the *Rule* expressly enjoins at least seven hours of manual labor in each day except the Sunday of rest. For able-

bodied monks when the weather is fit, outdoor labor is required.
When the weather is too rough, and for those too frail for heavy
labor, work in the library and the copying room is later enjoined,
with two hours of reading in each day besides the hours of heavy
labor. Even for noblemen, not a few of whom became members
of Benedictine houses, the rough garments of toilers and the
stiff toil of farmers and builders were a requisite part of the
monastic life.

Among these men, especially after Gregory I (590-604) began
to promote the Benedictine way far and wide, something of the
knowledge of systematic agriculture and sound architecture that
Rome had developed now slowly became available for the rude
fighting men of the Germanic tribes. A spreading network of
monastic settlements, founded by preference in the open country, came to be at once a model and a school for skilled, civilized
living. Chief stress was still laid upon the hours of devotion—
stated periods of prayer and praise (not passive meditation)
spaced throughout the twenty-four hours of every day. Devotion
to God was the ruling principle of life. But the stated times of
work were the indispensable correlate to periods of worship. In
this context, for the new warrior peoples who were to become
the substance of European civilization in the age of Christendom,
work acquired new dignity and meaning.

When at the end of the sixth century the ancient order had
crumbled even in the Roman Campagna itself, Gregory brought
the monastic ideal into the center of church life. The beginning
of a new cycle of European history is a thrilling story. Gregory
well deserves to be called "the Great," a statesman of rare gifts
and a humane, imaginative leader who boldly undertook the all
but impossible task of making the Church the pioneer and trus-
tee of a new civilization. Contemporary accounts of the state of
Italy after the Gothic and Lombard conquests show a picture of
stark desolation. Gibbon's summary is familiar.[28] In the golden
age of Augustus, the population of Rome had been somewhere
between one and two million people (allowing for a wide margin
of error in primitive statistics). When Gregory became pope in
590, it had shrunk to between forty and sixty thousand—some-

where between 2 and 6 per cent of the earlier total. Partly, this was the result of disease that followed the breakdown of aqueducts that had brought clean drinking water from the surrounding hills, the crumbling of the great sewers that had carried off the city's waste, and the clogging of ditches that had drained the malarial swamps around the city's walls. Partly, it had resulted from stoppage, under the vigorous but rough and ignorant new rulers, of essential grain shipments from Egypt and Sicily. The hard, straight Roman roads that had carried imperial messengers swiftly with news of trouble, and made possible the prompt movement of the legions to places of danger, were falling into disrepair. The physical conditions of complex civilization were fast breaking down. The result was far-flung chaos, decay of the imperial schools, and breakdown of commerce and of effective government. From the walls of the city, one could look out across miles of the surrounding plain and see deserted marble villas of the old nobility, inhabited now by jackals and bats.

To this welter of rude vitality, ignorance, and wreckage Gregory brought the devoted will of one who had desired to be a monk and a missionary,[29] and the administrative tact and organizing genius of one who had been in fact a skilled diplomat and public servant. Since the Church alone, of all the major institutions of the broken empire, had come through the wreck without fatal disruption, Gregory set about making the Church and its clergy and lay officials, great and small, the pioneers of a new age—though not its political governors.[30] A devoted follower of Augustine, the pope urged that no one should hold a position of authority in the Church who takes delight in domination, but only one who would have preferred a life of humble service, and who even as responsible officer (*rector*) regards himself as the equal of his brothers.[31] Moreover, "the rector should not relax his care for the inner life in his occupation with external affairs, nor neglect to provide for outward needs in his solicitude for things that are within."[32]

Following these principles, Gregory re-established regular shipments of grain from the Church's estates in Sicily, at fair prices and just measures under the guaranty of the Church.[33] Unfair taxation and graft were condemned,[34] the rights of Jews protected,[35] disputes judged,[36] and social counsel given. Secular governors were urged to bring about just arbitration of injuries,[37] weak churches were merged[38] and new churches, monasteries and hostels were built.[39] Captives were ransomed,[40] and estates settled.[41] Public defense and personal discipline alike were the concern of the indefatigable pope, and far-ranging missionary and educational activity went on under his patronage.[42] At the same time, Gregory refused for himself and denied to John and to Cyriacus, patriarchs of Constantinople, the title "Universal Bishop," maintaining that all true bishops (or priests?) are spiritually equal.[43] The great pope's temper is rightly understod by the Spanish bishop Licinianus who writes in admiration of Gregory's *Pastoral Care* that Augustine himself had understood the title *episcopus* (supervisor, bishop) as "a title denoting work, not dignity."[44]

3. CRAFTS AND THE THOMIST HIERARCHY OF WORK

It is well known that as medieval society developed, and a new feudalism established new patterns of inequality and aristocracy in which the warrior had first place in the secular world, the early temper of monastic leaders became corrupted again and again in the lives of their followers. The taste for idleness which even Augustine had felt it necessary to rebuke in his treatise *Of the Work of Monks*, and the spiritual pride against which Gregory argued so vehemently came to be all too characteristic of monastic establishments. In this climate of thought and taste, the claims of vigorous constructive labor became more and more subordinated to a preference for privileged leisure in quest of "perfection" as a higher order of Christian virtue. Reform after reform within the monastic movement itself—at Cluny, at Citeaux, at Clairvaux—brought at length the heroic and devoted efforts of Francis of Assisi, as the thirteenth century began, to recall a Church grown prosperous and powerful to the demand for simplicity and devoted service.[45] It is ironic and tragic that before the end of his brief journey, "the little brother of the poor" saw his vision rejected and his devoted way of life corrupted by some of his own friars.

By this time, however, the character and the needs of medieval society had changed profoundly, and new movements within and without the Church were rising to express, to mold, and to redirect the change. Western Europe was no longer a sparsely peopled wilderness, learning the rudiments of Roman civilization from monks and clergy, with a frail fabric of social order trembling always on the brink of chaos and repeatedly upset by some new mass movement of barbaric peoples. Once the marauding Northmen, the last and toughest of her conquerors, had planted themselves in France, in England, on sundry Mediterranean coasts, devoured and adapted with astonishing rapidity the culture they had invaded, and become its belligerent defenders and propagators, western Europe had emerged as a new fast-growing civilization, full of turbulent vitality. There was still disorder and violence in plenty, but no longer the frustrating aimlessness and confusion that repeatedly blighted life in the Dark Ages between A.D. 500 and 1000. Society now had a stable framework, relative security and a strong urge to adventure, dramatized and partly fulfilled in the Crusades.

In these circumstances, both the intellectual and spiritual life of clergy and "religious" (the members of monastic communities), and the development of new forms of life for the laity were strongly stimulated. For our present purpose, both were of vital importance, and the latter—the new forms of activity and organization among laymen—have quite special interest.

From one point of view, it can be said (much too simply) that patterns of life already long familiar in the monasteries are now adapted and vigorously developed for the whole church membership, clergy and laity alike. On the one hand, Pope Gregory VII —another Gregory "the Great"—in 1074 and thereafter sought to enforce the monastic rule of celibacy on "priests, deacons, and all clergy," and to free the Church as completely as possible from control by laymen, even princes and emperors, who must acknowledge their subjection to the clergy in all matters of Christian faith and discipline. A practical basis for enforcing this demand had long been developing through the extension of the originally monastic practice of frequent confession and penance to lay members of the Church, under penalty of excommunication for obstinate disobedience. This practice now came to be undergirded by a thoroughgoing doctrine of sacraments covering every major aspect of life, under full control of the higher clergy. On the other hand, laymen now developed, largely on their own initiative, quasi-monastic military orders (the Templars, Hospitallers, and various others) for the fighting nobility, and self-governing guilds of merchants and skilled craftsmen—armorers, goldsmiths, weavers, masons and many more—among an increasingly important middle class. With the rise of cities as growing centers of economic, political, and cultural life, these guilds advanced in prestige and corporate self-consciousness—and, it must be said, in conservatism. Their carefully graded and disciplined organization, with apprentices, journeymen, and masters arrayed in a hierarchy of skill and seniority, their rules of membership, and their pride of craft made them in many respects an active lay counterpart of the monastic and clerical orders. Moreover, laymen's reform movements and quasi-monastic lay brotherhoods, some orthodox, some heretical, seeking a renewal of simplicity, integrity, and even democracy in church life, together with local demands that the Mass be celebrated in the language of the people or that Bible-reading be freely permitted to the laity, bespoke a rising spirit of protest against too sharp a division between laymen and the hierarchy. When Christian universities (Bologna in 1158, Paris in 1205, and scores of others within the next two centuries) began to be chartered as guilds of scholars—students, bachelors, masters, doctors—many of these turbulent currents were channeled through them. Clergy and laity, orthodoxy and heresy, systematic research in the humanities, civil and church law, medicine, and theology, defense of the existing order and demands for a new one—all found place in these tumultuous growing points of medieval life.

A magnificent exemplar of the fusion of conservatism and radicalism in this new age was Thomas Aquinas (d. 1274), student and teacher in the University of Paris, author of two monumental "synopses" (*summae*) of thirteenth-century Christian philosophy and theology as well as many smaller works. In his tremendous system, both Church and civil State are close-knit hierarchies, in which authority is granted from God through. Jesus Christ to the pope as successor to Peter, chief of the apostles; and by the pope granted to bishops and priests, on the one hand, as spiritual guides of the people, and to the emperor as chief worldly ruler, on the other. In Church and in civil society alike, authority is delegated from the top of an ordered pyramid downward, through rank after rank, and exercised at length upon the plain folk at the bottom. On the face of it, this is ultraconservative defense of the feudal *status quo* and the papal claims to supremacy. But the defense rests on an act of great boldness: the adoption into Christian thought of the newly discovered and widely distrusted philosophic writings of Aristotle, that had actually been prohibited by the bishop of Paris in 1209 for study and teaching in his diocese. The hierarchical theory of society just described was developed by Aquinas from Aristotle's conception of social order in the *Politics* (which in turn owed much to Plato's analyses in the *Republic* and the *Laws*). Basic in Aristotle's account (and in Plato's) is an appraisal of work that foreshadows Karl Marx's thesis that economic activity is primary in human civilization. Uniquely among the animals, man works because he is rational, and thus able by suitably organized labor to supply his own needs for food, clothing, weapons, and shelter, and so to provide conditions suitable for humane living. A human community is in many respects like a great living organism, with its activities graded and interrelated to serve the life of the whole social body. Each useful sort of work, suited to the natural abilities, inclinations, and training of diverse workers, finds its significance in this context. So Thomas also holds, with the crucial further affirmation that all this is ordered at bottom by the providence of God.[46] In the hierarchy of work, "spiritual works"—prayer, preaching, and the like—rank higher than "manual works" in their contribution to corporate life; though all are necessary. This view is reaffirmed and elaborately developed by Antoninus of Florence (A.D. 1486-87)[47], who elsewhere says that God *calls* (*vocat*) men to various occupations. It well represents the fully matured hierarchical thought of the medieval Church.

4. BIBLICAL FREEDOM FOR LAYMEN

But within fifty years of Aquinas' death, Marsiglio of Padua in Italy and William of Ockham in England were developing a theory that sought to reverse this perspective. Both held that the Bible alone, interpreted when necessary by a general Council of the Church, holds the truth necessary for man's salvation. By it both laity and clergy must be guided. Marsiglio insists, on Biblical grounds, that all bishops have equal authority, "directly through Christ, nor can it be shown, in accordance with divine law, that in either spiritual or temporal matters one stands over or under another." "Neither bishop nor priest," moreover, has any "coercive jurisdiction over any cleric or layman, even if he be a heretic," but in all secular affairs all clerics are subject to "the human lawgiver (*legislator*)," to wit, "the total body of citizens or the major part thereof."[48] Ockham, less radical in defining the source of political power, was even more drastic in asserting the dependence of both clergy and councils on the whole membership of the Church. For in his view the Church is not an organism, but precisely the aggregate of its individual members. Taken together (as the two men in fact worked together) it can fairly be said that their thinking, based like that of Aquinas on teachings of Aristotle, defined in principle a democratic conception of both Church and State.

In England, the great successor to Ockham was another Oxford man, John Wyclif, who lived, thought, and worked in a society reeling under the terrific impact of the Black Death and the violent social disorders that followed it. He carried out in a succession of powerful works both Ockham's insistence on the supreme and sufficient authority of the Scriptures and his championship of the rank and file of believers.[48a] In his fundamental doctrine of divine dominion or sovereignty, Wyclif reaffirms the Augustinian view that every believer holds his title to "all things" directly from God. "By this formula," says R. L. Poole quite accurately, "all laymen became priests, and all priests laymen. They all 'held' of God, and on the same terms of service."[49] The universal condition of human tenure of authority, great or small in extent, was faithfulness of service to God and man. For prince and priest and pauper alike, if each is a true believer, it may be said that all things are his, so long as he continues faithful. As regards his ultimate status among men, no human person is dependent upon any other for dignity or freedom. In the final analysis, God is the sole Ruler of heaven and earth, and human authority is at best official and functional, neither hereditary nor inalienable. The claims of the priesthood to open or close the gates of salvation by miraculous powers to absolve mortal sin and to speak the words necessary for transformation of the bread and wine in the Mass are utterly rejected. Whatever spiritual authority a priest or pope may rightly claim is just as properly to be claimed by any faithful Christian. The plain people should have access to the Scriptures in their own tongues, and Wyclif's energetic sponsorship of the work of translating the Vulgate into English bore practical witness to his conviction. At the same time, like Luther in a comparable situation, he refused to support the political insurrectionary preaching of radicals like John Ball and some of his own Lollard followers, and disavowed responsibility for the Peasants' Revolt of 1381. Through John Hus and others in Bohemia, where a request for public worship in the people's language had been denied a full three centuries earlier,[50] Wyclif's essential ideas were transplanted to the Continent; and many of his basic writings were carried to Prague and assiduously studied as documents in a growing demand that the laity be given a more ample place in the Christian Church. None of this newer theology, as far as I know, expressly revaluated everyday work in theological terms, but it helped directly toward that further step.

5. CHRISTIAN VOCATION IN FOURTEEN CENTURIES

During these fourteen hundred years, from the end of the apostolic age to the verge of the Protestant Reformation, the Church's understanding of Christian vocation in its bearing on daily life had been narrowed and then broadened again. We recall that in Pauline thought the words for *calling* had meant (1) the *summons* from God to each man and woman to the life

of faith and love, (2) God's choosing or *election* of each believer
for his place in the corporate body of the Church, and (3) the
earthly *station* of the Christian, allotted to him by the divine will.

In the writings of the Church Fathers, the first two senses persist, with varying frequency and emphasis. Occasionally the principle of divine calling is examined closely, in an argument against
some erroneous view.[51] But much more often the words denoting
vocation are used in so matter-of-fact and unemphatic a way as
to indicate that the idea was familiar and generally accepted.[52]
This broad usage continued long after infant baptism was customary (extending the covenant to those not consciously called),
and after monasticism (setting up a special calling) was established in both East and West.[53] These changes in the over-all
pattern of church life no doubt tended to restrict more or less
sharply the use of the language of vocation. But Christianity continued to be a missionary religion through most of the Middle
Ages, and the dominant role of monasticism did not ever really
obliterate the conviction that each Christian is chosen and summoned to sonship (Rom. 8:28-30) by the word of God.[54]

At the same time, use of the word "calling" in its derivative
sense, to mean the earthly status "in which each was called" (I Cor.
7:20), was almost if not quite absent from Christian literature.
Tertullian[55] translated the word *klēsis* in that verse as *vocatio*
(or found it so rendered in an early Latin translation), but in
his current mood of fierce contempt for ordinary life, he used
the passage for his own negative purpose and made no effort
to look below the surface. Clement of Alexandria, a contemporary almost completely opposite in temper, used the Pauline
idea without the specific word. If a Christian be a farmer, a
sailor, a soldier, let him recognize the presence of God in the
perspective of his daily work.[55a] This idea in one guise or another,
without the specific word "vocation," is not hard to find in later
writings, even among the leaders and supporters of monasticism.
Cyril of Jerusalem[56] sees an analogue to Christian faith in the
trust displayed by partners in marriage, by farmers, by seamen—
a widespread secular "faith" by which "most of men's affairs are
held together," and that can serve as prelude to Christian faith.

Basil uses more than once Paul's word: "Whether you eat or drink, or whatever you do, do all to the glory of God" (I Cor. 10:31; cf. Col. 3:17, R.S.V.). Gregory Nazianzen[57] urges that at all times and in all sorts of occupations, "the work of your salvation is one upon which you should be engaged." Gregory the Great[58] urged the claims of both the contemplative and the active life, while frankly stressing the superiority of the former and the burdens of the latter.[59] But in these passages the word for vocation was used only once.[60]

It began to be used often, on the other hand, to signalize the entrance of one already a Christian, at least formally, into the status of one seeking "perfection." This meant commitment to lifelong ascetic discipline; and this, in turn, came to be equated practically with joining a monastic order. Taking monastic vows was often called a "second baptism," beginning a new kind of life. Monks thought of themselves as, in a special sense, "soldiers of Christ"; and like Abraham who had left home at God's call (Heb. 11:8), they too accepted the command to "become perfect" (Gen. 17:1) and sought to walk as "friends of God" (Wisd. 7:27; cf. James 2:23).[61] Moreover, in seeking to chart the way of perfection, they followed the lead of Antony in taking Matt. 19:21 (and 19:11-12) as a direct guide.[62] The eventual result was the widespread acceptance of a double standard of Christian living: for ordinary Christians, obedience to the "commandments" (Matt. 19:17-19); for the seekers of perfection, the harder "counsels" of poverty and celibacy, and the contemplative life. Although every Christian was indeed called, in the most general sense, only the monastic life deserved, as an earthly status or order, to be named *a vocation*. At least so it came to be held by a large body of medieval opinion.

At first the picture was not so clear-cut. Basil offers his sketch of the ascetic life as a pattern for *all* genuine believers ("The Christian ought to be so minded as becomes his heavenly calling," etc.[63]), and speaks of his friend Gregory Nazianzen as practicing "the poverty of a Christian."[64] Gregory himself, preaching on Matt. 19,[65] begins by urging that Jesus, the one truly perfect among men, "is made all things to all"—a fisherman, a wayfarer, acquainted with weariness and tears; proceeds to honor both mairiage and celibacy, the latter of which "is given to those who are called and . . . who incline that way" by the providence of God; concludes that the real intent of Jesus' cryptic word in Matt. 19:12 is—"like the verse, Depart from evil and do good"—to enjoin "spiritual chastity" that shuns all evil; and ends, "I enact this for laymen too." In the same key writes his younger friend Gregory of Nyssa[66] on "the holier life, the calling of virginity," "this high calling," which is not a physical state but the cultivation of a single and steady mind, balanced, moderate, and sober, intent on "no other goal than . . . the power . . . of seeing God" and becoming "a holy priest standing before God." It can be practiced in marriage, with great difficulty, and it can be distorted by misguided asceticism: but the distractions of "the secular life" (such as his own![67]) make the quest impossible for anyone who yields to them. Gregory the Great uses the terms "called" and "recalled" (*revocavit*), and much more often the term "converted" (*convertitur*[68]), with respect both to becoming a Christian and to becoming a cleric or a monk. The vivid figure of enlisting as a "soldier of Christ" (II Tim. 2:3), moreover, preempted for monasticism perhaps by the ex-soldiers Pachomius and Martin of Tours,[69] had been used freely by their contemporaries for any and all good Christians.[70] Nevertheless, the distinction between the monastic "vocation" and the life of the ordinary Christian grew sharper and wider, as feudal society developed its hierarchies in Church and world. Ordinary work and Christian vocation in its now restricted sense seemed very far apart.

Two converging lines of development prepared the way for a revolutionary change. One has already been noticed: the revaluation of the life of the plain people, resulting partly from the vigorous thought of men like Marsiglio, Ockham, and Wyclif, and partly from actual shifts in the social scene. There is no need to rehearse here the familiar inventory of changes in secular practice that helped bring about the new turn: the decline in wealth and power of the nobility after the Crusades and dynastic wars, the corresponding rise of a prosperous middle class of mer-

chants and skilled craftsmen, the economic and social dislocations that resulted from the Black Death and succeeding droughts
and famines, the introduction of gunpowder and the printing
press. These factors and many more helped to break the prestige
and strength of feudal aristocracy, and to stir the middle classes
and even the serfs of Europe to demands for a larger place in
the sun.

The other major development was the growth and spread of
mysticism, both inside and outside the cloister. Its intensely
earnest effort, disciplined or reckless, was to "see God" in this
life, and not only in the life to come. *This* is the quest of perfection, the true way of those who seek to be "God's friends." It
involves a paradoxical and often confused attitude toward the
created world and its everyday duties. On the one hand, since
God is wholly other than everything created, to seek Him means
to renounce the world, human loved ones, and most of all oneself as a distinct individual, for the sake of the one True Good.
On the other hand, since everything created is from God, the
man who by divine grace sees and loves God will love and serve
His creatures also; doing in love whatever work is necessary, but
quietly, humbly, without ever letting the work become an end
or a source of pride.[71] Through this whole development, in its
purest forms, there is evident the principle vividly stated by
Gregory of Nyssa: In every "virgin" soul, Christ comes to live.
"What happened in the stainless Mary . . . happens in every soul
that leads by rule the virgin life."[72]

In the Western church, from the time of Augustine through
the high Middle Ages, mysticism grew in prevalence and per-
suasiveness. The twelfth-century school of St. Victor, the passion-
ate and powerful example of Bernard of Clairvaux, and the
tranquil saintliness of Francis and Bonaventure brought the
movement to a new peak of honor and influence. The characteristic form of mystical teaching during this time stressed, on the
one hand, the need for careful, persistent self-discipline of body
and mind and will, in preparation and hope for the vision of
God; and, on the other hand, the impossibility of reaching the
vision by effort, however sincere and steadfast. If the vision came,

it came as a gift of God and not as an achievement of the believer. But those who engaged in the quest, and especially those to whom the vision was granted, might properly be thought of as *called*, in the most profound way, to be friends of God.

The monastic life was still regarded as the best preparation and the most promising status for those who craved the ultimate gift. But the very nature of the mystic way makes it ultimately a threat to any sort of formalized and dictated life pattern.[73] This became especially clear in the great flowering of Western mysticism in the fourteenth and fifteenth centuries. Not only the multiplying brotherhoods and sisterhoods of "the Free Spirit," often irresponsible in both morality and doctrine, but the ablest leaders used language that moved out beyond the traditional bounds. Partly under the stress of a radically new cultural and ecclesiastical development, partly in logical fulfillment of the genius of mysticism itself, seers like Jean Gerson, a busy man of affairs, university chancellor and ecclesiastical statesman, and John Tauler, a powerful popular preacher, began to urge that the vision of God may come to the ordinary layman as well as to the devoted cleric or monk. The determining factor, after all, was not the activity of man but the gracious will of God. The vision then may be granted, Tauler said, to a field hand or a kitchen maid as well as to monk or priest. Since this is so, this earthly status itself may be termed a commandment (*Ladung*) and calling (*Ruf*), in which it is well to remain.[74]

6. THE GENIUS OF LUTHER: WORK AS VOCATION

The two themes, daily work and divine vocation, long separated where the double standard of Christian life prevailed, and in the late Middle Ages beginning once more to converge, were brought together with startling emphasis in Luther's teaching, and in Calvinism (especially in England and North America) to 1660. Thereafter they fell apart once more, with unhappy results.[75]

Revaluation of the plain man and of the occupations of the laity was carried forward in a great sweep of power when the Protestant Reformation rose to full tide. Luther's bold attack on the abuses of the sacramental system began by following what seemed to be well-established lines, but ended in a profound re-direction of currents of both thought and life in the modern world. In many details he had indeed been anticipated by Ock-ham, Wyclif, and Hus. His doctrine of the sufficient authority of Scripture, the common priesthood of believers, and the need for drastic reform in the organization and practice of the Church had already found voice in his predecessors. But the basis on which all these rested, in Luther's experience, was radically new: a rediscovery of the Pauline understanding of Christian faith, to be worked out now in a world passing beyond feudalism into a new age.

On the one hand, this involved a new assertion of the abso-luteness, the transcendent holiness and sovereignty of God, that ruled out any supposition that men, high or low, righteous or unrighteous, could have any just claim upon God. The whole system of sacramentally infused virtues and acquired merits is abolished, root and branch. In God's presence, the demand that confronts *every* man is the demand for perfection. There is no possibility that any merely human being, in a monastery or out, with whatever title to sainthood, can possibly fulfill—let alone exceed—this requirement. On the other hand, the God of abso-lute, transcendent holiness, the Ruler and Judge, is at the same time the ever-present, immediately accessible Redeemer and Life-giver to those whom he has chosen to be men of faith. In faith alone, the complete, unreserved, inescapable commitment of the whole self to God, is salvation to be found. But faith itself is God's doing, not man's; and no earthly organization or disci-pline can lay claim to a preferred status in the life of faith and grace. There simply is no such thing as humanly earned merit, let alone surplus merit. Here the ax goes to the root of the feudal and hierarchical scheme.

Luther had learned much from the mystics, although he did not take unreservedly their way. They were content to stay within the system of ecclesiastical and sacramental piety in practice, despite the radicalism of their theory, and to pursue quietly their own quest for perfect vision. But Luther, who had found in the system of churchly discipline not a stairway toward the vision but sheer frustration of his deepest need, found himself compelled to challenge the whole medieval system. For him, the life of each individual person is set in a new double perspective. On "the right hand" is God's kingdom of grace, in which believers are enabled to live in faith and love, sustained and renewed daily by repentance and forgiveness, keenly aware of the immediate, uncompromising presence of God as Redeemer. On "the left hand" is the created kingdom of nature and history, ordered according to God's will in its fundamental structure, and good except as men and devils have corrupted it and made it bad. The believer is compelled to live in both kingdoms. He cannot withdraw from either, to simplify his living. Moreover, he cannot oscillate between them. The uncompromising demand for faith and love is binding upon him in his relations with the family, the State, and the institutional Church, even when his corporate responsibilities in the natural and social orders compel him to express his faith in hard, violent ways that seem to deny love. At the same time, if he is a genuine believer he will recognize God as present also throughout nature and history, and in all the detailed situations of everyday social life. The word of God will come to him in all his human relationships, and his work on behalf of his fellow men will be at the same time an affirmation of trust and praise toward God.

In this context, Luther adopts and develops much further the insight of the later mystics, that any sort of serviceable status in society, through which one may serve his neighbors, deserves to be regarded as a divinely ordained calling (*Beruf, vocatio*). There are diversities of gifts, of responsibilities, and of services, some very small, some very great in range and complexity. But whether one be a simple householder, a magistrate, or a prince of the realm, each believer can know his status in the perspective of Christian faith as, equally with every other, a calling appointed by God. There is no such thing as a profane or merely secular order from which God is absent, and in which God is not to be served.

7. REFORMED SUCCESS AND DECLINE

This conception of calling becomes characteristic also of the Reformed wing of the Protestant movement. Calvin uses the term "vocation" as frankly as Luther and in essentially the same sense, although with less exuberance and imaginative fervor. Among the Calvinists, moreover, in Geneva, in Scotland, or in England, Christian vocation was understood to require active social and political reform. Affirmation of the sole and total sovereignty of God and the common obligation of man carried over into a steady onslaught upon political as well as ecclesiastical autocracies. The doctrine of Marsiglio and of Wyclif is put into living action. Government must be carried out as a trust from God, and rulers must be fellow servants, not despots, in relation to those whom they rule. The rank and file, wherever the Reformed churches become strong, move toward the establishment of "Christian constitutionalism,"[76] embodied in some more democratic political order. John Knox denouncing Mary Stuart in Edinburgh and Cromwell in the field against her grandson bear witness in their different ways to the rising demand for freedom from human tyranny, as a demand that stems from the will of God. But even these leaders were not proof against the temptations of power. Calvin in Geneva and Cromwell in London displayed all too clearly the soundness of Lord Acton's aphorism. They could break autocratic authority to better purpose than they could wield it. There was need also for George Fox, refusing to take off his hat to any man living, or to employ the ceremonious "you" in place of the familiar "thou" in addressing his would-be superiors; and stubbornly arguing against all comers for the understanding of the Scripture that had been "opened" to him as a simple Christian.

Fox, indeed, rather than Calvin, foreshadowed the next major stage of Protestant development. In Luther and Calvin, the medieval understanding of human community as an organic whole, a living body of diverse members, was still strong. They rejected the claims of the papacy and of the Holy Roman Empire, and found their main support among sober middle-class folk—burghers, yeomen, magistrates, local princes, and gentry—against the feudal autocrats in Church and State. But they retained much of the feudal sense of solidarity and of the need for due order in civil society. The more unbridled sorts of individualism, whether doctrinal, moral, or political, they resisted. "The freedom of a Christian man" did not mean freedom to follow any course that seemed good to oneself. But the tremendous social pressures that preceded, entered into, and followed the Reformation were too strong to be held within traditional bounds. Especially after the disrupting blows of the Thirty Years' War on the Continent (1618-48), and the Civil War and the iron years of Cromwell's dictatorship in Britain (1642-58), the old sense of organic unity and readiness to accept the old restraints on individual action had largely broken down. Before the turbulent seventeenth century ended, the victorious Protestant middle class in the Netherlands and in Britain—one the chief commercial power in Europe, the other her fast-growing rival for supremacy—had impatiently shrugged off diminishing efforts at control of business enterprise by either parsons or parliaments. The traditional condemnations of "usury" (that is, money-lending at fixed interest), of "enclosure" (private purchase of public lands), and of hard trading for high profits (against the old doctrine of a "just price") grew weaker, and at length changed to general approval. Poverty came to be regarded not as a special claim to generous help from the community, but as at once a mark of moral delinquency and an economically useful fact to be exploited, not cured. The eighteenth century dawned on a vigorously expanding commercial economy in western Europe and North America, whose successful members felt that the Church, and presumably the Lord, was on their side.[77]

The terms "vocation" and "calling" had a conspicuous place in this change of perspective. The Reformers' rejection of the double standard for Christian living, and the declaration that every man's work and place in society is for him a divinely ordained vocation, was followed by a series of steps that led further and further from Luther's great insight. For him, daily work and all the everyday relationships of men, women, and children form a medium in which the Word of God comes to each person, and in which his response of love for his neighbor can be offered to God, in whom he trusts with all his heart. The primacy of faith in God and the requirement of love for neighbor made it impossible to regard daily work as an end in itself, and even to view with favor an outstanding degree of worldly prosperity. But seventeenth-century Calvinists and sectarian individualists, busily engaged in bringing a new economic order to birth and conquering a new world of unexplored resources, saw no impropriety in judging that prosperity for one who labored diligently in his calling was a mark of divine approval, not a sign of the deadly sin of avarice.

The next step in this fateful modern development was still more drastic and decisive. As the business world of the late seventeenth and the eighteenth centuries freed itself from churchly and governmental control, it insisted on regarding itself as free also from liability to criticism on grounds of Christian morality. The will of God was either equated with successful business practice, or it was excluded from any effective relevance to worldly affairs. The logical end of the process, for more and more busy people, was to disregard or deny the reality of divine will altogether. Faith in human progress replaced faith in God. The terms "vocation" and "calling" were still retained, but they came to mean little or nothing more than worldly activities pursued with diligence for their own sake, and for the sake of worldly rewards.

This reduction of the once religiously powerful words to secular dimensions, having meaning only in terms of the present world of affairs and its standards of success, continued through the nineteenth century and into our own time. The economic and political movement of which it has been one aspect has brought immense gains for human welfare, along with less widely recognized losses. Return to a feudal society, of autocratic rule, hereditary privilege, and serfdom, is unthinkable. But recovery of the lost sense of living human community under God is imperative.

NOTES

[1] See the selected and helpfully edited bibliography in *Laymen's Work*, May, 1952, pp. 26-35 (World Council of Churches). The indispensable brief study of the changing uses of *vocation* exists only in German: Karl Holl, "Die Geschichte des Wortes Beruf," in his *Gesammelte Aufsätze*, III, 189-219. The most familiar studies in English are Max Weber, *The Protestant Ethic* (Eng. tr. Talcott Parsons), R. H. Tawney, *Religion and the Rise of Capitalism*, and various sections of Ernst Troeltsch, *The Social Teachings of the Christian Churches* (Eng. tr. Olive Wyon). Holl's study has been the mainstay of my own efforts to understand the development; but he deals much too hastily with patristic and early medieval thought. In citing source material for this chapter, therefore, I have given disproportionate emphasis to that section.

[2] This seems to fit best the testimony of the oldest Gospel record, Mark 16:1-8 (esp. v. 7; cf. Matt. 28:7), and the strange epilogue to the Fourth Gospel (John 21:1-23), if this can be regarded as originally independent of John 20. The oldest record of all, I Cor. 15:3-8, fits better with this picture than with one taken in detail from Mark 16:9-20, Matt. 28, or John 20. The sequence in Luke 24–Acts 1-2 looks like a combination of various traditions, including that represented by I Cor. 15:3-8.

[3] *To the Corinthians*, xix.2-3; xxi.1; xxxiii.4-8.

[4] *The Shepherd*, Vis. III; Sim. IX.

[5] Mand. II.4; Sim. II; cf. Vis. III.ix.2-6.

[6] Mand. IX.i.4-5; Sim. I, IV.5, IX.xx; Vis. III.vi. 5-7.

[6a] *Exhortation*, X.

[7] On this whole subject, see H. B. Workman, *The Evolution of the Monastic Ideal*, and for a much less favorable view, G. G. Coulton, *Five Centuries of Religion*.

[8] Athanasius, *Life of Antony*, 3, 50, 53; 14, 89, 93. Cf. The somewhat earlier injunctions of the *Apostolic Constitutions*, II. S3; IV. Z, 3, 11.

[9] *Ep.* ii, xiv; ccxxiii; xciv, cc, cciii, etc.

[10] Gregory Nazianzen, *Oration* xliii.63; Basil, *Ep.* xciv, cf. cxlii, cxliii.

[11] Basil, *Hexaemeron* III.1.

[12] *Longer Rules* or *Reg. Fus. Tract.* 7.

[13] *Ep.* xxii; *Reg. Fus. Tract.* xviii, xxii, esp. xxxvii-xxxviii; *Shorter Rules* or *Reg. Brev. Tract.* cxxviii, cclviii.

[14] *Reg. Fus. Tract.* xxxvii.

[15] H. Reuter, *Augustinische Studien*, 477 (quoted somewhat differently by K. E. Kirk, *The Vision of God*, 274, n. 2.). Karl Holl disagrees (*op. cit.* III, 200, n. 1).

[16] *Ep.* xxii; cf Augustine, *op. cit.*, 14, 16, 19-20.

[17] *City of God* XIX.v; cf. iii.

[18] XIX.xxiv; XIV.

[19] XVIII.ii, xxvii; etc.

[20] V.xi, xxiv; cf. xii-xv; XIX.xiv-xvii.

[21] XV.iv; XIX.v-ix, xxviii; XXI *passim*.

[22] XIV.xxviii; etc.

[23] XVIII.xlvii, xlix; etc.

[24] XVII.xlviii; XX.viii, ix.

[25] XV.iv, i-ii; XVII.xvi-xvii.

[26] *Rule* xxxiii-xxxiv, xlii, xlix-lv, lxxiii.

[27] viii, xxii, xxxv-xxxvi, xxxix-xli, xlviii, lxvi.

[28] Cf. Gregory, *Ep.* IV.xxxi, c.594—ed. Paris, 1675. The numbering of the Letters differs in various editions. See Gibbon, *Decline and Fall*, Ch.xxxi, xlv.

[29] Cf. *Ep.* I.v, vi, vii, xxiv-xxvi; XII.xxv.

[30] *Ep.* VIII.xi; XI.xxxi.

[31] *Pastoral Care* I.vii-ix; II.vi; cf. *Ep.* IV.viii.

[32] *Past. Care* II.vii.

[33] *Ep.* I.ii, xlii, lxx; XI.xli; XII.xxx.

[34] *Ep.* IV.xxxiii; VI.xx; XI.xxxiii, xli.

[35] I.xxxiv, xlv; III.xxxi; IV.vi; VII.xxvi; etc.

[36] I.ix, lxxi, lxxiii, lxxx; II.xxx; III.xliii; VI.xxxv; XI.xv-xvi; XII.ii-iii.

[37] I.xxxi; II.xvii, lviii; XI.xxvi, xxxviii; XII.v.

[38] I.viii; II.xxxi, xxxv; V.ix.

[39] III.viii, x; V.xxii; IX.xx; X.x-xi, xxiv; XI.x, xxiv; XII.x.

[40] III.xvii; V.xxiv; VI.xiii, xxiii, xxxv; VII.xxiii; X.1.

[41] II.xxi; III.x, xxxvi; V.i; VII.xiii; VII.Ind.II.xvi, xlv, liii; X.xv, xlii.

[42] I.xvii; II.ii, lx; III.xxiii, xxv-xxvii; IV.vi; V.x, cf.v-vi, lii-liv, lvii-lix; VII.11, xxiv, xxx; VII.Ind.II.lxiv, cxiii; IX.lii, lvi, lviii-lx; XI.ii; esp. XII.xxxi—a long letter to Augustine, his missionary bishop in Britain, answering many detailed questions.

[43] VII.xxx; IV.xxxii, xxxiv, xxxvi, xxxviii; VI.iv, xxiv, xxviii, xxx; VII.Ind.II.lxx; XI.xlvii.

[44] See *Nicene and Post-Nicene Fathers,* 2nd series, XII.120. The quotation from Augustine is in *City of God,* XVIII.xix. Cf. Gregory, *Ep.* V.xxix.

[45] Cf. his *Rule,* 2, 5, 6, 10.

[46] *Summa contra Gentiles* III.134; *Sum. theologiae* II.ii. q. 187; especially *Sum. de quolibet* VII.17—which Holl, in a rare lapse from accuracy, misunderstands, *Gesam. Aufsätze* III.203 n. 3.

[47] In his *Sum. theologiae moralis,* part III—e.g., III.viii, introd.; 2; etc.; cf. Holl, *op. cit.,* III.207 n. 6.

[48] *Defensor Pacis,* c.1384, Pt. III.ii. concl. 1, 2, 6, 8, 9, 14, 17, etc.

[48a] See especially his drastic treatises *On Divine Rule, On Civil Rule,* and *On the Church.*

[49] *Illustrations of Mediaeval Thought and Learning,* 255.

[50] By Gregory VII in 1080 (*Ep.* VII.xi, quoted in Mirbt, *Quellen zur Gesch. des Papsttums,* 2d ed., p. 112). In 1199, Innocent III refused permission for Bible reading by the laity in the Rhineland (*Ep.* II.141, 142, 235, in Mirbt, pp. 125-27); and similar actions were taken by popes,

emperors, and councils during the next three centuries (cf. Mirbt, pp. 142, 143, 153 f., 154 f., 173).

[51] E.g., Irenaeus, *Against Heresies,* IV.lxx; Augustine, *On the Predestination of the Saints,* xxxii-xxxiv, xxxviii-xli.

[52] So, e.g., before A.D. 225: I Clement xlvi.6, lix.2, lxv.2; II Clement i.8, ii.7, v.1, ix.4, 5,x.1; Barnabas xvi.9; Hermas, *The Shepherd,* Mand.IV.iii.4, 6; Sim. IX.xiv.5, xvii.4; Irenaeus, *Against Heresies,* IV. lxxvi, V.xxviii; Epistle to Diognetus vii.5; Tertullian, *To His Wife,* II.ii; *Scorpiace* xii; *On Monogamy* vi.

[53] Thus: Cyril of Jerusalem (d.c.386), *Catechetical Lectures,* procat. 9, II.1, III.2, cf. XVIII. 24; Basil of Caesarea (d.379), *Ep.* xxii.1; Gregory Nazianzen (d.391), *Oration* XXXVII,13,XL.20,25 (cf.17,28, on infant baptism), XLII.9; Gregory of Nyssa (d.ca. 395), *On Virginity,* introd.; Augustine (d.430), *On the Spirit and the Letter* xl, lviii, lx; *On Nature and Grace* v, xxxv; *On the Grace of Christ* xiii, xiv; *On the Predestination of the Saints* vii; *Retractations* I.xxiii.3, 4; Gregory I (d.604), *Homilies on Ezekiel* II.xiv (on Rev. 22:17, on Isa. 26:1, on Acts 1:1, on John 6:15); but cf. for a different interpretation of calling, *Homilies on the Gospels* II.xxxviii (on Matt.22:14).

[54] Karl Holl's word must not be taken literally: "This conception must have faded out completely when infant baptism developed" (*Gesam. Aufsatze* III.190). On this whole development, with especial reference to the "double standard" in medieval ethics, cf. Kenneth E. Kirk, *The Vision of God,* V, VI.

[55] *On Monogamy* xi.

[55a] *Stromata* VII.vii.

[56] *Catech. Lect.* V.3.

[57] *Or.* XL.14, 19.

[58] *Hom. on Ezek.* I.iii; II.xiv.

[59] Cf. *Pastoral Care* I.iv-vii.

[60] *Ibid.,* I.v, where men chosen as working pastors are *vocati.*

[61] On all this and the following section, Holl's discussion is of especial importance, and may well be read in conjunction with corresponding passages in Kirk, *The Vision of God.*

[62] Athanasius, *Life of Antony,* 2.

[63] *Ep.* xxii.

[64] *Ep.* xxxii.

[65] *Orat.* xxxvii.

[66] *On Virginity* xi, xxiv, viii, xxiii.

[67] *Ibid.,* introd. iii.

[68] *Ep.* X.xxxvii; cf. V.xlix, IX.xxxix, xliv, XI.lix.

[69] Cf. Sulpicius Severus, *Life of Martin,* iii.

[70] So Cyril of Jerusalem, *Catech. Lect.* I.3, III.3, 13; cf. X.1, XVII.33, 36-37; Gregory Nazianzen, *Orat.* XL.17; XLII.11—"being all soldiers of God."

[71] This paradox is characteristic of all Christian mysticism. A convenient brief example can be found in the late fourteenth-century

Theologia Germanica (Eng. trans., 1949), chaps. XIX-XXI, XXIII, XXVII-XXXIII, XXXIX, XLIII-XLVI, L-LIV.

[72] *On Virginity*, ii; cf. above, pp. 103-104.

[73] A brilliant statement of this principle in the terms of contemporary thinking forms a major part of Henri Bergson, *The Two Sources of Morality and Religion*.

[74] Holl, *op. cit.*, III, 205-8.

[75] The most convenient discussions in English include Max Weber, *The Protestant Ethic*, with various criticisms by H. M. Robertson and others; and R. H. Tawney, *Religion and the Rise of Capitalism*. In German, various sections of Holl's *Gesammelte Aufsätze*, I,239-87, 468-518, III,213-19, 385-436; and on Luther, the admirable study of Gustav Wingren, *Luthers Lehre vom Beruf*, much the best account that I know.

[76] H. R. Niebuhr, *The Kingdom of God in America*, 59 ff.

[77] On this development, see Tawney, *op. cit.*, chaps. III-IV; Holl, *op. cit.*, I,277-81, 500-518, III,279-82, 385-436; Max Weber, *The Protestant Ethic*; etc.

III

Work and Vocation
in American Industrial Society

ROBERT S. MICHAELSEN

Two essays of the Roman Catholic philosopher, Josef Pieper, have recently been translated from German under the title *Leisure—the Basis of Culture.* Dr. Pieper speaks on behalf of an ideal which has found very little acceptance in the American community. It would appear, rather, that the ideal of the American has been *"Work—the Basis of Culture."* No virtue has been so widely or consistently extolled in America as industry or diligence. Some have attempted to account for this by reference to our origins in an activistic Protestantism—a Protestantism which has stimulated the growth and expansion of an even more activistic capitalism.[1] It is no doubt true that Protestantism has never been able wholeheartedly to embrace the ideal "Leisure—the Basis of Culture." Protestantism—especially in its Reformed branches—has placed much more stress on the active life than on the contemplative life; and insofar as American origins are Protestant and Protestant activism has blessed the activities of economic enterprise, the American ideal can be explained in terms of our Protestant background.

It is necessary to add, however, that *economic* factors themselves have contributed to the development of the ideal. The growth of America can be understood in part in terms of the challenge of a virgin continent and an abundance of natural resources. The American who has met this challenge has not had time for leisure—nor has he had the inclinations to pursue the contemplative life, even if he had the time. If he has drawn upon an activistic Protestantism to support his work, he has shaped that Protestantism to meet his own needs. It might be more accurate to say, then, that out of the background of Protestantism *and* the pressures and challenges of the environment, the American has formulated an independent ideal which might be labeled "Yankee Enterprise" or the "American Gospel of Work." Thus the early Protestant ideal of capturing the world of work for the glory of God was replaced by the "Yankee" ideal of working for man's glory—or for one's own enhancement. Christian vocation became secularized. A Protestantism which set out to "spiritualize commerce" became so corrupted by the pressures of practical economics that it ended up by "commercializing the spirit."[2]

1. VOCATION IN AMERICA

In order to understand what has happened to the doctrine of Christian vocation in America, and what impact it has had on the approach to work in America, we need to go back at least to the Reformation. As has been indicated in the previous chapter, the leaders of this movement placed a renewed emphasis on the role of vocation in the life of the ordinary Christian, and—at the same time—they developed a different understanding of the meaning of vocation from that most commonly held in medieval Christianity. The distinction between religious and secular callings was no longer made by the Reformers. Man's response to God's call was understood in terms of worship and work. One becomes aware of God's call to him—or of his election by God—through the reading and hearing of the Word in Scripture and in the Christian community. He responds with acts of devotion and thanksgiving, and with the dedication of his whole being to the glory of God and the service of neighbor. All aspects of one's life are caught up in this response. One exercises his Christian vocation, then, as father, mother, son, or daughter, as citizen and as worker. Thus common work received a new importance by becoming integral to a person's total religious life.

This interpretation of Christian vocation came to be an accepted element in what can be called Reformation theology. Men like Luther and Calvin did not treat it systematically, but it occurs again and again in their writings. Many of those who followed these men were even more thorough and systematic in their treatment of Christian vocation than the Reformers themselves had been. Many of the confessions and catechisms of the Reformation period deal with vocation or calling—most frequently in the framework of God's acts in relation to men, but also in terms of man's response to those acts.[3] The early Puritans considered the idea of Christian vocation to be of sufficient importance to merit special treatises or lengthy discussions in their theological and devotional works. They distinguished between the general calling—God's Word expressed in and through Jesus Christ—and the particular or personal calling or vocation. The latter has two sides: (a) the individual awareness that God has addressed him, and (b) his response in terms of worship and the "practical" areas of daily living, including work. They insisted that the call is mediated through the community which stands in covenant relationship with God. Therefore, the personal calling is neither apprehended apart from the community of faith nor does it involve leaving that community—a community which lives in the midst of the world and carries on its work in the world. Among other things, this subjects the individual to community guidance and discipline in his calling—and therefore in his work. "Vocational guidance" is exercised by the community which stands in covenant relationship with God. Thus these men differed quite radically from the late medieval mystics referred to in the previous chapter. They were both less mystical and less individualistic. They were more concerned with God's acts—as revealed through His Word—than they were with practicing the way that leads to the vision of God. Thus the active life—not the contemplative life—was exalted. In this, I believe they were true followers of the Reformers, although they went beyond the Reformers in their understanding of the role of the community in covenant relation with God and in their systematic development of the doctrine of vocation.

Work, in early Puritan theory, was understood first of all as an area of the individual's calling, as a primary means of grateful response to God's grace in Jesus Christ. Second, it was considered to be an area for service to the community. The early Puritans consistently warned their fellows against the vicious temptation of covetousness and the pitfalls of prosperity. They did not accept the latter as being a *clear* sign of God's favor; it might be that, but it might also be a broad road leading to corruption and eventual destruction. The worker of this world must labor hard, but he must deal gingerly with the fruits of his labor. The notion that the worker should be free to go his own way, to pursue freely his own wealth and happiness, was soundly condemned by the early Puritans. Work—together with all other areas of life—should be subjected to divine sovereignty as known through God's Word and as interpreted by the community of the called.

Changes took place within seventeenth-century Puritanism, however, which paved the way for a sanctification of commercial activity in the late seventeenth and early eighteenth centuries. Industry came to be identified with righteousness, and idleness with sin. Utilitarianism as a primary motive to work—i.e., work as a way to heaven or to wealth or both—replaced an attitude of grateful response to God as primary incentive. Sensuality came to be regarded as a more fundamental sin than pride or covetousness. A communal ethic was supplanted by an individualistic ethic, as the covenant theology disintegrated.

In the eighteenth century, despite the pervasiveness and intensity of the Great Awakening in the thirties and forties, the Christian doctrine of vocation was even more fully secularized. Poor Richard's *Way to Wealth* is an indication of the ultimate extent to which this secularization went. The theologians of the period were little concerned with a doctrine of vocation. Their attention was turned increasingly toward what a later generation came to call "religious experience." Their ethic tended to be individualistic. This was especially true of those who were strongly influenced by pietism.

By the nineteenth century American Protestantism had almost completely succumbed to the American gospel of work. The religious life was freely and openly advocated as assuring (or even demanding) success. Service to God and service to Mammon were harmonized, as far as this was possible. "Calling" was interpreted almost entirely in terms of a highly emotional and personal experience of conversion—an experience which really had little direct bearing on one's daily work. Insofar as a change of ways was called for it was conceived of largely in terms of "religious" work, i.e., doing good through charitable, missionary, and reform organizations, or in terms of personal and petty morality —swearing, drinking, etc.

Toward the end of the nineteenth century the leaders of the Social Gospel Movement began to call a halt to the sanctification of wealth-getting. They discerned a distinct incompatibility between the gospel of work and wealth and the gospel of Jesus Christ. They were also aware of the inadequacies of the individualistic ethic of previous generations. They called for a renewed appreciation of the social nature of sin and salvation. Although they did very little directly to reconstruct the doctrine of vocation they did help to lay some of the ground work for that reconstruction by their criticism of the individualism, optimism, and materialism of the gospel of work—and especially of the theories of classical economics—and by renewed appreciation for man's social nature.

Recently American theologians have turned increasingly toward the task of revivifying the doctrine of vocation, being spurred on by the work of their European brethren, by a renewed interest in the Reformers, and by the needs of our industrial society. This task is a difficult one, especially in view of the problems created by industrialism and the prevalence of a secular doctrine or secular doctrines of vocation in our past and our present.

2. THE AMERICAN GOSPEL OF WORK

In America the doctrine of Christian vocation gave way to the American gospel of work. This gospel has played an important role in American life and economy. It is central to our discussion since any attempt to reinterpret the doctrine of Christian vocation for contemporary American industrial society must take the gospel of work into account, and also because of its influence in the development of American industrialism.

The basic affirmation or assumption of the gospel of work is that hard work will gain all that one needs in this life—the needs of life usually being thought of in materialistic terms. The gospel is optimistic and individualistic. Any hard-working man can make his way without the help of society, the state, or his fellows. Society is so constructed that the "way up" is always open to the man of ability and determination. Thus it is obvious that anyone who does not make it is either lazy or inefficient or both. This gospel has been well buttressed in America by the prevailing tenets of the classical or *laissez-faire* economists: (1) the assumption that the economic sphere is primary in man's life and work and that all that a man does is guided basically by his selfish desire to enhance his material welfare; (2) the confidence that the individual can gain his way by following his selfish urges; (3) the optimism that society's interests will be best served when individuals are allowed or encouraged to pursue their own selfish interests; and (4) the view that the primary function of the state is to "let the individual alone" in that pursuit and to protect the property which he accumulates.

The industrial system which has grown so rapidly in America in the last seventy-five years, and which now plays such a dominant role in the American economy, was organized in large part by men who were converts to the gospel of work and believers in the theories of classical economics. Thus the worker has been approached as a selfish individual who would pursue rationally his own material interests if given the proper opportunity. Industrial managers and executives have frequently looked upon the worker as an "economic man" or a "slot-machine man."[4] They have accepted the "rabble hypothesis"[5] in their view of man and society. Thus the worker has frequently been regarded as little more than a machine to be reconstructed as a single-purpose, high-speed machine tool. He is an automaton which responds to monetary stimulus like a candy-vending machine. Therefore, if work is to be drained from him, he must be constantly enticed by ever better wage incentives.

Labor has been approached as a commodity which is offered for sale by the working man and paid for by the employer. Its sole usefulness has been seen in terms of what it can produce economically. It is true there is a real sense in which labor is a commodity—that is, a part of the production costs of any enterprise. But to persist in treating the laboring *man*—the flesh-and-blood human being—as a commodity is to cheapen his own idea of the importance of his work and to drive him into a rebellious state which will ultimately prove harmful to management and to all of society. Labor is another name for a human activity which goes with life itself and which "in its turn is not produced for sale but for entirely different reasons, nor can that activity be detached from the rest of life, be stored or mobilized. . . . Labour power . . . cannot be shoved about, used indiscriminately, or even left unused, without affecting also the human individual who happens to be the bearer of the peculiar commodity."[6] The tendency of the concept "economic man" has been to dispose of the physical, psychological, and moral entity "man." This working man needs to be recognized as a *citizen* in the industrial enterprise and made to feel that he has a role in the total process which is not merely economic. His work needs to be recognized as an integral part of his total life, and to be given some status beyond that which results from its place as a highly specialized and minute contribution to the total production and profit of the industrial enterprise.

Both the gospel of work and classical economics have been highly individualistic. The industrial manager who has been raised under their influence has generally approached his workers and his industry in individualistic terms. Traditionally, industry —from scientific management on—has used individual production quotas and individual incentive wages; has, in other words, approached the worker in terms of his highly specialized task rather than in terms of his role in a collective process. Undoubtedly it has been and is necessary for industry to use production quotas and incentives of some sort, but much damage is done—in the form of worker hostility, lower production, etc.—by setting these quotas and incentives wholly in terms of the *individual*. This tends to cut him off from his fellows, or to set him in competition with them. Competition may act as an incentive in production, but individual competition does not always produce this result. The individualism of a preindustrial era has, in many cases, blinded the industrial manager to the fact that his enterprise is a social community, and that his workers are members of that community—looking upon their work, or attempting to look upon their work not only in terms of their own individual effort and gain, but also in terms of their membership in the "team" and their relationship to the total production process.

Another aspect of the gospel of work and classical economics which has been influential in the approach to the industrial enterprise is an abundant optimism—an optimism regarding the individual's abilities to lift himself by his own bootstraps and about the present and future state of society. Thus it has sometimes been pointed out that any worker could make his way to the top of the enterprise if he worked hard enough, just as any American boy might anticipate the possibility of becoming President of the United States. The industrialist could point to the dramatic examples of such men as Andrew Carnegie and Henry Ford, just as the citizen might cite those of Abraham Lincoln or James Garfield. The leaders of the Scientific Management Movement liked to point out that under their system of job specialization and individual incentive and enterprise, the worker was, as it were, set up in business for himself and could prove his worth as he pursued his specific task with all his diligence—being assured that a bonus awaited him. Furthermore, they asserted that in this type of setup the best interests of the worker, the management, and society as a whole would be served. The worker would receive his bonus and the chance of advancement, management would make a substantial profit which might be used to expand the industry, and society could look forward to an ever higher standard of living. In a sense, many felt that the new age—the new Utopia—had dawned or would soon come.

Finally, because of the overwhelming emphasis upon the economic sphere which characterized much of the American "ideology" of the nineteenth century, and because of the deep involvement in mechanical matters necessitated by the rapidly advancing industrialism of the late nineteenth and early twentieth centuries, the organization of work in the industrial enterprise has been approached almost entirely from the standpoint of the most efficient use of the machine in the achievement of the highest level of production and the best rate of profit. To use Scientific Management as an example again, the leaders of this movement concentrated almost entirely on the technological or physical aspect of the plant against the background of production and profit. The introduction of scientific management methods into a plant meant more and more concentration on the work process itself. Little consideration was given to the most efficient use of man the worker—to his needs, interests, and attitudes. He was approached as a solitary individual to be geared into the total process, and to be appealed to through economic incentives. But, unfortunately, the most efficient use of the machine may result in a highly inefficient use of the man—and thus eventuate in harmful psychological and physiological effects and a lower rate of output.[7] One of the largest problems which needs to be faced in the industrial enterprise is that of giving the worker a sense of his participation in the whole, of giving him a feeling of status and function, of cultivating in him what has been called "the managerial attitude." Very little effort has been made in this direction. It is true that as the century advanced, more emphasis was placed on "the human side of industry" by the Personnel Management Movement, for example, and by other movements or developments emphasizing human relations in industry. In many cases, however, these movements have been more concerned with schemes of an "extra-curricular" nature designed to make workers "happy" than with the problem of human relations *on the job*—although increasing consideration has been given to this problem in recent years. It is a hopeful sign that more and more managers are recognizing the importance of approaching workers as total human beings rather than just as "hands." At a postwar convention of the National Association of Manufacturers, Clarence Francis, chairman of General Foods, observed:

> You can buy a man's time, you can buy a man's physical presence at a given place; you can even buy a measured number of skilled muscular motions per hour or day. But you cannot buy enthusiasm; you cannot buy initiative; you cannot buy loyalty; you cannot buy devotion of hearts, minds, and souls. You have to earn these things. . . . It is ironic that Americans—the most advanced people technically, mechanically, and industrially—should have waited until a comparatively recent period to inquire into the most promising single source of productivity, namely, the human will to work. It is hopeful, on the other hand, that the search is now under way.[8]

Thus today, for example, an increasing emphasis is being placed on the magic word "communication" in an effort to win over the worker's enthusiasm, loyalty, etc. Still it is difficult to overcome the atmosphere of hostility which has come about as a result of seventy-five years of predominance of a certain type of approach to the worker. Furthermore, too much of the recent interest in the "human side of industry" suggests the *manipulation* of men as workers for ultimate ends to allow one to have a wholly confident attitude as to its beneficial possibilities.

Progress is taking place, no doubt, but looking back over a century of industrialism, it appears that the problem of fitting the worker to the job and the job to the worker, and the related problem of integrating workers as individuals and as members of social groups into the total enterprise, have received little consideration as compared with the question of the most efficient use of the machine and the levels of production and profit. As a result the worker's opportunities for creativity and freedom in his work have noticeably declined, up until recent times at least. This again would seem to indicate that many of the problems connected with work in contemporary industrial society are not inherent in industrialism itself, but have resulted from the ways in which the industrial enterprise has been organized and operated. I do not wish to suggest that a change in approach to the industrial enterprise will solve all the problems. Far from it. As we shall indicate, many problems remain and will undoubtedly continue to remain in various forms. But it does appear that there are certain ways in which we might move to infuse more meaning into work in the industrial enterprise. These ways we shall also consider more fully later.

3. INDUSTRY FABRICATES THE WORKER

An understanding of the conditions of work in American industrial society is even more important to the attempt to make the doctrine of Christian vocation relevant for contemporary America than is some awareness of the nature and role of the American gospel of work. We need to begin, insofar as this is possible, with some comprehension of the facts—with a real appreciation for the context in which millions of Americans work.

The social historian, looking back upon the United States, recognizes the fundamental significance of two revolutions in American society—the political revolution of the eighteenth century and the industrial revolution which really took hold of American society during and following the Civil War and which reached its fullest fruition in the mass production process of the twentieth century. It is possible that future historians will find that the latter was far more profound in the changes it wrought and much more pervasive in its world-wide influence than the former.

Between 1860 and 1900 America leaped from fourth place as a manufacturing nation to first in all the world. During this period the machine rose to its dominant place in industry, capital or economic and industrial power came to be concentrated more and more in the large corporations, the trusts, and the holding companies, the number of wage earners increased in much greater proportion than did the total population, and the rift between capital and labor grew in width and depth. The turn of the century saw the extensive development of the mass-production process—i.e., the centralization and rationalization of machine production in the factory system. Thus the two primary factors in the growth of industrialism have been the extensive development of the machine and the centralization and rationalization of machine production in the factory system. In America these factors have been accompanied by the use of capitalistic methods in both manufacture and marketing and by the rise of a large industrial laboring class and the continuing growth of a capitalist class.

The mass-production process is characterized by the production in quantity of a standardized product by means of a rationalized, specialized, and integrated system of production. The production of the product is broken down into a number of operations. Each of these operations is performed preferably by a machine—since the efficiency of the total process depends in large part upon the extensive use of labor-saving machinery—or by a machine and a worker, or by the worker himself. The total process is so integrated that a great number of individual and highly specialized operations contribute to the assembly of the final product. The gradual perfection of this process has accounted in large part for America's tremendous advance in manufacturing in the twentieth century. This is most evident in that area of manufacturing which has shown the most phenomenal growth—the automobile industry.

Any consideration of the conditions of work in the twentieth century must begin—and, one might add, end—with an analysis of the effects which this advancing industrialism has had upon work and the worker. By doing so we may well expose ourselves to the charge of partiality, i.e., concentrating too much upon industrial work and the industrial worker to the exclusion of many whose work is outside the industrial realm. Our justification for this apparent exclusiveness is twofold: (1) Whereas the "industrial enterprise" actually comprises no more than approximately one fourth of the total economic activity of the United States, it is the most symbolic, representative, and decisive aspect of that economy, and its influence penetrates far beyond the immediate enterprise itself so that even the nonindustrial worker has not escaped the influences of industrialism.[9] Many large-scale nonmanufacturing enterprises now utilize the methods of industrial organization, i.e., rationalization of organization and equipment. (2) As a practical matter of procedure, it is much easier to generalize about the worker in industrialism than about workers not immediately employed in industrial enterprises. We shall attempt, however, to discuss some of the nonindustrial groups.

What then have been the effects of the growth of the industrial enterprise and the mass production process upon work and the worker?

The philosopher A. N. Whitehead[10] observes that with the advance of industrialism we have witnessed the gradual coming to an end of "a mode of sociological functioning which from the beginning of the sixteenth century onwards has been slowly rising to dominance within the European races. I mean," he continues, "that trend to free, unfettered, individual activity in craftsmanship, in agriculture, and in all mercantile transactions." The "sturdy individualism" which was fostered by conditions in the west from the sixteenth century on is gradually giving way under the pressures of an advancing industrialism which has, in many ways, seriously undercut or limited the freedom of the individual worker. Thus, today, in any large city in the industrial west, "almost everyone is an employee, employing his working hours in exact ways predetermined by others. Even his manners may be prescribed. So far as sheer individual freedom is concerned, there was more diffused freedom in the city of London in the year 1633, when Charles the First was king, than there is today in any industrial city in the world." This is a serious charge. If it is true it is certainly the most damaging effect industrialism has had on work. The validity of Whitehead's observations will no doubt be challenged by those who are sincerely convinced that modern industrialism has enhanced rather than circumscribed the freedom of the individual. It must be admitted that it is next to impossible to compare, in a "scientific" manner, the conditions of work in one generation with those of another. We who would bring some standard of judgment to bear upon our contemporary scene are constantly tempted to idealize some period in the past (most frequently the era of "craftsmanship") and to regard subsequent development as being something of a fall. Nevertheless, we cannot discount the opinions of such shrewd observers of history as Whitehead and others. In what sense do the conditions in contemporary industrialism bear out these opinions?

The mass-production principle is a social as well as a mechanical principle. It is a principle of human organization. The environment of work has been greatly changed. The worker has been brought into a large, complex, and impersonal organization. Whereas in a former and earlier period he may have worked for himself on a farm or in a small shop or hired out to an employer alongside of whom he worked day by day, or at most worked with a gang of ten to one hundred employees, today he finds himself part of a labor force frequently running into the thousands.[11] In this situation he has no direct contact with the "big boss," being hired by a personnel director or by one of his assistants and working under a foreman or a gang boss. He may be little more than an industrial private far removed from the general and with little or no contact with the colonels, the majors, and the captains. This is true even of most of those workers who are employed in small plants of one hundred employees or less. Their plants are parts of larger organizations. They depend on a larger productive process and chain of command for the materials they work on, the nature and amount of their output, and the usages to which the products they form will be put. Their work means little apart from that productive process and chain of command to which they are related.

The atmosphere of the industrial enterprise is impersonal, as far as the work process itself is concerned. The worker is geared into the production process. It is true that he is thrown into contact with a large number of fellow workers, but this contact may be intimate and personally rewarding only on an *informal* basis, or in organizations outside the plant itself. Furthermore, the worker is not doing *his* work; he is not working on his property and with his tools. That with which he mixes his labor does not become his; nor does he put his mark on it, since a highly standardized form of work is required of him.

The mass production process, then, changes the type of work a man may do, and also requires him to adjust himself to an entirely new social environment. This process shatters cultural patterns, traditional forms of relationship between man and his society, and between man and his family. He is thrown into a new, complex, and interdependent society or community of work. In such a society opportunities for personal initiative have not always been abundantly in evidence.

The worker in the industrial enterprise finds himself attached to but a small segment of that enterprise. The task upon which he works is greatly narrowed in contrast to a former period. If he runs a machine, he most likely does not service and repair it— this being a job of other specialists. If he takes away from a machine, he does not run it, and he has little opportunity even to know how it runs—except what knowledge he might gain from observation.

In this situation only the most shrewd and wide-awake observer will be able to understand how his task fits into the whole and to approach some comprehension of the total process. The ordinary worker will not be encouraged to gain this kind of insight—thus he will have neither the incentive nor the opportunity to do so. It is not necessary for the private to understand the details of the battle plan. He will serve well if he understands his own task and performs it with dispatch. This fragmentation of work would appear to make it exceedingly difficult for the individual to gain satisfaction from the daily task in itself.

The mass-production process has been effective only insofar as it has maintained a high rate of production and has produced at a profit. These appear to be inherent requirements of the industrial enterprise. Thus the worker in the industrial enterprise has frequently found himself subordinated to production and profit. His work has meaning in the eyes of his employer only as it contributes to the end product. Frequently this has meant that *he* has meaning only as he enhances productivity.

The worker who would identify himself with his work has thus faced the necessity of attempting to identify himself with the total process. This has been difficult if not impossible to accomplish—both because of the size and complexity of the enterprise, as we have indicated, and because of the fact that the worker has had no easily visible stake in the level of production or profit. Some industrial managers have attempted to surmount this barrier by showing a greater interest in the worker as a person and by devising schemes of profit sharing. In recent times more interest has been shown in the "human factor" in industry in an effort to give the worker a fuller sense of his own identity and his stake in the industrial enterprise. In some cases, no doubt, personnel management programs, profit-sharing schemes, and other devices, have enhanced the worker's identification of himself with the productive process. Unfortunately, however, many of these real improvements in industrial relations made by management have been regarded by workers as gifts extended to them rather than actions based on a recognition of workers' rights. Thus they have not always accomplished the end of securing a fuller identification of the worker with the industrial enterprise.

It is true also that certain labor unions have shown an increasing interest in the areas of production and profit and have been somewhat successful in bringing about a closer identification of the interests of the worker and manager. Nevertheless, the fact remains that anyone who would speak to the industrial worker about exercising his Christian vocation in his work must first begin with an understanding of his subjection to a large production process over which he has little or no control and in which he is able to find little opportunity for the expression of his whole self.

4. WORK AS A MACHINE OPERATION

Frequently the worker in the industrial enterprise is closely attached to the machine, and he may find himself not only subordinated to production and profit, but to the machine as well. It must be indicated, however, that the effects of the machine on work and the worker have been varied and complicated.

They are difficult to assess accurately, but an attempt to get some idea of those effects must be made.

Possibly the most obvious effect of the use of the machine is the replacement of manual labor. On the one hand, this has meant a decrease in the amount of sheer physical drudgery associated with work in a preindustrial society. It has also made possible the shortening of the hours of labor and thus has afforded an opportunity for more leisure time. Furthermore, by enhancing productivity many times, it has reduced the amount of work necessary in fashioning the product. On the other hand, the machine has replaced many, if not most, of the skills of preindustrial society. At the same time new skills have become necessary in the manufacture of machinery and in its operation and organization. The use of the machine in the mass-production process has required the development of many new skills. Some of these are manual. But perhaps a majority of them are not manual but technical and theoretical—consisting in knowledge of the principles and processes of mass production. Some of the required skills are also social—consisting in skill in the organization of men for work in a close group and in fitting together their operation, their speed, and their abilities.

In many cases, the use of the machine has meant a subordination of all but the most skilled workers and those in executive or administrative positions to the machine itself. The machine operator must adjust himself to the "demands" of the machine. This is even more necessary in the case of the worker whose primary responsibility consists in "taking away" from a machine which is operated by someone else or entirely automatic in its operation, and of the worker who has a specific task in the assembling of products which machines have shaped. The situation of the assembly worker is worth special notice since "among . . . factory occupations, assembly jobs are by far the most numerous."[12] Such a worker has little or no control over the speed and manner of his work—and thus little or no opportunity for the use of his own initiative. Thus it has been argued that the violation of the essential human rhythm by trying to conform it to machine rhythm constitutes the real degradation of mechanized industry.[13] Man the worker is not master. He must adjust himself to the machine; he is not in control. It is necessary to point out, however, that workers have always had to adjust themselves to the "otherness," the giveness or factuality of their materials. Nevertheless, in a preindustrial society, many have had some choice as to the way in which the work was to be done; they have not been forced to subordinate themselves to an "iron master." Furthermore, what mechanical assistance they made use of—in the form of tools, for example—enabled them to extend their own control over the materials upon which they worked and to enhance their own skill and productivity. The automatic machine, however, leaves little choice to the worker. It is not an extension of him; he is an extension to it. The same thing applies to the assembly-line worker. On the other hand, the operator of the semiautomatic machine, or even more the user of the "mobile" machine, may have more of an opportunity for an extension of his own power and control. The crane operator or the train engineer may enjoy a sense of power and prestige because of the nature of his machine and his relationship to that machine.

Some of the severest critics of industrialism have charged that man's relationship to the machine and the whole industrial enterprise almost inevitably produces monotony, and, in many cases, mental collapse. One may conclude that boredom and mental breakdown both are to be found among workers in modern industry, but one need not conclude that they are caused solely, or even principally, by the conflict between man and machines. It is also necessary to point out that it seems almost impossible to eliminate an element of drudgery in any occupation. Work suggests the overcoming of a resistant force of some sort, which is outside the self. This almost inevitably will have its boring aspects, although it is evident that the amount of boredom will vary with the "atmosphere" or setting in which the work is done.

The evidence gathered to date is not conclusive on the amount of detrimental influence caused by the worker's association with the machine. Wyatt and Fraser concluded that "the amount of boredom bears some relation to the degree of mechanization of the task. It is less liable to occur when (a) the work is entirely automatic. . . ." It is also less likely (b) "when attention is entirely concentrated on the task. . . . It is most marked in semi-automatic processes which require enough attention to prevent mind wandering, but not enough for the complete absorption of mental activity." Therefore, the conclusion is that the amount of boredom bears *some* relation to the degree of mechanization and not that boredom is caused by mechanization, *ipso facto*. Mayo has added that these conclusions reached by Wyatt and Fraser can be "extensively confirmed by the experiences of industry in the United States."[14]

On the basis of one of the most extensive research projects in an industrial plant—that carried on by Mayo and his associates at the Hawthorne Plant of Western Electric in the early '30's—Mayo concluded that there is no great evidence "of that 'deadening' effect of machine-minding or routine work which literary critics commonly suppose to be the chief problem of a mechanical age."[15] One of Mayo's associates, F. J. Roethlisberger, also pointed out that this study failed to sustain the assumption that mechanization has made a bored automaton of the worker. "Most of the tests," he pointed out, "were conducted with workers engaged in semi-automatic tasks in which boredom, according to some, is most likely to appear. Yet there was little evidence, from a study of either their work behaviour or verbal behaviour, that monotony in any simple sense could characterize their response to the work."[16] Thus the evidence is inconclusive.

Undoubtedly it would be instructive to add to this rather impersonal account by the scientific ("objective") observer the personal testimonies of those who have worked in the industrial enterprise. Many have found this type of work to be very deadening in its effects, and some of these individuals have given rather full and dramatic expression to their feelings on the subject.[17] On the other hand, it is impossible to say exactly how many people have not been particularly bothered by boredom and monotony but have found a real sense of satisfaction in their work in industry. Nevertheless, the problems of boredom and monotony in the industrial enterprise cannot be lightly dismissed. Furthermore, boredom and monotony in themselves are merely the negative aspects of something which is more fundamental. Their existence in any appreciable degree points to the more serious charge that much of the work of the industrial enterprise is of such a nature as to fail in calling forth the best that is in the worker, and to fail to give much opportunity for the satisfaction of the desire or urge to do something meaningful, stimulating, and satisfying in one's work.

5. LEISURE, UNEMPLOYMENT, AND CLASS

Since, in many cases, it has been impossible for the worker to find much real emotional satisfaction in his highly specialized task in the industrial enterprise, he has frequently turned outside of that enterprise in search for that satisfaction. He has turned to leisure-time activities, to voluntary associations with his fellow employees, and to his paycheck. The concentration upon leisure time and association with one's fellows may have some beneficial results. Many interpreters of the industrial scene have looked to leisure-time activities as the primary source of meaning and satisfaction in the worker's life. Is the worker bored by his work? Does he fail to find meaning there? Let him turn to leisure-time endeavors. This type of approach appears to me to be an escape hatch without too much merit in answering questions about the meaning of work. It appears to me that the right use of one's leisure cannot solve all the problems that arise from one's work. Furthermore, the sundering of work itself from all meaningful activities is not healthy—especially in view of the central importance of man's work for his psychological satisfaction.

Because the worker in the industrial enterprise has had to rely upon that enterprise for his work, and indirectly for any social prestige which might be attached to that work—because he is dependent upon, and subordinate to, the productive process of the large industrial enterprise—the fact or possibility of unemployment has been an almost constant threat to his economic and emotional security. Apart from the enterprise he has found it extremely difficult to exist. He possesses none of the essential tools of production except his own labor and that is of no value to him apart from a functioning industrial enterprise. He finds it next to impossible to strike out on his own in an effort to support himself and his family. Subsistence farming, for example, is all but impossible in an industrial society even if the industrial worker might have the skill for it—which is a slight possibility.

The threat or reality of unemployment is not only economic in its effects; it is psychological or emotional as well. The worker who has been cut off from the enterprise faces the loss of status and prestige in his society—since these still are in large part attached to one's work—as well as order and stability in his own life. Studies of the unemployed have shown this to be a large factor in their lives.[18]

A problem closely related to that of unemployment is that of technological displacement—which may or may not result in loss of work, but which certainly results in a change of work, a change which also involves a psychological and frequently an economic adjustment. As the use of machines increases, and as machinery is constantly reorganized and reordered in the industrial enterprise, so as to achieve the fullest efficiency in production, technological displacement remains an ever-constant threat and reality.

To these threats to the security of the worker one might add the element of "factory mobility." This is evident in the conversions that take place within factories to meet new requirements of production—a new model car or a tank instead of a car—and in the actual movement of a factory from one place to another. These and other factors compel the worker to move here and there both within the plant and outside of it.

Finally, the growth of the industrial enterprise has given rise to new classes or groups—collective units in society, the distinctive nature of which is determined by the type of work done in the new enterprise. Most obvious, perhaps, is the growth of a large class or group of mass-production workers—the industrial "proletariat." The members of this class or group consist of those laborers on the lower rung of the industrial enterprise—the tenders of semiautomatic machines, the assembly-line workers, etc. Less obvious, but almost as noteworthy, is the rise of an industrial middle class—the technicians, the foremen, accountants, middle managers, etc.[19] As the industrial enterprise becomes more highly specialized, an increasing number of "middle men" or middle managers becomes necessary to its efficient operation. At the top, so to speak, are the industrial executives on the one hand, and the union executives or leaders on the other hand.

The effects of industrialism upon work and the worker have been many. We have attempted to list some of them. One's ultimate conclusion as to their beneficial or detrimental nature would appear to depend a good deal upon one's personal judgment. Undoubtedly, the initial effects were quite detrimental to the worker. Fortunately, the "satanic mill" of the late eighteenth and early nineteenth centuries is no longer with us. The conditions of the worker have improved immeasurably in the last one hundred years. But many problems remain. Many of these may not be entirely inherent in the industrial enterprise itself, but may stem in part from the manner in which the machine and the techniques of mass production have been utilized. There are those who claim that industrial mechanization itself is neutral, but that the manner in which it has been and is used is of utmost importance. Mayo has written, for example, that, "mechanization itself is of no great importance in an industry that sets itself, intelligently and diligently, to discover what human changes of method must accompany the introduction of repetitive methods of work. . . . With the institution of adequate researches, physiological, psychological, social, society has nothing to fear from industrialized mechanization."[20] Mechanization is a dangerous or a beneficial weapon, depending upon its use.

Some are inclined to place the blame for many of the inadequacies of the work situation in contemporary industrialism at the door of the capitalistic system as much or more than at that of industrialism or the machine. The Hammonds, for example, concluded—perhaps overoptimistically—that if the machine system had been introduced in an age when the workers con-

trolled the means of production, the results would have been
much more beneficial to both worker and community. Stuart
Chase has written that "so long as the force which owns the
factory has no interest in labour, save as a commodity, the workman is distinctly worse off than before. If, however, the force . . .
regards the workman as a human being for whose benefit the
wheels of industry are principally turning, he may well stand
to gain more than he has lost."[21] It is highly possible that the
human factors surrounding work, including the ways in which
it is organized socially as well as mechanically, and the relation
between employer and employee, are more important than the
mechanical factors in their direct effect upon the work and the
worker. For example, Ellsworth concluded on the basis of his
study of the "New Freedom Products Company" that, "despite
the evidence that changes in equipment—so-called technological
changes—have been at the roots of social change on a large scale
in western society, this element seems to have had relatively
little effect upon the social relationships within this company.
On the whole, changes in the *use* of machines, that is, in technological norms and rules, seem to have been more important
than changes in the machines themselves."[22] Further analysis of
worker reaction supports this conclusion.

6. HOW THE WORKER REACTS

Few workers can escape the influence and demands of industrialism. Obviously some are more involved than others. Those
who are most intimately involved in the industrial enterprise
have been forced to swim within it or sink outside of it—have
been forced to submit their work to its demands or lose their
livelihood and citizenship outside of it. How have they reacted
to this demand?

Some have attempted to resist industrialism in an effort to
maintain a grip on their vested interest in a particular type of
work which may be called preindustrial or to preserve the *status
quo* at a particular stage of industrial development. The most
dramatic instance of this type of resistance is found in the case
of the early machine breakers—those who invaded the plant and

attempted to destroy it. This radical type of action has not been very common, however. For the most part resistance has been far more subtle and less direct. The workers have resisted the speed of the industrial enterprise through adherence to informally agreed upon quotas of production. Even the nonunionized workers have restricted output under the pressure of this informal type of agreement. Workers have also expressed some fear of the machine, fear stemming basically from the fact that it might invade their work, changing it or doing away with what they have adjusted themselves to. Technological advance has been resisted, or if not resisted wholeheartedly, efforts have been made to control it so that acquired skills would not become obsolete. In general it would appear that the worker is not basically opposed to mechanical advance—he may, on the contrary, be all for it—but he fears it when he is not certain what it will do to *his* work, his place in the enterprise, his status in the industrial community, and his income. Unfortunately, in some cases, technological advance has been forced upon the worker without any effort to obtain his understanding and co-operation. When this has happened he has resisted, and if he has failed in this resistance, he has done all in his power to maintain his place, his vested interests—by forcing upon management, through his union, rules which protect him as the advance is made.

The worker in the industrial enterprise has found himself subordinated to production and profit, regulated by the tempo of the machine and the assembly line, with little ownership of the means of production, and in a very unequal relationship to the employer. He might be told that he has the power—in the possession of his ability to work—to work where he wants, to bargain for the purchase of his labor, and to climb the industrial ladder by his diligence. On the other hand, the realities of his situation frequently have failed to convince him of the truth of these confident assertions. He has had to work where he could at the wage he could get. He has frequently been persuaded that advance in the industrial enterprise occurs more in terms of favoritism than in terms of reward for genuine effort. He has been confused, disillusioned, and frustrated. To find strength which he has not possessed in himself, he has turned to collective effort—to joining with his fellow workers in a common attempt to get meaning from work, assurance or order, and economic advance. On the one hand, this collective approach has taken the form of an informal social organization in the industrial enterprise. On the other hand, it has taken the form of a formal organization in the trade or labor union. Almost every industrial plant will have several of the informal type of organizations.[23] Any new worker soon learns that there are certain group standards and practices to which he must conform or become a social outcast. For the most part these represent efforts to find strength as a group which cannot be found individually. The industrial manager who hopes to get some real co-operation from his workers will not be wise to resist this organization. He will probably have much more success as he attempts to understand it and work with it.

The formal organization in the labor union is much more obvious. As is commonly known, the number of unionized workers has increased greatly in the last half century, with the most spectacular growth taking place within the last two decades. Early efforts at organization in the period following the Civil War were not at all successful except among a few of the skilled workers. The most successful labor organization up to the 1930's was the American Federation of Labor, a federation of craft unions. In the '30's most of the large-scale industrial enterprises were successfully organized on an industry-wide basis. The Congress of Industrial Organizations has been most successful in bringing these industry-wide unions together in one large organization. Today the largest unions are those connected with such industries as steel and automobile manufacture. According to latest census reports, the number of unionized workers ranges between fourteen and sixteen million—this out of a total labor supply of approximately forty-five million in nonagricultural pursuits. Thus it can be seen that still only a minority of workers belong to labor unions. Nevertheless, most of the large-scale manufacturing industries have been organized.

The most obvious goal of the unions has been the improvement of the economic status of the worker and the regulation of hours of work. The leadership of the American Federation of Labor has consistently emphasized "trade-unionism pure and simple," that is, hours and wages. Beyond this, the unions have been concerned with such matters as job protection, regulation of output, control of technological change, seniority, and many other items which come under the heading of "the rights of the worker." It would appear that union leadership has generally operated under the assumptions of the hypothesis "economic man." It has concentrated on questions of wage rate with the confidence that this is the area of fundamental concern to the worker and with the certainty that if the worker can receive more and more of the economic pie, he will be happy. Thus the interests of the workers frequently have been set in opposition to the interests of the industry. This has brought about an almost continuous state of civil warfare—hot or cold—in many of the industrial enterprises. In many instances, union leadership has made little effort to come to grips with the basic nature of the industrial enterprise, and to help fit the worker into that enterprise in meaningful fashion and in co-operation with management. It must be admitted, however, that unions have not been encouraged by management to do this sort of thing. Furthermore, certain present-day union leaders are showing an increasing interest in the total productive process and its relation to the worker.

Much worker reaction to industrialism can be described in terms of an almost constant quest for security through whatever means could be used—and especially through the union and government. Apparently one of the primary needs of a man is some sense of certainty that his work has some permanence as well as significance. This need is felt both in economic and psychological terms. The worker's experience in the industrial enterprise has been such as to persuade him that opportunity is not unlimited, that success is not always the reward of industry or diligence, that the work situation in which he finds himself is not an open situation but one with fairly prescribed limits. Any effort to persuade him that he has kinship with the pioneer who faced unlimited opportunities if he were willing to exploit them would probably be scoffed at by the industrial worker. He is concerned with security. He wants to do all that he can to be certain of his work, his income, his future.

Finally, it seems evident that the worker's reaction to industrialism cannot be fully understood in terms of the concept "economic man." Possibly we have seen the "end of economic man" and now must think in terms of the "future of industrial man."[24] At any rate, it appears that although much of the approach to the worker—both by industrialists and union leaders—has been guided by the "myth" of "economic man," still the over-all reaction of the worker has demonstrated his basic recognized and unrecognized interest in far more than material reward. He seeks much more out of work than his paycheck. He wants some sense of his role in the total enterprise—a feeling that his work means something in itself, and that there is a future in it beyond the tangible financial return. He longs for a place in the industrial community—some satisfaction of his urges as a social individual. Possibly he would also like a fuller voice in the decision-making that takes place in the industrial community, and some sense of responsibility for the condition and use of industrial production.[25] Studies of industrial workers —such as that made at the Western Electric Plant—seem to indicate that when the worker feels that he is getting some of these things, he finds meaning and joy in his work almost regardless of economic incentive. It is interesting to note, for example, that when the workers who were approached in this particular study at Western Electric became confident that the researchers were not interested in getting more work out of them, they reacted by producing more merely because they felt that at least someone was concerned about them, their problems, and their work. This appears to give some indication of what needs to be done in helping to give more meaning to work in contemporary industrial society.

To sum up to this point, industrialism has been revolutionary in its effects upon work and the worker. On the one hand, there can be little doubt that in many ways it has greatly limited the opportunities for freedom and creative endeavor in work. The worker in mid-twentieth-century America lives in and depends for his very existence upon a much more complex and highly organized society than his counterpart of a hundred or a hundred and fifty years ago. His work is much more specialized and subject to a narrow routine, and his job much more dependent upon forces outside himself. On the other hand, his material welfare has been enhanced, the physical conditions surrounding his work are better on the whole, and his standard of living has improved as a result of the growth of industrialism. And it is also highly possible that his opportunities for cultural and educational advancement have been increased over those of the preindustrial worker.

There are many indications that we have not handled this industrial revolution as well as we might have, especially in terms of its influences upon people. We have employed the methods and ideologies of a preindustrial and highly individualistic age to deal with a phenomenon which has so radically changed our conditions of life that there is probably much more difference between the American society of 1950 and that of 1850 than there was between the society of 1850 and that of 1630. No doubt, when it comes to methods and ideologies in approaching work and the worker there are many things which "abide eternally," but these underlying principles need constantly to be readjusted, reinterpreted, and applied in new ways to rapidly changing circumstances. Before suggesting directions in which we might move, however, it might be well to give some consideration to other groups than the industrial worker.

7. EFFECTS IN NON-INDUSTRIAL WORK

So far we have concentrated almost entirely upon the predicament and the reactions of the industrial worker because he appears to be the most representative in contemporary American society, but some fuller treatment is needed of the conditions of work which face other groups than the industrial worker. First of all, it is evident that industrialism itself has created many types of work which do not come under the heading of "common labor." Or, to put it another way, there exist in the industrial enterprise many workers who are in no sense members of the "industrial proletariat." As a matter of fact, the idea that the industrial enterprise consists almost entirely of the mass-production worker or the "industrial proletariat" on the one hand and the industrial executives on the other, appears to be quite inaccurate. Between the common laborer and the top executive there exist many groups on many levels and with differing functions. Perhaps the analogy of the army is of some use in understanding the industrial enterprise. There are, it is true, the generals and the privates, but there are also all ranks in between. Furthermore, in addition to the infantry there are the engineers, those concerned primarily with supply, the office workers, and a host of others. We have already pointed to the existence of an industrial middle class: the foremen, the junior executives, the technologists, the draftsmen, the accountants, etc. This "class" is growing with the advance of industrialism. For the most part, it is a class without membership either in the labor union or in the select group of managers, top executives, and owners. It has elements in common with both groups. And if the members of this group are to achieve meaning and function in their work, they too must be given full opportunity to become citizens of the industrial community.

Beyond those workers directly connected with industrialism, there exist many groups whose work has not been immediately identified with the industrial enterprise. These include professional groups, clerical workers, workers in trade and finance, service workers, and farmers. It is next to impossible to generalize about these groups, but one can point to certain problems or realities which apply to most if not all of them. First of all, it is evident that industrialism has had some influence upon them— either in terms of their work as such, or certainly in terms of their daily living. Farming, for example, has been increasingly mechanized in the last half century so that the farm worker, too, must adjust himself to the machine. Obviously his situation is not entirely comparable to that of the industrial worker—although there is an increasing similarity between the conditions of the industrial worker and the worker in the large industrialized farm which concentrates upon the turning out of one product. Farming is becoming more and more a large-scale operation comparable to an industrial organization. The introduction of the machine in farm work has had varied results— both harmful and beneficial to the worker. It has greatly enhanced his productivity, while at the same time it has reduced the number of farm workers needed. It may mean fuller opportunity for the development of creative tendencies; on the other hand, it can lead to a greater boredom, monotony, and a decrease in the freedom of the individual worker.[26] These same generalizations can be applied to some extent to other types of work upon which the machine is having an increasing influence.

Second, insofar as other than industrial workers—such as clerical, service, and to a certain extent farm workers—are a part of a large and complex enterprise in which many of the techniques of the industrial enterprise ("rationalization," assembly line, etc.) have been adopted, they too face similar problems in their work to those of the industrial worker. These are the problems of finding personal meaning in their work, identification with the enterprise, and a sense of citizenship in the work community of which they are a part. Insofar as these workers have been unionized, their problem may have been helped some. At least they have not found themselves in a completely unequal bargaining situation. But, lacking a union, and depending upon the attitude of their employer, they may well find themselves in a frustrated state as far as their work is concerned. Possibly this is most evident in economic terms, for it is frequently the nonunionized worker who has been squeezed out as unionized workers have won higher wages. It is also evident in psychological terms, especially in the case of the service workers. The condition and life of the industrial worker has been dramatized by the union and also by writers and social scientists. His job now enjoys some status in the public eye. This is not true of the service employee. (The farm worker probably enjoys a prestige which has carried over from an earlier time and the clerical worker has status bordering on "white collar" even if he (or she) does not have a high degree of economic security.)

I would like to call special attention to the clerical workers. According to *The Occupational Outlook Handbook*, "In 1870, only one out of every 160 workers in the United States was in a clerical occupation. In 1950, one worker out of every 8 was doing this type of work."[27] These workers are connected with all types of enterprise—industrial, business, financial, governmental, etc. Many of them are parts of stenographic or typing pools where their work is highly specialized and totally dependent upon a chain of command in which they have no voice. This type of specialized and dependent work creates the same type of problems for the clerical worker as those faced by many industrial employees. Furthermore, when this type of work is done in an atmosphere which requires the appearance of work whether real production is taking place or not, the effects can be very demoralizing.[28]

Although the vast majority of workers in this country are employed by others, there still exists a large group who are more or less their own employers, such as those who own and operate small grocery stores, drugstores, garages, farms, etc. These individuals do not face the same type of problems as those faced by the employee. Although they too have been influenced by the advancing industrialism and they must deal with it in their own situation, many of them face the threat of extermination as independents as industrialism advances. In this age of an increasingly more complicated social and economic structure, the lives of the independent workers have also become more complex. The independent businessman must conform to many community and government regulations, as must also the independent farmer. In many cases we have reached the place where the demands upon the independent worker are so onerous that only those with courage and financial resources can even think of setting themselves up in business independently. This is rather unfortunate in terms of the welfare of the community. In the past the independent worker has been one of the community's staunchest citizens.

Two or three things can be noted with reference to the professional groups. They, too, have not escaped the influence of industrial techniques. Mills writes:

> Most professionals are now salaried employees; much professional work has become subdivided and standardized and fitted into the new hierarchical organizations of educated skill and service; intensive and narrow specialization has replaced self-cultivation and wide knowledge; assistants and sub-professionals perform routine, although often intricate tasks, while successful professional men become more and more the managerial type.[29]

Nevertheless, professional men and women probably still have fuller opportunity than others to find a sense of meaning and prestige in their work. They have deliberately chosen and prepared themselves for that work. The community accords prestige to most professions. Possibly in an inflationary period they may receive more prestige than real income. The professional man faces the same types of temptation in his work that any other workers face, but since his is a job which requires far more skill and personal concern than many jobs and since the community has accorded him prestige, his temptations are heightened. In this complex industrial society with its impersonal elements and its economic pressures, the professional worker may well be tempted to use his skill solely for his personal advancement regardless of his influence upon the community; or he may be strongly tempted to do his work in a haphazard fashion—as long as he can get by. On the other hand, improved industrial techniques and scientific advances have meant that certain professional men can now increase their skill over a former period and can be that much more useful to the community.

Finally, a word on women workers. Statistics would seem to indicate that more women are working outside of the home than ever before in American history.[30] They are working in the same types of employment as men, although a larger proportion of women than men work in clerical occupations. Approximately one third of the women who work outside of the home are married. This is especially significant for marriage and family life. It is one further indication of the changes which an advancing industrialism has brought about in the lives of Americans.

Meanwhile "occupation-housewife" continues to be an important category in the lives of American women. Work in the home is more varied in its requirements of the individual than most any other type of work in modern industrial society. Fortunately, the products of industrialism have contributed immeasurably to the ease with which *much* of that work can be done.

8. BARRIERS AND BRIDGES AHEAD

We turn now to some consideration of the potentialities in the present industrial situation, the realization of which might improve the conditions of work of the industrial worker. At the same time we want to consider those realities of the present industrial situation with which we must deal. In other words, what are the facts we must face, and in what direction may we move to make work more meaningful in industrial society?

There has existed an articulate minority which has urged that in essence we must return to a preindustrial society if we hope to recover for the worker a genuine sense of wholeness and meaning in his work. Actually, this does not appear to be a very live or even desirable alternative. The achievements of industrialism in the past century have been very extraordinary. Recognizing that the rapid growth of this system has brought about many undesirable results for the worker still it is obvious that the worker and all of society have benefited in countless ways. Furthermore, there remain many beneficial potentialities which might yet be realized. Our way, then, lies not in a denial of the machine and mass production in favor of a return to a premechanical and preindustrial age, but in a positive use of the machine and of industrialism for the good of society and the individual. But it would appear that many of the standards and assumptions which have guided us in the use of the machine and in the establishment and operation of industrialism, must be either denied or redeemed. We have seen, for example, some of the havoc wrought by an overdependence on the myth of the "economic man," by the treatment of labor as a commodity, and by a too-extreme individualism. The industrial enterprise is economic of necessity, but it must be recognized and approached in much broader terms than the economic. Social and human factors need to be recognized. Labor must be approached as a primary and human resource and not just a commodity.

Some indication of the positive ways in which we might move in giving work more meaning in contemporary industrialism can be gained from the studies of the industrial worker which have been made in recent times.

> Every study of workers shows that they consider the social function of the enterprise the most important one. . . . [The] major demands of industrial workers appear as demands for good and close group relationships with their fellow workers, for good relations with their supervisors, for advancement, and above all, for recognition as human beings, for social and prestige satisfaction, for status and function. Wages, while undoubtedly important, rank well down on the list.[31]

We hear more and more about the industrial enterprise as a social community and about the importance of worker citizenship in that community. It is pointed out that if the worker can find a role as a "citizen" in the plant rather than as a "subject," then many of his desires will be fulfilled. Apparently the worker in modern industrial society cannot find sufficient satisfaction in his work alone, but only by an identification with the industrial process as a whole and with the industrial community. If this is true, then any approach to work in modern industry must be broadly social in character; it must take into consideration the whole organization and control of the plant, and not just the individual's work. The assumption of the adherents of the gospel of work that the individual can find his way in his work and by himself appears to be almost entirely irrelevant today. This is true also of most workers who are not so closely identified with the industrial process.

Again, if the primary need of the industrial worker is that of status and function in the industrial community, then the approach of the union leader as well as the industrial manager should be guided by this point as well as by others. Furthermore, since management's basic function and primary allegiance is economic, that is, producing at a profit and keeping the enterprise afloat, it cannot be *primarily* concerned with the likes and interests of the worker. This would appear to be one of the main functions of the union, and it is a function that goes far beyond mere economic concern—that is, interest solely in wages and hours. The union needs to be concerned, in as responsible a fashion as possible, with the full rights of the worker—political and social as well as economic.

The union has accomplished much on behalf of the worker. Many workers have found a certain sense of vocation in and through their unions and may continue to do so. On the other hand, there are certain dangers inherent in the present state of the labor unions. Increase in size, and a relative degree of success have opened the way to the possibility of an excessive attachment to the *status quo* and to a loss of interest among rank and file workers in the affairs of the union. Union leadership in the large unions tends to become permanent, sometimes creating a chasm between union leader and worker, and also leading to an increased centralization of power. This factor, combined with the size and strength of the unions today, has given birth to a new power group—a group which could do much harm or much good in the contemporary scene. Thus anyone who is concerned about the worker and his work in contemporary industrialism will want also to be concerned about the caliber of union leadership as well as industrial management.

We underline, then, the facts that the worker needs to find a sense of identification with the industry, citizenship in the industrial community. It is necessary, however, to point out that identification with the industrial enterprise is not sufficient. The worker's work may take on much more meaning when he feels that he is a citizen of the industrial community, but there is also a danger of becoming overly identified with the community of work of which he is a part. It is important that the worker feel that his work has some significance in terms of a much larger community than the industrial enterprise, just as it is important for the citizen of the state to feel an identification with a much larger community than his own particular state or nation. The worker who belongs to the Christian Church should feel a sense of identification with the church universal and should become aware that his work in some sense has significance for that church universal and even more important, that it has relevance in the eyes of God. It would appear to be one of the primary duties of the church and of the professional workers within the church to make clear to the worker his place as a member of the church universal and to indicate to him that his ordinary work has a significance which goes beyond the industrial enterprise. Too frequently the church has asked the worker to identify himself with the church universal only in his specifically "religious" work, and thereby has failed to meet him on the level on which he lives most of his life.

We have emphasized the necessity that the worker find status and function in the industrial community, that he be enabled to achieve full outlet for his needs as a social individual. At the same time, we have stressed the fact that industrialism has impeded the freedom of the individual worker, and that much of the individualistic ideology characteristic of the American gospel of work appears to be irrelevant under modern industrial conditions. While recognizing these factors, we do not wish to underrate the importance of the freedom of the individual worker. But, here again we must attempt to be realistic. The individualism of nineteenth-century America tended to overlook the fundamental truth that man achieves fullness of self-development only in society. Furthermore, individual freedom is not easily realized in industrial society. Still, this is an area which must be of concern to us in our approach to the worker. We need to ask not only how may he achieve status, but also how may he have the fullest possible opportunity for his development as an individual worker. Whitehead has suggested the possibility that "the great corporations in various ways should interweave in their organizations individual craftsmanship operating upon the products of their mass production."[32] The whole tendency of modern industrialism is toward mass production of standardized goods. The plant is geared almost ruthlessly to this end. But perhaps we need again to be concerned with quality and variety as well as with quantity. And, although mass production thrives on the standard way of producing great quantities of identical products, perhaps there are ways in which the process and the end product might be varied so as to give more play to creative and craftsmanlike workers. Standard procedures and standard products require standard workers, but men are not all cut of the same cloth. Possibly modern industrialism can give more consideration to individual differences and even benefit in the long run by doing so.

Finally, when the realities of the present industrial situation are considered, two primary factors emerge: one, the constant conflict—open or masked—between management and labor, and two, the pump-priming effects of a war and defense-dominated economy. Tension between labor and management is almost inevitable. Undoubtedly, there is a possibility that this tension can become creative. On the other hand, it may become quite destructive. Questions of wages and hours, amount of work, management prerogatives, "ownership" of work, control of work, the relative role of government as a peacemaker, etc.—all of these and more are sources of irritation in the relationship between labor and management. Any consideration of work in contemporary industrial society must take this background of conflict into account.

We need to be reminded that our present situation—and the one in which we have lived for the last ten to twelve years—is an abnormal one. Our economy is stimulated by the constant demands of a nation at war, or a nation concerned primarily with expenditures for defense. Production, therefore, has been maintained at a fairly high level. Industrial workers—and others—have not faced the problem of unemployment. Wages have been fairly high. Morale in the actual war period was quite high. If and when the time comes when this artificial stimulation is removed, then we will undoubtedly be faced with a whole new set of problems. In the meantime, just what ultimate effects production guided by the needs of a nation at war or preparing for war will have upon work and worker, it is difficult to say.

9. THE CHRISTIAN NOTE

It has become common practice among theologians to point out that the word "vocation" has lost entirely its religious significance in contemporary parlance. This may be as much the fault of the Christian as of the secular community. At any rate, it is symbolic of our contemporary approach to, and assumptions about, work and vocation.

Among the ancient Israelites, the Reformers, and the early Puritans, vocation was judged primarily in terms of the calling of the community and the work of God. Today we judge it entirely with reference to secular standards of success. These standards are income, prestige, and status. One has "arrived" if he owns a certain make of automobile, if he can keep a house in the right neighborhood, if he can employ his leisure time in certain ways, and if he can send his children to the right schools—with the assurance that they have the opportunity even to surmount his achievements. Standard of living is a primary test of accomplishment in work and vocation. To a certain extent freedom is measured by what one can command with his income. If the worker can afford an automobile with which to roll along the highways on the weekend, he has more freedom than the man who must stay at home or ride by bus.

We assume that the power for achievement in our vocation comes from ourselves—perhaps with a bit of luck thrown in. If God merits attention at all as a source of power it is as kind of a junior partner who enhances the prestige of the senior member of the firm and fills in the little crevices in the structure of success.

The confidence in a "rugged individualism" which characterized our attitude in earlier periods has subsided somewhat. We are more willing to rely upon group effort and to find satisfaction in community achievement. The individual worker finds some satisfaction in his community of work, and he seldom cares to leave it. There is an increasing tendency for the factory community, the labor union, the sales force, and other types of work communities to become self-conscious and to find a certain completeness in themselves. But, few of these communities want to give the appearance of a "public-be-damned" attitude. They want at least to give the impression—and perhaps even to convince themselves—that they are contributing to the general welfare. The corporation makes it clear that it has contributed its share and more to the total community. Identification with the national destiny, a secure role in the "American century"—these are increasingly becoming sources of motivation and satisfaction in vocation. America has a "calling." It is difficult for the Christian community to compete with this sense of community vocation.

An attempt to revivify the sense of Christian vocation in our time will need to proceed within a framework somewhat like the following: The first necessity is rootage in a vital and realistic theology; or, stated in less abstract terms, in a vivid sense of the divine initiative such as that felt by the Reformers and the early Puritans. Whenever the Potestant emphasis on the value of common work has been severed from this framework or sense, it has been appropriated by or in some other framework and has been greatly distorted in the process. There is much power in a meaningful philosophy of work and vocation, but its real value depends upon what it stresses as the *sources of motivation* and the *goals of work*.

One of the most common dangers which has beset and will beset any American philosophy of work and vocation is the danger of an excessive emphasis on prudence. Calculation of gain with a close eye to personal advantage, never being overly religious but just enough to help one along—these are among our most common temptations. There is, on the contrary, a radicalness in the call of the gospel of Jesus Christ which bursts this old wineskin. One hesitates to answer the question as to how the Christian worker might pursue his calling in an attitude of going the second mile. But the reality of divine grace assured in that gospel implies that the Christian worker give of himself without an eye constantly cocked toward personal gain. This should not mean that he cannot join in an organized effort to protect himself and others from injustices, to better his lot and the lot of others, or to reshape his society. Such activity, however, stands under judgment and should constantly be guided by a basic attitude of love. This suggests the maintenance of a delicate balance between the Scylla of excessive prudence and the Charybdis of excessive innocence.

A second necessary element in the process of revitalization is a recovery of the sense of community. Christian vocation can have no basis apart from that community which feels itself called of God.

Third, we must face realistically the conditions and ideals of work in contemporary industrial society. If the Church is concerned with the revival of Christian vocation in our time, it will need to consider the worker in his total environment and not only as an individual, the effects of industrialism upon his work, his relationship to the industrial enterprise, and his citizenship in an industrial or other type of work community. It will need also to consider the common motivations to work in our time, and the possibilities of changing or redeeming these motivations. It will need to see these and many other questions in an effort to be as realistic as possible about the worker in his present situation.

NOTES

[1] The thesis that the "Protestant ethic" paved the way for the development of the "spirit of capitalism" was first set forth by the German sociologist, Max Weber. (See the Bibliography for a listing of his works, and others, which deal with this subject.) This thesis has become widely accepted in academic circles. In my opinion, it is open to criticism at two points: (1) the failure to put sufficient emphasis on the place of economic factors in influencing Protestantism, and (2) the overlooking of significant changes which took place within Protestant theology.

[2] Cf. Richard B. Schlatter, *The Social Ideas of Religious Leaders, 1660-1680*, p. 197. Schlatter refers to English Puritanism, but what he says applies to America also. (Full information on books cited can be found in the bibliography.)

[3] See the Bibliography, pp. 214-215.

[4] Both these phrases are used in various places by Peter Drucker.

[5] The phrase is Elton Mayo's. See *The Social Problems of an Industrial Civilization.*

[6] Karl Polyani, *Origins of Our Time* (London, 1946), pp. 78, 79.

[7] Ellsworth reports that the introduction of a wage-incentive system based on time-motion studies into the "New Freedom Products Company" meant an increased depersonalization of work, or of the specific job. Wage rates, standards of output, etc. were no longer set in a rule-of-thumb fashion in which much account was taken of individual differences—of the worker as a person. It now became the worker's task to fit himself to the job. Furthermore, the introduction of this system meant that an increasing number of managers or "bosses" came between the worker and the top officials. It also brought about a decline in the frequency of official visits to the plant. He traces many of the subsequent difficulties in this plant to the time when the new system was introduced. See John S. Ellsworth, Jr., *Factory Folkways*, chap. III *et passim*.

[8] As quoted in *Time* magazine, April 14, 1952, p. 97.

[9] Cf. Peter Drucker, *The New Society*, pp. 29 ff.

"Four out of ten workers in the United States are in the trades and industrial occupations—skilled, semiskilled, and unskilled. These are the men and women who . . . mine the coal and ore, run the railroads, build the houses, bake the bread, make the clothes, and keep the Nation's machines in running order." (*The Occupational Outlook Handbook*, Bulletin No. 998, Supt. of Documents, U.S. Gov't. Printing Office, Washington, D. C. As quoted by Cameron P. Hall, *The Christian at His Daily Work*, p. 7.)

[10] "The Study of the Past—Its Uses and Its Dangers," in *Essays in Science and Philosophy*, pp. 151-65.

[11] "In 1939, 1 per cent of all the firms in the country—27,000 giants—engaged over half of all the people working in business." On the other hand, "the 1,500,000 one-man enterprises made up almost half of all non-farming businesses, but engaged only 6 per cent of all the people at work in business. . . . No matter which year is studied, or what criteria are used, the fact of extreme business concentration is clear." (C. Wright Mills, *White Collar: The American Middle Class*, p. 24. Mills apparently uses the term "business" in this context to refer to all incorporated nonfarming enterprises.)

[12] As quoted by Cameron P. Hall, *op. cit.*, p. 7.

[13] See, e.g., J. A. Hobson, *Work and Wealth,* New York, 1914, chap. V.

[14] See Elton Mayo, *The Human Problems of an Industrial Civilization*, pp. 32, 33, for the citation from Wyatt and Fraser and for Mayo's comments.

[15] *Ibid.*, p. 118.

[16] *Management and the Worker*, p. 573.

[17] The following, e.g., is an account given by a former student at Wayne University of her experiences as an automobile assembly-line worker:

"At the gate you push your way in because there are 20,000 other guys who want to get to work at 7:00 too. Inside you wait for the cattle car (technically known as the 'freight elevator'—the smaller 'passenger elevator' is reserved for white collar workers and bosses). After what seems like a ten minute wait, the elevator comes and you push your way on in the best 'survival of the fittest' form. . . .

"Now your job is really something. Maybe you're greasing every fourth door that comes down the line, or maybe you're putting in the bolt that holds the vent window in place on every second door. Chances are you'll be doing something even less creative, like running a lathe or a punch press. If the work is hard and the production standards are high, at the end of the day you'll be exhausted. If it's not hard, you'll be just very tired.

"For the first day or the first week or month, incredible as it sounds, your job will be quite interesting. An assembly line is, after all, a remarkable thing. At first you'll be curious not only about your own job, but the jobs of others and even operations in other parts of the plant. This will wear off. In a few months you'll find other things to think about, or I should say, dream about, for by now you can do your operation blind-folded, leaving your mind to wander where it will. Then after a year or so, you'll find another strange thing happening to you. You'll find that your mind has little or nothing to think or dream about. At this point, you'll begin to know for the first time what it's 'really' like to work in a shop.

"During your dreamy stage, maybe you'll bring a book to work to read during your lunch hour or relief. But you'll run into a snag here too. You'll find yourself dreaming while you read. Other barriers to concentration will be clock-watching and the terrific noise of hammers and machines and the distraction of the conversations along side of you. This inability to concentrate will carry over into your after-office hours, too, and it will take considerable prodding on your part and the part of your friends to keep yourself mentally alert. . . . At this point you will understand, perhaps, why sensationalist literature has such an appeal for workers. At the end of the day, you'll realize also why movies, particularly the light, happy-ending, refreshing ones enjoy such popularity. . . .

"The most frightening thing about the job is that you may very well come to like the grim side of your work. You may come to like the very monotony of the job, in a strange, contradictory sort of way. Nobody really likes monotony, but it's easy to fall into the routine of a monotonous job, and that routine can often be comforting and security giving. And, because the job involves doing the same thing over and over, you become efficient enough at it to get out your production and have a little time left over for yourself. If you change jobs you'll lose this time. So you will begin to resist change on your job. You'll want to work at the same operation, in the same spot, with the same people. By now your job is a reflex motion, and it's a lot of trouble to change reflexes. Besides, if you go on another job, after a few days, it will be the same story, the same monotony."

Pat Cayo, "A Student in the Auto Industry," *Outlook*, Fall, 1950, pp. 20 ff.

[18] See especially the studies by E. Wight Bakke.

[19] Drucker claims that this group constitutes 25 per cent of the enterprise, and that it is increasing in number proportionately at a greater speed than the first group. (*The New Society*, p. 41). Cf. C. Wright Mills, *op. cit.*

[20] "The Human Effects of Mechanization," *The American Economic Review*, Vol. XX, #1 supplement, pp. 156-76.

[21] *Men and Machines*, p. 329.

[22] *Factory Folkways*, p. 146.

[23] See, e.g., Stanley Mathewson, *Restriction of Output among Unorganized Workers*.

[24] These are titles of two well-known books by Peter Drucker.

[25] For an excellent list of the needs of industrial workers see E. Wight Bakke, *Principles of Adaptive Human Behavior*, New Haven, 1950, p. 10.

[26] For a short description of what has happened to the farmer in the last half century, see C. Wright Mills, *op. cit.*, pp. 15-20. See also A. Whitney Griswold, *Farming and Democracy*, New York, 1948.

[27] As quoted by Cameron P. Hall, *op. cit.*, p. 7.

[28] For example, see the lively and damaging criticism of the conditions of clerical work in governmental service in Deula Counts, *Why Work: Inefficiency in Federal Service*, New York, 1952. See also C. Wright Mills' description of "The Enormous Files," *op. cit.*, chap. 9.

[29] *Op. cit.*, p. 112.

[30] "In 1949, 28% of those in the civilian labor force were women 14 years and older; about one third of these women workers were married. Looking at this in another way, in that year nearly one out of every three women had a job that paid a cash income." As quoted by Cameron P. Hall, *op. cit.*, p. 7, Mr. Hall refers to "Handbook of Facts on Women Workers," Bulletin No. 237 (1950), p. 1; and "Facts on Women Workers," March 31, 1951, p. 1; both published by the Women's Bureau of the United States Department of Labor, Washington, D.C.

[31] Drucker, *The New Society*, pp. 47, 48. Drucker refers especially to the studies carried on by Mayo, Roethlisberger, Dickson, and Whitehead from Harvard; Bakke of Yale; A. W. Jones' study of Akron, Ohio, published under the title *Life, Liberty, and Property*; and the "contest" which General Motors conducted in 1947 and which resulted in 175,000 individual essays on the topic, "My Job and Why I Like It."

[32] *Essays in Science and Philosophy*, p. 161.

IV

Work as Christian Vocation Today

ROBERT L. CALHOUN

1. The antiphony of worship and work. 2. Work as medium of divine command and promise—a. Demand for technical, social, moral responsibility; b. Promise of growth, and the joy of sharing with God. 3. Work as vehicle of Christian response—a. In service to men; b. In gratitude to God. 4. Marks of work as Christian response—a. In the task: direction to real needs, enlistment of individual gifts, opportunities for growth; b. In the worker: integrity, creativity, imagination, love, social contributiveness. 5. Christian presuppositions—a. The triune God; b. Jesus Christ as Savior; c. Man in covenant with God and fellow men.

PRECEDING chapters have made clear the nature of our problem. The life of modern man has been broken once again, as so often before in times of widespread confusion, into disunited parts. This has come about partly by reason of the increasing specialization and complexity of modern civilized living. It has resulted partly from the breakdown of traditional and familiar patterns of behavior and of thought. There is no good reason to suppose that either of these tendencies will diminish in the near future. Specialization and complication will almost surely increase as mankind becomes more numerous, as pastoral and agrarian cultures become industrialized, and as the economic and political tasks to be performed everywhere reflect the results of continuous research, invention, and multiplied human contacts. How long it may be before a new pattern of equilibrium in thought, feeling, and social action may be achieved to replace the simple confidence in progress that marked the nineteenth and early twentieth centuries no one can say. But it is clear, at least, that we live now in a period of revolutionary upheaval and transition, and there seems little likelihood that long-term stability will be reached again for many years.

Religion should be an integrating force in both tranquil and stormy periods of human history, as well as a source of continual remaking of men and societies. But today religion too often fails to provide a principle of unity and confidence. On the one hand, as in the ancient world, there are too many gods and churches competing for man's devotion. There are national, racial, class, and party loyalties which here and there are raised more or less explicitly to the dignity of religions. There is, moreover, even where Christian faith is professed and the organized Christian Church is maintained, a sharp division between clergy and laity, and between areas of life regarded respectively as sacred and profane. Many men and women of our civilization no longer even profess Christianity, because it has come to appear irrelevant to the concerns that really enlist their interest and devotion. But even for professing and practicing Christians, religious life is likely to be identified with churchgoing, with occasions of private or public worship, and with the particular kinds of jobs that involve professional service in some form of organized church life—the jobs we ordinarily have in mind when we speak of religious vocations.

This isolation of clergy from laity, and of places and times regarded as set apart for God from the places and times in which men and women spend most of their waking time and energy, has resulted in a way of life intolerably divided against itself. In it too many men and women miss the guidance and strength that religious devotion should provide. In it the activities they take most seriously are left largely barren of profound moral and religious significance. Their professions of Christian commitment and conviction, meanwhile, have tended to become largely formalized and futile. Christian faith has come to be regarded as a luxury, not as a vital necessity for human health and the source of hope for salvation here and hereafter. There is urgent need to realize once again, more effectively than ever before, in both thought and practice, "the priesthood of all believers," and the full meaning of Christian vocation.

One way to try to make clear what this means, for our present concern, is to start with a statement of Christian theology, and to show what understanding of work it involves. In essential respects, this is the approach that is worked out in Chapter I, in which the Biblical foundations of our understanding of work are examined, and human work is treated always in the context of Hebrew and Christian faith. Similarly, in Chapter II, the developing life and thought of the Christian Church is the explicit framework within which work and vocation are defined and interpreted. In Chapter III, the order of presentation (but not the underlying presuppositions) is changed, and work as we know it in modern industrial society is examined, with especial attention to actual conditions that make it difficult to see in much ordinary work today what the Church has meant by vocation, or calling. In the present chapter, both ways of approach are attempted. On the one hand, the place of work in man's total response to the presence of God is briefly indicated. Then some of the familiar characteristics of everyday work are reviewed, to see how far work in fact can and does serve as a medium of divine calling and human response. Finally, a brief sketch of the Christian convictions directly underlying this interpretation of work as vocation is offered, to suggest that the interpretation is grounded not in some particular doctrine alone but in the whole fabric of Christian affirmation. The intention of the whole book is not to derive a Christian theology from the fact of everyday work, but to show how the fact of everyday work can be illuminated, judged, and redeemed in the living context of Christian faith.

1. THE ANTIPHONY OF WORSHIP AND WORK

Religion is man's total response to the overwhelming presence of God. For Christian believers, it is response to the God and Father of our Lord Jesus Christ. In such response, work can never be the whole nor even the primary reality, but it has its own indispensable, wholesome, divinely appointed and positive place. Our immediate concern is to identify and appraise the role of work in the Christian life, recalling both the way in which its place has been recognized in the development of Christian tradition and experience, and the conditions of work in our own time.

Genuine religion is never a human invention, device, or instrumental activity. It is a profound and total answer, willing but inescapable, to the demanding presence of a Being that confronts man as overpoweringly great and good. Such response, as uncalculated as the response of seeing eyes to light, of the mind to evident truth, of the heart to an object of loyalty and love, has two interrelated moments or phases: worship and devoted work.

Worship is the mood of one who finds himself irresistibly moved, first of all, to the deep, self-denying reverence we call awe—a response touched with wonder, self-abasement, even fear, and fascination—before an Other too great and good to be borne. Such response is neither a reasoned conclusion from argument, nor a simple feeling or emotion, nor a deliberate act of will. It involves all these and much more. For it is a sort of opening and yielding of the whole self that underlies and outranges thought, feeling, and voluntary choice. Only when the deep springs of a man's being are moved and redirected, and the hidden sources of his thinking, feeling, and action are set in motion and carried out beyond the customary bounds of their routine behavior can we properly speak of religious response. In such response, the worshiper is at once constrained and set free. He cannot do other than to answer with the depth of his being, yet he is not cramped and confined but fulfilled in a way that he could not foresee. The response is not of his making. It comes in answer to an impact upon him that may well shock him and fill him with dread for the comfortable ways and cherished values of his life hitherto. God comes upon men at first, even if it be in the gentle figure of the suffering Christ, as an Other unforeseen, inescapable, uncontrollable, and unbearable—a terrifying threat to one's self-centered self and one's cherished world.

But this is only the first moment of worship. By itself it would bring death, not life. The first strain in the mighty symphony of worship is consciousness of alienation—alienation through weakness and unworthiness. And so long as it is God in His full holiness that confronts man, this strain will never cease to sound. But in genuine worship, it is taken up into a powerful movement of reconciliation and communion. Not by man's own resources but by the power and grace of the One who confronts him, he is assured, as it were in spite of himself, of acceptance, renewal, and fulfillment. Alienation is not annulled, but it is overcome, and new dimensions of life are opened. The very truth and holiness that terrifies and convicts man, that threatens him with destruction, proves in ways that he could not have foreseen a powerful source of life. In high worship there is no place for complacency or self-glorification. The worshiper is filled with the cleansing fire of repentance. But in repentance he is made to know himself forgiven and accepted, and the God of unbearable truth and righteousness calls forth from him a surge of unutterable self-devotion. This is religious faith. This is the total and unreserved commitment by which, as St. Paul says, a man is justified—forgiven and vindicated—before God. Here is the center and core of worship and of Christian life.

But such faith is never content to stop short of active, grateful acknowledgment of God's bounty through some concrete, appropriate expression. Characteristically, it seeks an outlet in devoted work. Work is no substitute for faith, any more than words are a substitute for living thought, or gifts for the love that prompts them. But just as thought seeks utterance and love seeks to serve the beloved, so living faith moves irresistibly to give appropriate witness to the worshiper's loyalty and love for the God who has given him new life. The almost inevitable and certainly the most fitting utterance of faith is enthusiastic and grateful activity of mind and hand. Faith is man's primary and indispensable answer to the call of God, and devoted work is the language in which that answer can most readily and continually become articulate.

Such work may be of endlessly varied kinds—manual, intellectual, social—but if it is to be fit for the service of God, it must

embody the integrity and the devotion that a God of truth and
life demands. Such work, moreover, will lead naturally, again
and again, to worship, in which the vision of God is renewed
and faith rekindled.

Christian faith and work belong in this pattern. The Christian
believer meets God face to face in Jesus Christ, and the call that
comes to him is the word of God's judgment and mercy embodied
concretely in the person who stands at the center of history. In
Jesus Christ "God speaks clearly," and the only sort of answer
appropriate for one who hears that call is faith and work formed
and determined by the spirit of the devoted, crucified, and risen
Lord.

2. WORK AS MEDIUM OF DIVINE COMMAND AND PROMISE

In talking of the place of work in Christian tradition, we have
given much attention to the basic concept of vocation. The term
means fundamentally, once more, the calling or summons of each
man to the life of Christian faith and service. The summons is
a word of command and of promise, directed to the springs of
each man's personal existence—to his capacity for personal response, for rational insight, and moral decision. To each man,
the word comes not in isolation, as a separate fact, but in the
concrete context of his living. It comes, as Luther insisted,
through the persons with whom one stands in responsible relationships—through parents to children and through children
to parents, through employer to worker and through worker to
employer, through the ruler to his subjects and through subjects to those who rule them.

The understanding of work as vocation, then, is most simply
to be stated in these terms. Very briefly, a person's work is or
should be, on the one hand, a medium in which the presence
of God may be recognized, and His summons may be heard. It
is or should be, on the other hand, a medium in which human
response to the summons may find appropriate expression. God
demands from man not merely verbal but active and actual
acknowledgment. The *primary and indispensable answer is Chris-*

tian faith. But genuine and transforming faith, trust, devotion, will *show itself in action.* For most people, the field of action that absorbs most of their waking thought and energy is the field of daily work. Here if anywhere a man's or a woman's faith in God should display its transforming power.

a. Demand for Technical, Social, Moral Responsibility

In its primary character, apart from particular defects and hindrances, work is peculiarly well suited to embody in one concrete form the demand and the promise that are involved in the divine word to men. In the first place, by its very nature work embodies inescapable *demands for responsible behavior* on the part of the worker. Whether his task be simple or complex, manual or oral or literary, productive or administrative or educative or therapeutic, it requires that the worker learn and fulfill inescapable technical requirements. Every job has its own characteristic structure, its mode of existence in the actual world, its distinctive goals and the instrumental processes by which those goals must be sought. The only person who can engage effectively in any sort of job is one who is ready to give himself seriously to the task of learning its character and mastering its skills.

But beyond that, each job that is fit to be called a vocation involves social responsibilities. No matter how independent and self-contained a particular task may seem, other persons besides the worker are involved in the success or failure of what he does. His actions must be so co-ordinated with the actions of fellow workers, of employers and consumers, of dependents and friends, that what he does as workman may become a fitting part of an undivided pattern of human relationships. One of the most striking intellectual developments of our time has been the sudden realization by some nuclear physicists and other research workers in the sciences that, in flat contradiction of a long-cherished assumption that workers in the exact sciences should be completely free from social and political concern, the social results of their work and its relation to public policy are in fact matters of urgent concern. The same thing has come to be true of policy makers in industry and finance. The time has gone by when intelligent business executives could suppose that they are free to follow any policy that may seem profitable in business, without regard to public opinion or social effect. Widely read periodicals devoted to the interests of business and finance now carry scathing criticisms of the use of paid bullies in labor disputes, a display of autocratic disdain for stockholders, customers, and public, or efforts to get special privileges from government officials through bribery or other underhand devices. Needless to say, there are still plenty of sinners against the principle of social responsibility, but the existence of the demand and the impossibility of complete isolation of any worker or executive from its claims is becoming increasingly clear.

But technical and social requirements are inseparable from moral requirements. As a matter of fact, in what has just been said the moral implications of work are already partly explicit. We shall have more to say on this point in a moment. It is sufficient here, perhaps, to say that the divine summons to men comes in part through the network of demands for responsible behavior on the job. For these demands are neither arbitrary nor escapable. They are intrinsic in the nature of work, properly understood. In them, each worker confronts an inescapable imperative that is grounded neither in his own preferences nor in the particular dictates of his cultural community, but in the complex and fluid order of existence itself.

There is need to examine more closely the moral dimensions of this imperative, to make even clearer the appropriateness of ascribing it to the Word of God. Every worker is called upon to work with humility and repentance, for no one is equal to the work that needs to be done. There are, no doubt, complacent or cocksure or indifferent or predatory practitioners of work for selfish gain. But such faults lie in the particular worker or the particular job rather than in the essential nature of work itself. To say that many men do not hear the voice of God is not to say that His voice is not sounding in the midst of their everyday activities.

It is significant that among men recognized as highly competent workmen, worthy of the respect and confidence of their peers, humility and self-criticism are likely to win added confidence and respect, and may take a more or less consciously religious form. A distinguished physician retired some months ago after many years as head of his department in a major university. During his years of active service, he had the affectionate, eager, almost reverent devotion of the younger men whom he has helped to train and who have become his junior colleagues or his enthusiastic emulators in private practice; and their admiration was augmented by his self-effacing modesty. One of his own comments after retirement was: "I have come to believe that my orientation has been religious rather than professional." More precisely, I think: religious *and* professional. Neither personal piety alone nor professional expertness alone could have drawn the kind of response he has won from tough-minded young medical men. They have been moved rather by unassuming piety expressing itself unmistakably in the language of their common profession. This principle applies not only in the practice of medicine, though doctors may face with unusual frequency the sort of emergencies that most obviously outdistance human resources. Humility and repentance are demanded of any worker, however fine and however admired, in any sort of work, who can recognize how great a claim his job makes upon him and the perpetual inadequacy of his response, even at its best.

In terms still more concrete, and still more directly related to the familiar imperative recognized by Christian faith, the demand that comes to the worker in any exacting task is a demand for devotion and trust. No worker is self-sufficient. No worker can supply the needed materials and conditions for carrying out his task or determining its ultimate effects. His dependence is evident at many different levels: dependence on natural resources, on cultural and social inheritance, on the co-operation and support of innumerable contemporary fellow men, on the steady maintenance and disclosure of technical standards and of dependable values that alone can make work possible and significant. But most profoundly and ultimately, each worker is dependent upon power not his own, beyond the powers of nature and of mankind, to take the work of his hands and mind and heart and to make it fruitful in ways that he cannot plan or control. Without such divine transvaluation of his work, a paradoxical acceptance, transformation, correction, and conservation of what he does through his whole life, there would be no good ground for assurance against the ultimate frustration of conscious futility. Every sober and thoughtful worker must say, in whatever terms are appropriate to his own situation, "Except the Lord build the house, they toil in vain who build it."

b. Promise of Growth, and the Joy of Sharing with God

Work which thus embodies a multitude of imperative demands, and in that sense is a medium of divine summons, can serve also as *a vehicle of promise*. The Word of God is always, to the one who has ears to hear, a heartening and liberating word, an assurance of fulfillment. The promise embodied in work, for one who responds as he can and ought to respond, is in the first place a promise of growth. Whatever be the ultimate meaning of the somewhat cryptic parable of the talents (Matt. 25:14-30), at least its obvious meaning fits some of the most certain and familiar facts of human life. Through the exercise of capacities, the vigorous exploitation of talents that are themselves a gift, a growing person comes to know in increasing measure the freedom and fulfillment of mastery—especially of self-mastery. "Unto him that hath shall be given, and he shall have abundance; but from him that hath not shall be taken away even that which he hath." If we remind ourselves that the man with one talent lacked any increase and lost his chance for reward because of his refusal to use what had been given to him in trust, the matching of the story with the hard facts of experience is clear enough. Only one who is faithful over a few things may hope to become master of many things—of skill, knowledge, strength, and endurance, of legitimate self-respect and the respect of others, of a widening range of freedom (always with added responsibilities), and a deepening understanding of the purpose of human existence.

Indeed, if we be permitted to read with some imagination the words of the returning Master to the men who have done his bidding, "Well done, good and faithful servant. . . . Enter thou into the joy of thy Lord," we may catch a glimpse of deeper meanings here. One may even venture to suggest that "the joy of the Lord" is the joy of creative and redemptive activity, and that the outcome of faithful work may be nothing less than admission to a share in that joy that no one but God can give. If something like this be a legitimate reading here, then the other parable—of equal payment for unequal work in the vineyard (Matt. 20:1-16)—will appear not as contradiction but as reinforcement of this same theme. For the joy of sharing in creation may be the same in kind for workers on the humblest scale and on the greatest, for veterans and for novices alike.

Once again, all this needs to be kept in true perspective. Work is no substitute for faith and love. Human salvation is to be found in these last, and cannot be had without them. Faith and love, moreover, are gifts from God and not calculated achievements of man. They are called into being by the Word of God in Jesus Christ. They are evoked in response to the demand that one be prepared to lose one's life, and the promise that so he may find it. At the same time, I have never forgotten the word of a thoughtful preacher years ago that for most of us, in ordinary circumstances, exacting work may offer one of the ordinary and enduring ways in which our self-regarding selves may be lost—may become absorbed, as we say, in doing what needs to be done. In that perspective, work may without sentimentalism or vainglory be held to embody the demand and the promise that in losing life we may find it.

3. WORK AS VEHICLE OF CHRISTIAN RESPONSE

Viewed from another side, the same task that brings God's call to us may even more naturally be regarded as a vehicle for our response.

a. In Service to Men

Most obviously, it is a concrete and inexhaustible way of *service to men*. Inasmuch as the second great commandment is that we love our neighbors as ourselves, the willing investment of our powers in persistent, responsible, devoted labor is almost self-evidently an appropriate way of showing that we take that commandment seriously to heart. In the course of the day's work, moreover, come our most frequent calls to deeds of mercy (Matt. 25:31-45).

It is true and right, of course, that "good works" have fallen under deep suspicion in the tradition of Protestantism. Surely one may find inadequate the conception of "pure religion and undefiled" in the first chapter of the Epistle of James. Surely one must reject the labored and artificial conception that through stereotyped routines of almsgiving, visitations, social services— let alone through deliberate working for prestige or profit—one may acquire merit in God's eyes, and a valid claim to the privilege of being saved. It remains everlastingly true that "the righteous shall live by faith" (Rom. 1:17; Gal. 3:11), and that "if I bestow all my goods to feed the poor, and if I give my body to be burned, but have not love, it profiteth me nothing" (I Cor. 13:3). The demand for perfection is genuinely relevant to human living, and the Protestant reformers were right in declaring that we live at every moment under the judgment of that demand. That is why lifelong repentance is necessary, and why the conception that men can acquire merit, to say nothing of surplus merit, is tragically wrong.

At the same time, as all of us well know, there is real danger that stress upon justification by faith alone may turn into another kind of legalism and ground for self-satisfaction. Whoever takes pride in being a man of faith, and rejects as valueless the simple, unstudied acts of kindness that his neighbor performs every day, gives ground for the judgment that his faith is "dead" (James 2:14 ff.). Genuine faith issues in repentance, and in works of love, not in pride. Likewise, there is great danger of unreality in any attempt to find salvation through pure altruism, that would love one's neighbor instead of oneself.[1] There are, no doubt, high moments when something like that rarefied and intoxicating height is actually reached. Happily, man is capable on occasion of genuine self-forgetfulness. Otherwise, "the way of the cross" would scarcely have a recognizable claim upon us. For our Lord Jesus Christ himself, the cross was the climax of "the whole course of his obedience,"[2] not a substitute for obedient living day by day. He who "came not to be served but to serve, and to give his life" (Matt. 20:28), has shown us the way of the cross in its true context. For us also it must be first of all a way of unpretentious service to our fellow men, embodied ordinarily in devoted work.

b. In Gratitude to God

Such work, moreover, can serve as a way of *response to the first great commandment* as well. He who commits himself to God in trust and gratitude can scarcely give adequate, overt evidence of that commitment except through what he does with the whole fabric of his daily living. The best expression of gratitude for gifts received is to use them fully and freely. The best expression of wholehearted trust is to risk what one has in the actual arena of human living. Trust does not show itself best in withdrawal, in retirement from the struggle, to practice unbroken contemplation. Bernard of Clairvaux, a master of contemplation, no less strongly than Gregory the Great, a master of action, insisted that the full commitment of love must necessarily pass from the blessed vision to the beggars awaiting bread at the monastery gate. Moreover, if we dare use quite frankly the insight and language of St. Paul, we shall think of such active commitment as co-working with God, participation in the perpetual task of world betterment. This obviously involves some theological presuppositions that must be examined more fully in a moment. Meanwhile, it fits well with the suggested reading of Jesus's parables, and with the view set forth again and again in the Fourth Gospel. Devoted work, on these terms, may be regarded quite straightforwardly as Christian vocation, in so far as it is a medium for the Word of God to man, and for man's response to God.

4. MARKS OF WORK AS CHRISTIAN RESPONSE

Not all human effort is genuine work, and not all work is fitted to be Christian response to God's call. No doubt the Word of God can come to man in any life situation. But work that can serve as a worthy response of man to God must be an authentic expression of faith and love. It must be directed, first of all, to the satisfaction of real needs.

a. In the Task: Direction to Real Needs, Enlistment of Individual Gifts, Opportunities for Growth

In a sense, this test goes back to a time before the beginning of the Christian era. The Stoics, for example, came close to it when they distinguished between desires that are natural and those that are artificial or unreal; and went on to distinguish among natural desires between those which are essential, and those which though accordant with the structure of human existence, are not in the strictest way vital to its continuance. In the perspective of Christian understanding, it seems to me that the basic distinction is still valid. Some occupations are almost obviously to be ruled out as exploiting human energy and ingenuity for the satisfaction of desires that are either trivial, artificial, and conventional, or actually harmful to the wellbeing of men. By contrast with these, work is requisite that genuinely serves the maintenance and improvement of physical and spiritual health.

No one will pretend that the line is easy to draw.[3] Especial difficulties arise, it may be, with regard to activities characteristic mainly of complex and sophisticated civilizations. Careers in the fine arts, in speculative thought and pure theoretical research, in the provision of various sorts of entertainment or of comfort and luxury beyond a fairly Spartan level of life need to be examined with especial sensitiveness, imagination, and candor. At their best, workers engaged in providing quite intangible and nonmeasurable contributions to human living may be among the chief benefactors of the human spirit. At worst, men and women professedly engaged in such occupations may be consciously or unconsciously poisoning the spiritual atmosphere with falsity, triviality, inducements to spiritual stagnation, and death. Often enough, a clear-sighted critic may see in the very jobs that are most highly honored in a given society—jobs involving management and administration, propaganda and salesmanship, office holding and political maneuver, academic or other professional activity, ecclesiastical leadership in pulpit, vestry, or conference chamber—some of the most wasteful deviations from the pattern of work directed to the fulfillment of essential need. Hasty, ill-informed judgment is always out of place; but heedless complacency, especially about one's own job, is at least equally bad. Neither God nor man is well served by the wasting of human resources. The actual load we must carry is too great to permit reckless dissipation of our limited assets.

Work that can serve as a man's vocation must, further, be adapted to his individual powers. Again, the principle can be stated but not examined in detail. The point is surely simple enough. If I am to offer a full response in my job, it must be one that subjects me to demands that call into active exertion at least a sizable part of the powers that are distinctively mine. That there are diversities of gifts, and that there should be diversities of function is again an old story. For Plato and for Aristotle it was central to any full-scale interpretation of human society. But no one has stated it more forcibly and succinctly than Paul (Eph. 4:1-16; Rom. 12:1-21; I Cor. 12-14). In the context of Christian faith and understanding, moreover, the principle can have a significance that is heightened and sharpened by the Christian appreciation of the concrete uniqueness of every individual self. The God of Christian faith speaks to each man by his own name, and each man's answer must be uttered in a way that is uniquely his own. In thinking of human work as a way of answer to the divine Word, therefore, we are committed to this characteristic Christian insight. A man can offer fitting response to God through work only if the work enables him to contribute his own unique voice to the universal chorus. If a man of quick imagination and insight is compelled to spend most of his life at a job that leaves no significant place for individual thought and action, that makes of him an interchangeable part duplicated by hundreds or thousands of others, his job can scarcely be for him the best vehicle for his answer to the divine summons and his realization of the divine promise.

Suitable work, finally, must provide opportunity for growth. The kind of fulfillment that is possible for men in this life is never a static and finished attainment. Rather, it is the concrete and paradoxical kind of fulfillment suggested by such words as participation and learning—experience in which one reaches continually toward a goal that lies beyond one's range and yet enters creatively and significantly into one's quest for it. Growth, as distinguished from mere change, is always a concrete interweaving of movement and stability, of what is and what is not yet. Growth, learning, personal participation involve always the transcending of the present self and its re-establishment or re-affirmation with new dimensions—one more instance of losing one's life to find it. Without this sort of growth or continual remaking, within the limits of each person's own capacities, a distinctive and indispensable characteristic of personal existence would be lost. Any work, then, that forces the worker into a fixed routine, in disregard of his personal capacities and needs, or rejects and at length defeats his imagination, or penalizes and deadens his initiative is work that cannot be for him what vocation ought to be.

b. In the Worker: Integrity, Creativity, Imagination, Love, Social Contributiveness

Such requisite conditions in the job are matched by similar requirements in the worker. No matter how exciting or spacious a task may be, its values will be lost for a worker who is himself not fit to realize them.

The first requirement, perhaps the most essential of all, is integrity. A prime reason why work can convey to men the commandments of God is that every genuine job involves the most direct contact between the worker and the real world order. But he will gain little from that contact, in the way of insight, discipline, and growth, if he does not open his eyes and his mind to the situation as it actually is, and direct his energies with honest regard for the claims of reality, to turn out work that is fit to stand. Any builder who puts in his time producing showy but unsound construction, any merchant who is content to market shoddy goods and pretend that they are fit for human use, any doctor or lawyer, teacher or preacher who is willing to be a plausible charlatan is violating the commandment of the God who made heaven and earth, and the injunctions of Jesus Christ in whom the mind of God was incarnate for our sake.

A second requirement, not easily labeled, is perhaps creativity—a delight in exploring and inventing and experimenting in new and promising ways. There is no need here to debate the suitability of the word "creativity," as applied to human enterprise. Obviously God alone is capable of that radical creation which brings into being and sustains from moment to moment the dependent existences of the world of nature and of men. But the very fact that men are able to recognize and take delight in acknowledging the creatorhood of God bears witness to their own capacity for participating, in various modest degrees, in the realizing of new situations and new values. This kind of spontaneity is, of course, present in widely differing measure in different persons. Some are more readily content than others to follow routine and to repeat again and again familiar patterns of work. As a matter of fact, the larger part of any skilled operation must be habitualized and stereotyped. Only so can complex skills be built up into dependable working equipment. But unless there be at least some measure of independence and daring, distinctive individuality, and delight in adding some fresh and novel turn that brings new significance to light, human work is too likely to approach the endless turning of gears and pistons, or at best the fixed ritual of a beehive, and miss one of the most life-giving characteristics of human activity.

The worker must have, in the third place, perceptive and resourceful imagination. The great artists, scientists, and statesmen, I suppose, are those who have in most impressive measure this capacity for seeing beyond the boundaries of the immediate situation. But for the simplest workers in any sort of productive task, there is both place and need for some measure of this power. When we are talking of work in the presence of God, we underscore the need that the worker shall be capable of seeing his task in the perspective of religious faith and devotion. Such imaginative vision can be cultivated and encouraged by reading and reflection—by exposing oneself to the history and tradition of one's own group and of other groups, large and small, present and past, near at hand and remote in place and in culture. Study of the Bible, of the poets and storytellers, of the dramatists and the seers who have always served as growing points and pioneers of imaginative insight, can help to widen the horizons within which any worker can live and carry on his job. Music and the other arts, free and candid discussion with like-minded and with unlike-minded neighbors, discerning use of newspapers, radio broadcasts, moving pictures, and television programs that are honest enough to hold up a true mirror to the life of men—education by all these means and many more can make of any man's job a more exciting and rewarding experience.

Another requirement, perhaps as imperative as fundamental integrity, is hard to label without risk of sentimentalism. The simplest and best name for it is love. If that word be used here, it must, of course, mean something very different from emotional glow or dutiful benevolence. It must mean the self-identification of the worker with his task, and with the various constituents that enter into it on every side. Whether he be working with raw materials or with living plants and animals, with human relations or with systems of abstract symbols, there is need that he lose himself, as we say, at least from time to time, in a vivid, concrete sense of their reality and distinctive natures. There is need for similar perception and appreciation of one's fellow workers, and of the social order that provides a place for one's working life. There is need for delight in the operations of the work itself, if that be possible, and for joy in sound achievement, whether it be one's own or that of a fellow worker or a competitor. This kind of love for one's job, not only in the simpler agrarian and handicraft civilizations, but in modern industry and wherever men work, is indispensable to discovery of the resources for the fulfillment of personal existence that work at its best can provide. If it be true that our work patterns have made it more difficult for many workers to achieve such outgoing concern and self-identification with their jobs, that is reason for seeking to modify the existing situation, not for ignoring or denying the primary need.

The worker whose task is for him a genuine vocation must experience, finally, real delight in contributive and co-operative action. Here the perspective is socialized, not simply individual. A major source of value and of satisfaction in any sort of work is the chance to work as a member of a team that becomes an object of the worker's loyalty. The importance of this factor even in highly mechanized industrial operations is coming to be highlighted in various studies of men and women at work. The *esprit de corps* of a gang, a factory, an industrial union, a professional association is of crucial importance for the attainment of humanly valuable results in the work. Members of a hospital staff, of a fishing crew, of a bridge gang, of a college faculty who respect and trust one another not only turn out better work with less fatigue and frustration, but find in the work a higher level of personal fulfillment than would be possible at all in a climate of mistrust or of mutual indifference. But beyond the working association itself, there should be for each worker some sense of participation in the working life of the entire human community. Efforts are being made in modern businesses to generate by slogans and by inspirational talks and various ritual observances—good, bad, and irrelevant—this sense of social significance and mission. The methods sometimes are deplorable, but the need is real, and its current recognition is encouraging. Almost certainly the need and the difficulty of meeting it have taken on new dimensions during the abrupt expansion of the social areas in which modern man is compelled to live, by comparison with even his relatively recent forebears. One of the tasks of the Church must be to find some pertinent suggestions for a sort of long-range education, to be carried out by the churches and by other suitable agencies, in order that the sense of participation in a common task for significant ends may be widened. Achieving a reasonable solution for this problem seems to me vital to a re-establishment of the plain man's confidence in the value of human life and of his own part in it.

5. CHRISTIAN PRESUPPOSITIONS

It goes without saying that no effort to interpret work in terms of Christian vocation can be acceptable unless it stands clearly within the tradition of Christian faith and understanding. To demonstrate in detail that this is true of the account here suggested is obviously a task that cannot be carried out within the limits of our present space. What is needed here, perhaps, is to indicate at some crucial points the presuppositions about God, about Jesus Christ, about man, and about history that underlie and support the present view.

a. The Triune God

The Christian doctrine of God as transcendent and immanent Creator of heaven and earth, as ever-present and active Sovereign and Judge, as powerful and merciful Savior, and as Sanctifier and Sustainer of human life is here presupposed from beginning to end. In line with a characteristic emphasis in Christian thought, especial stress is laid here upon understanding God as perpetually at work.

As Creator and providential Sovereign, it is He who has established and who maintains the conditions in nature that make human work at once possible and necessary. On the one hand, without dependable structure in an inconceivably intricate and diverse physical universe, it would be quite impossible for man to learn and to carry out systematic operations involving the natural order. Since man is himself not capable of radical creation, but must depend upon materials and upon natural processes already given or in course of being given, the creating and governing activity of God is at the very outset discerned by Christian faith in the fact that man can learn to work.

On the other hand, it is no less directly the outcome of God's way of ordering and maintaining the world that man is compelled to work in order to live and to seek fulfillment. However the story in Genesis 2 be understood, it is surely clear that it was written in an effort to account for a number of evident facts. One of these is precisely that man must earn his bread with sweaty toil. The story indicates that the requirement that man's work did not begin only after his disobedience. Rather, he was created and put into the garden "to dress it and keep it." In other words, work as such was a part of God's plan for men, and the effect of human disobedience was not to make work necessary but to make it needlessly hard. That perspective seems still to fit the essential facts as we know them.

Moreover, the God of Christian faith, Creator and Sovereign, is not one who finished His work trillions of years ago and exists now in a perpetual Sabbath of rest. Rather, He is one whose world is unfinished even now, and whose creative and sustaining energy never ceases to uphold the existing order and to produce continually new reality throughout the whole fabric. No doubt in some sense rest and blessedness are to be ascribed to Him, but His rest and beatitude is found not in inaction but in the steady flow of divine energy.

Moreover, the God who makes and sustains the world is at the same time its Judge and its Redeemer. We have referred repeatedly to the way in which a Christian believer may find in his daily work a medium through which the commandments of God are made known to him, and his failures to meet those demands become plain. If one take into account the entire range of relationships involved in a typical human task, technical, social, and normative, there is perhaps no more inescapable and convincing judgment upon human inadequacy than can be found in the refusal of a working situation to tolerate careless or dishonest response. Untutored fellow men may be fooled, but God is not mocked. His word of judgment is spoken silently, perhaps inaudibly to the heedless listener, in every sequence of work and in every human career. Sometimes the word crashes like thunder when a cumulative mass of human failure brings down in ruin, under the uncompromising pressures of the real world order, a bridge or a dam, a business or a government, an empire or a civilization. These calamities come about for no abstract or mysterious reason. They come about when men through some combination of ignorance and inability, inadvertence and willfulness, have failed to meet in large-scale programs of concrete action—

of work, in its properly inclusive sense—the requirements that God lays down.

At the same time, as we have urged again and again, a man's work can provide a way of experiencing not only the commands and the judgments of God but also His mercy and redemptive power. In principle, this does not happen apart from the impact of Jesus Christ upon the life of the worker, and the opening of his eyes to discern the forgiveness and grace of God even in the exacting demands which apart from such insight might seem to him indeed a way of imprisonment and frustration. We shall give more attention to this point in a moment. Meanwhile, we shall do well never to forget nor to let our neighbors forget what Luther so clearly saw and affirmed: that God's Word to us comes not ordinarily in isolation but rather most intimately and pervasively involved in the human relationships in which we live. The relationships of the working world constitute for each of us a major source for the understanding of God, if we have the wit to look and listen. The other side of this same insight is that our working situations themselves sadly need to be redeemed, transformed into more appropriate vessels for God's will and man's response. To view the situation in this double perspective, seeing in the task at once a means for the transformation of the worker for the better, and a human reality that needs the redemptive grace of God, is one way of doing justice to the complexity and indivisibility of concrete human situations. In work, we both find and need God as our Redeemer.

The Holy Spirit, for Christian faith the Sanctifier and Sustainer of the Christian life, must be thought of as supplying the very life-breath of all devoted work. Whether we speak of learning or growth, fulfillment or transformation, discernment or devotion, we are speaking of dimensions of human life that cannot be conceived at all except as the work of the Holy Spirit. Moreover, for Christian faith the Spirit that is to be discerned in the redeemed life is the same Spirit that moved and still moves through the darkness above the primeval abyss, and through the groping and growing struggles of an unfinished world. Through the presence of God, what every man does at his workbench or in his study or in the working hours and days of his home becomes a living part of the age-old, world-wide work of creation and redemption.

b. *Jesus Christ as Saviour*

In all of this reading of the way in which our doctrine of work presupposes the living triune God, the indispensable focus is the centrality of Jesus Christ for Christian faith. In the quick survey of Christian tradition and the place that work has in it, we have already noticed the significance of Jesus' status as son in a working household, perhaps himself an apprentice and worker before he began his public ministry, a man of the people, surrounded by and concerned for those who toil. It is not, of course, his social status that makes him our Savior and Lord, but the power and wisdom of God incarnate in him for our salvation. Moreover, if we are to do justice to the sound doctrine that all men must be saved through Jesus Christ, we must be always on guard against the tendency to understand that word too narrowly as regards his earthly life. As all of us are keenly aware, there is an exceedingly difficult and delicate problem involved in seeking to find the right way between a too literal particularism that would make salvation depend upon some detailed acquaintance with the man of Nazareth, and a too vague and complaisant universalism that would abandon all concrete historical reality for general moral and religious good will.

I presume most of us would concur at least in the traditional judgment that revelation through Jesus Christ did not begin at the time of his incarnation, but had been a reality also for patriarchs, lawgivers, and prophets throughout the time of the Old Testament. This does not diminish but rather enhances the significance of the revelation in the earthly life of Jesus Christ; for what it affirms is that the redemptive power then become incarnate was the same power that had worked throughout the history of the people of Israel. But if this principle be accepted, as I think it should be, then it is not unnatural in further extension of the principle to hold, with Clement of Alexandria and with other Christian Fathers and Schoolmen, that the same divine Word has been actively present in the lives of other peoples throughout history. If it be true, as Augustine and Calvin agreed and as I think we must agree, that the incarnation was not the beginning nor the crucifixion a precondition of God's love for men, but rather the conclusive historical revelation of that love, it seems necessary to hold that men everywhere and in all times have opportunity to hear God's word of command and of forgiveness, and to respond to that word in faith.

If this be true of civilizations remote in space and time from the earthly life of Jesus Christ, it seems to me more inescapably true of a civilization like ours that has been permeated in all sorts of ways, conscious and unconscious, open and hidden, by the influence of the Christian community. One may give full weight to the deplorable fact that Christian faith and life have been perverted almost beyond recognition in much of Western civilization. It remains true, nevertheless, that work carried on in any ordinary situation in the Western world can scarcely avoid being affected in various concrete ways by the historic life of Jesus Christ and its results in the Christian Church, as well as by the eternal Word of God in its more general manifestations. The Christian ethic has made consciences uneasy over conditions and practices in the working world that once would have passed without comment. The Christian community has taken active and explicit cognizance of the need for fresh affirmation and wider practice of responsibility to God and brotherhood for men. Under the threat of destructive secularism, the Christian gospel and tradition are being studied with a new assiduity and eagerness, and the authority of Jesus Christ is being proclaimed more widely than ever before around the globe. It is in this context that one may think it right to urge that every Christian believer should see his work, as well as other aspects of his life, in the perspective defined by the central revelation.

c. Man in Covenant with God and Fellow Men

Very little need be said here about the conception of man that is implied in our whole account. We have in view the whole traditional affirmation, that man is created according to the image of God, corrupted through sin, and restored in Christ. Man as creature is not self-sufficient, but dependent upon the sustaining bounty of God mediated to him in part through the resources of the natural world and the opportunities for social communication and co-operative living. In his working life, we have urged steadily, these resources and opportunities are present in concrete and inescapable forms. Man as free and responsible creature can find in this context the appropriate setting for exercise and development of God-given powers and the quest of those proximate goals of physical, intellectual, and social effort that find their significance in the will of God.

This is another way of saying that man lives in covenant with God and his fellow men. The covenant relationship, I take it, has been understood in Christian tradition not primarily as positive and external legislation imposed upon man but rather as a profound and intimate involvement of man's very nature with the divine order of existence and right, and with the needs and hopes of his fellow men. This inner, essential covenant has found articulate expression in the Scriptures and in many a legal and moral code, many a venture in co-operative living, many a recorded vision of good beyond what individuals and societies have yet achieved. But the essential bond is not in a written word nor in any actual pattern of social custom. It is in the living dependence of man as creature upon his Maker, and of each man as member of a social body upon the vast hierarchy of human communities. Once again, the working life of the Christian believer is in essential ways an embodiment of this covenant and an opportunity for the worker to acknowledge and affirm it as his own way of life.

The sin that corrupts men and societies is refusal or failure to acknowledge this covenant relationship, and to carry out its obligations. The commandment is to love God and neighbor, a commandment rooted in the very existence of human life, so that disobedience to it becomes inevitably a way of corruption and of alienation from oneself as well as from God and other men. If then by the grace of God a man or a society be redeemed, that redemption is in a profound way, as Irenaeus expressly affirmed and as many others have implied, the establishment of a new covenant in which the old is essentially fulfilled in new dimensions. This is not to say that man is saved by moral effort or virtue or merit acquired by obedient service. It is to say that the transformation of an unbeliever into a man of faith and love is not a kind of annulment of his responsibility to God and neighbor, but rather a forgiveness that reaffirms his responsibilities and gives him new insight and new energy—through "God's power and God's wisdom"—to meet them. The believer is not set free from the obligation to work faithfully. On the contrary, he is enabled to work with vision and devotion such as he had never known before.

In this view, finally, the whole of history is a communication between God and man. In it there is no division between sacred and profane, no sharply restricted "sacred history" separated off from a surrounding wilderness of "world history." All history is a continuing encounter of men with the creative and redemptive presence of God. This is not meant, once more, to minimize the crucial significance of that segment of history recorded in the Bible, nor to suggest that the working presence of God could be discerned with equal facility and clarity in any part of the turbulent human enterprise. It is to say that God is not absent from any part of that enterprise, but everywhere in it is working as Creator, Redeemer, and Lifegiver. Inasmuch as the concrete activities of men, more specifically their working hours, have in this view the character of confrontation and communication between men and God, all history—and all nature, too—becomes surcharged with moral and religious meaning. Here, for Christian faith, is the "vast and varied workshop of divine creation"[4] in which men are discovered as fallible co-workers with God. But here too is a vast living fabric of communication and communion, in which every event can become, in Augustine's sense, sacramental—a "symbol and occasion" of the working of the Holy Spirit in the life of men. The workshop is or should be, at the same time, an altar.

NOTES

[1] Cf. Kierkegaard, *Works of Love*, tr. Lowrie, 15-18, 38-42.

[2] Calvin, *Institutes*, II.xvi.5.

[3] Tertullian examined with searching the problem of trying to draw it by excluding, for Christians, all the arts and crafts that contribute to idol worship. See *On Idolatry*, iv-xii, xvii, etc. His conclusion is that a sensitive conscience, not a rule of thumb, is the only safe guide. The whole treatise is worth close study.

[4] Basil of Caes., *Hexaemeron*, IV.1.

V

A Christian Strategy

ROBERT S. BILHEIMER

IT WILL already have become clear that our purpose in this book is to be suggestive, to break open large realms of thought and their implications for life. Yet some basic principles and facts emerge with a force which cannot be denied.

1. IN SUMMARY, TWO CONCLUSIONS

From the side of the Christian faith, it is first of all clear that what we find in the Bible is the exposition, or revelation, of God's great calling to mankind. We do not find, and should not look for, a specific "doctrine of work and vocation" in the Old and New Testaments. It is not necessary here to recapitulate what was said in Chapter I, but it is important to stress the fact that as we turn to the Scriptures we should expect there to hear the voice of God calling all sorts and conditions of men back to obedience to Him. This obedience is to take place within a community of men called by God to perform service to Him and to mankind; this obedience has important implications for all that men do, including their work; but the formulation of a doctrine of calling or of vocation according to the Bible must always be in terms of God's calling to men to follow and to serve Him.

Second, from the side of Christian faith, it is inescapable that

186

God's calling connects inevitably and inextricably with the work which men do in the world. The Bible makes this clear. As recorded there, whether in the Old Testament or in the New Testament, the calling of God to all men is answered where they are, in their ordinary life and in their work. This has its own implications, as we have seen in Chapter I, for the substance of their work and for the way in which they do their work. The precise character of these implications will be a matter of debate, and should be. It cannot be gainsaid, however, that the Bible understands that men must live out their response to God's calling in their work in the world.

This Biblical claim has been recognized by the Church throughout the ages. Chapter II has indicated the different ways in which God's call has been thought to be relevant, in the different epochs of the Church's history, to the work of men at those times. Some of these patterns of earlier Christians we would reject for various reasons. In some of them there is much of value for our own problems. The central factor is inescapable: in Christian history as in the Biblical times, the great call of God has been directed to men's work.

The same lesson is driven home as much by theological thought as by Biblical study and historical survey. What we have been given to know, as Chapter IV points out, of the nature of God and of His purposes and His will, and what we have been allowed to understand of His calling to men, indicates with undeniable force that a chief arena in which men must work out their response to God's call, their appreciation of His character, and their following of His will is the work which they do in the world.

A single conclusion must be underlined: God has a concern for our work, so that work must be carried on by the Christian in direct reference to his faith as a Christian. Any conception which separates God and faith in God from work is false.

The preceding chapters indicate also some basic facts on the side of work. However we may describe it, and whatever causes we may assign to the fact, it is clear that industrial patterns are pervasive in modern Western society. Not all work is carried on in industry. Yet even those vast areas of labor which seem remote from the factory have been pervaded by the atmosphere, methods, and tools of industry. To deal with work in the modern world, therefore, means to deal with the industrial form of work, with whatever variations in the basic pattern may be appropriate. Yet this is a complex pattern, shot through with good and bad, possessing potentialities for future good and existing circumstances of evil. A simple damnation or commendation of industrial life will not do. This is the more true because, especially in America, we have given great prominence to work. Even if economic circumstances permitted, the gospel by which most of us live—the "gospel of work"—would not let us yield to the kind of indifference which a simple answer to the problems of the worker would indicate. Any approach to work in the modern situation must take account of complex, often contradictory, factors.

Two of these contradictory factors have emerged with such prominence in the preceding pages that they must be singled out. The first is the fact that, although the gospel of work in America had—in part at least—Christian roots in the Puritan doctrines of the founding fathers, it has now become almost wholly secularized. Work proceeds in the American scene without decisive reference to the will of God. The success which work brings, or is maintained to bring, to the individual and the corporation and the nation, is success measured by non-Christian standards. The motives, therefore, for work in our present scene are largely non-Christian motives. Yet, contrasted with this existing state of affairs, we have seen it demonstrated in Chapter IV that work in itself contains specifications and characteristics which make of it a vehicle on the one hand for God's communication with us, and on the other hand for our response to Him. In the deepest sense of the word, work *should* not be secularized, however much we may be wayward in making it so. It is something designed—a Christian theologian will say designed by God—but nevertheless designed, to accomplish for and with men, what God wants to accomplish.

Again, a single conclusion must be underlined: In the complex pattern of secular, industrialized work, our failure is not that we have neglected to Christianize work, but rather that we have perverted the basic design underlying all work in the world.

The conclusion from the side of Christian faith and the conclusion from the side of work define a part of the mission of the Church. The full mission of the Church, in whatever language it may be put, is to bring men into the calling of God. If this is to be done in any complete sense, men's work is involved. There have been times, as Chapter II has pointed out, when the Church saw this part of its mission more clearly than at other times. The days of vigorous monasticism, when work and prayer were the alternate points of each day's disciplined living, was one of these periods. Another came to birth in the Protestant reformation when men understood afresh the relationship between God's calling and their earthly work. There have been times also when the Church neglected this part of its mission, and probably in our own day this neglect is as widespread as it has been at any time. But a more subtle fact is that the Church undoubtedly has fulfilled its mission at certain times without primary reference to the connection between daily work and God's call. One thinks particularly of the days of the Christian resistance in Europe, starting with the Confessing Church movement in Germany and spreading throughout Europe during the years of Nazi occupation. At this time, so far as we can judge, the Church had a different mission from that concerning work and vocation. To be sure, its mission then was very directly relevant to events in the world. Yet its primary focus was directed toward maintaining the freedom and integrity of the Church against those who would limit it or stamp it out or pervert it beyond recognition. While it must, on the basis of Biblical and theological evidence, be maintained that the full mission of the Church must be directed toward the daily work of men, this is not the only part of that mission, and there are times when the Church must direct its primary attention elsewhere.

In the present condition of American society and in view of the situation of the churches in that society, however, it can be forcefully argued that a primary element—one might say the primary focus—of the mission of the churches does lie in this area. On the one hand, if the churches fail to insist upon the relevance of God's Word for work, they are untrue to that Word. On the other hand, the deep perversion of the practice and goals of work in the American scene constitute a challenge from which the churches cannot escape. The moral fabric of this working nation cannot be upheld; it cannot be redeemed unless it is brought within the wisdom and purpose of God. This is a decisive element in the mission of the Church in America.

There is, therefore, a need for a new conception of the strategy of the churches. By a new strategy, however, we do not mean simply an adjustment of techniques, whereby customary church thought and practice and programs may perhaps be made more effective and far reaching. For one thing, the churches are too burdened now with suggestions for program to carry out any more. The pastor receives envelope after envelope, several a day, from the city council of churches, the state council of churches, the boards of his denomination, and societies concerned with social work of various sorts, all containing pleas, challenges, and suggestions for the betterment of his program. Denominational officials, and officials of interdenominational bodies are so weighted with new ideas for getting various things done that the whole seems to be frequently a burden. In short, a good case can be made that the institutional structure of our churches is so freighted with the demand to make that structure efficient, that no more additional weight can be borne. A strategy, therefore, to deal with the problem of work in modern society should not be attempted in these terms. A new strategy is demanded, however, and we suggest that it should involve a fundamental rethinking of the pattern of operations in contemporary church life.

2. THE CHURCH IN TWO WORLDS

Any consideration of the setting in which we consider a strategy for the churches must start from the base line of Christian faith. We do not mean that kind of faith which simply involves a certain knowledge of Christian doctrine, a certain assent to the validity of the doctrine, and a certain willingness to go through the forms of Christian observance. This is a dead faith, and such knowledge, assent, and observance as it requires neither heal nor disturb the soul's anxieties, but rather are laid over upon a person's life without marked influence upon it. True faith, however, strikes deep into life, and means that a person has a working loyalty to God, a fidelity which makes him think of God in every decision of life, and seek in those decisions to do what God would have him do.

The Bible speaks of the people of God as strangers and pilgrims, aliens and exiles. These terms suggest something of importance concerning the Kingdom of God. They denote a strangeness which the citizen of the Kingdom of God must ever feel in the kingdom of the world—the strangeness which is felt by the man whose impulse is to sacrifice when others around him grasp for power; the strangeness of mercy amid cruelty both subtle and gross; the strangeness of moral principle when morality is spurned or ignored. They denote too a different loyalty and purpose. There is but one supreme loyalty for the people of God and that is God Himself. For many, family, self, ambition, the nation or race, or a host of other things may demand final loyalty. At this point, too, the Christian is strange: his loyalty is to the unseen Spirit and Truth, to God. He is involved in a movement. As a pilgrim, he goes on toward a goal, a goal not seen but tasted, a goal not proved but promised. As an exile, he is an alien who cannot go back. Belonging to God, he has made a decision which is irrevocable. The touch of God upon his soul has in a final way broken him away from his past, and his movement is now always forward to a future controlled by God's purpose. This strangeness, this loyalty, this movement, this break with the past mean that the Christian is always in a certain type of conflict with his world. He is still in one sense a citizen of this world, subject to its claims, its opportunities, and its temptations. But in another sense he is not a citizen of this world but of the Kingdom of God, and in conflict with all that this world holds and means. He moves through it toward a new city, and in the motion is involved in conflict both in his own soul and in his relations with others.

We are concerned with a particular portion of this conflict. In this book we are dealing with the kingdom of work, of which the Christian is a citizen at the same time he is a citizen of the Kingdom of God. In the realm of work, economic pressures and the drive for security, the attractiveness of material ease and the urge to success, the demands of the employer and the demands of the union, the need for efficient mass production and the desire for creative work—these and other pressures, needs, and the loyalties which they inspire—all operate upon people. The factory is the epitome of industrialized work, and here work is carried on in a tightly organized, self-conscious community, based on secular presuppositions, using secular means, seeking secular ends. Its loyalties press upon a Christian, with a power which cannot be denied and with characteristics which are antithetical to his loyalty to God. This does not constitute a general condemnation of industrialized work, as distinguished from work in a different type of society. It rather is a description, in contemporary terms, of the eternal tension in which a Christian is placed. He is a citizen of the city of this world and the city of God at the same time.

The resulting strangeness, conflict, and movement can never be removed, short of the final consummation of God's purposes. Church strategy should not be based upon the assumption that it can. To do so is to augment frustration and despair, or to be condemned beforehand to irrelevance. Rather than to seek to remove the conflict, the solution is to recognize it for what it is, and to make it creative rather than destructive.

It is precisely at this point, however, that the most serious problem of our present setting arises. On the whole, our churches are so constituted that they do not recognize the radical difference between the Kingdom of God and the Kingdom of this world with seriousness, with the result that the lives of the millions of people who are members of churches are not noticeably different from the world in which they live. We live in one of the most "religious" eras of American history. The churches have rarely, if ever, been as prosperous; they have rarely, if ever, been as respectable; they have never been as well populated; they have rarely, if ever, been as active in promoting their programs. Yet if Christian pride mounts up at these facts, one fact alone will cause it to crumble. This is the fact that up and down this great industrial land, where work is part and parcel of our manner of life, the patterns, the methods, the goals, and the presuppositions of work are on the whole formed without decisive reference to God. Religion is carried on in compartments of life, and if there are connecting doors with other compartments, they are rarely opened, and then only with great self-consciousness and effort. Christ's love rarely animates the range and depth of the whole person, nor permeates the working structures of life.

3. CAPTIVE RELIGION

What is it that makes it possible for this prosperity of church religion and this secularism of work to exist at one and the same time? Exhaustive analysis would need to lift up many causes, but we must point to one element in the situation which seems conclusive. This is the fact that in our contemporary scene Christianity has become captive to the spirit of the age and culture and become almost wholly specialized. Our civilization puts a high premium upon specialization: industry and the professions call for a high degree of specialized knowledge and competence. Machines are built for increasingly specialized functions. The tendency has been augmented by the extraordinary success which such concentration has provided; in realm after realm human knowledge and human welfare have been increased by it. Yet, specialization applied to religion, and among religions, especially Christianity, is fatal. The habit of mind which has advanced so far in scientific and technical fields has tended to push religion to one side of life, holding it in a special compartment, withholding it from life in general. Men do not normally expect religion to have anything to do with work, or politics, or economics, because religion is for the spiritual side of life, or at best for the moral side of life. People who profess religion are not expected, for that reason, to have anything to say, nor any right necessarily to say it, about these matters. They have habitually been reserved for specialists in other fields. Not only has this prevailing temper of mind tended to put religion on one side, but it has also been a powerful factor in confining religion to the boundaries of the institutions of religion. Church organizations are regarded as the proper sphere for the exercise of religion, and what might be expected has in fact happened. Churches urged on by this concentration of religious interest have grown and become large. A full-fledged Christian institutionalism has been developed. In four important ways this can be readily illustrated.

The very faith of the churches is in itself in a certain sense specialized and institutionalized. In the first place, the rigidity of the denominations has caused a type of restriction of the distinctive elements in the faith, a desire to perpetuate certain leading ideas in and through the denomination. The tendency of denominations to justify themselves to some degree in terms of a particular aspect of the faith, puts that faith into the confines of a specialized institution. In many ways, this is a great good, for thus important elements in the faith are preserved. The evil tendencies of self-sufficient denominationalism, or an absolute self-justification in terms of distinctive tenets of the faith, are fortunately widely recognized and fought against. The association of the churches together in the ecumenical movement has been of great value at this point. A more important factor however, lies in the inability of the churches to enunciate their faith in categories and terms relevant to the lives of the people. In congregation after congregation, the faith and its exposition is the preserve of the institutional representative—the minister. The layman who can give a good and convincing statement of Biblical faith is rare. Theology is a private preserve of the technically trained, and the laymen are not only content that it is so, but enthusiastically endorse the situation. The Bible, widely bought, less widely read, and rarely studied, is the book of the church and Sunday school, not the book of the common life. Religious books, even those which do not deal with the faith, much less those which do, reach a wide circulation if they go as high as five thousand total sale. An inner circle of professional representatives of ecclesiastical institutions seems to have pos session of the faith, in the sense that any informed and articulate awareness of it is absent en masse from the laity in general.

Second, discipline has become almost wholly specialized in the sense that its demands are mainly those of the institution. What makes a good Christian in any generally accepted sense of the word? The mark of a Christian in any wide usage of the term is that he supports his church. The discipline of the Christian community at the present time is an institutional discipline, according to which men to be good church members must live up to the demands of the organization. Fnancial support is a must. Attendance at Sunday service—which is the nearest thing we have to spiritual discipline—is not required with any force, but is expected at a fair rate of regularity. Participation in weekday activities is neither demanded nor on the whole expected as a matter of course, but it is always urged, and the quality of a man's church membership is generally determined by the number of activities in which he is regular. In Sunday schools, regularity of appearance on the part of teachers is generally more appreciated by the superintendent than intellectual depth and understanding of the subject matter. In distinction from Christian practice in the early days of our country, we have substituted for a moral and spiritual discipline, a discipline of the institution.

Third, Christian morality has come to be defined in practice more in terms of institutional demands than in terms of the demands of the Gospel. Except that Christians are very busy in their church organizations, there is little to distinguish the Christian from any decent citizen. Christian morality does not stand out in the nation as a light to guide its wanderings. On issues of national moral policy, the churches are either silent, or their pronouncements are so hedged about with qualifications as to make them acceptable and safe to all readers, or are regarded, if they have a prophetic ring about them, as the irrelevant or questionably radical statements of the clergy who do not know what they are talking about anyway. Clear pronouncement on national issues is hampered, to be sure, by the fact that Christians disagree, but this by no means accounts for the total situation. Christian family life in many a congregation is not different from the general pattern of family situation throughout the community. Christian relationships within the congregation do not distinguish themselves notably from the "fellowship" which exists in many a club. Moral demands are made, but to such an extent in terms of petty morality that larger issues are lost. Yet Christians spend time and money and effort in church work. Good will is not lacking; man hours are not lacking; economic resources are not lacking; brain power is not lacking. All of these are found in our churches and in abundance. The root of the trouble is that Christian morality has been "let off" with the maintenance of a certain respectability and with the demands for "stewardship" within the organized churches, on behalf of the organized churches and for their benefit.

Fourth, the activity of a Christian, at least the activity demanded of him by his church, is activity directed at the upbuilding of a church organization. It is the rare preacher who urges his people to stay away from a church function in the interests of making a witness in a community organization, if this means harm to the church program. It is a rare congregation which expects any accounting of its individual member's time, beyond what he puts into church work, providing he puts a reasonable amount into church work. Activities regarded as essential to the Christian—except for the conventional morality expected of all respectable people—are those which relate to the growth of the church organization. The whole structure of denominational program and procedure is geared to making the local congregation an effective instrument for its own development and that of the denomination. The reports demanded of the congregation by the higher ecclesiastical agencies; the program suggestions which are handed down from them and from the boards and agencies of the churches; the pressures upon the ministers; the appeals to the pride of the congregations, all conspire to specialize Christian energy, to direct it into the development of the institution, and therefore to discourage the diffusion of Christian energy into surrounding community life.

This specialization of Christianity has had a double effect. On the one hand, it has drawn Christians out of the world about them into the organizations for which their loyalty and energy are demanded. This is a quite different type of withdrawal from that which took place in the monasteries. There Christians were bodily as well as spiritually transported into a community closed off from the world. Not so with us. Our pattern is rather that subtle withdrawal from the world whereby Christianity is associated in laymen's minds with what one does in church, and is not associated with what one does everywhere. It is an intellectual and spiritual separation of Christianity and the Church from everyday affairs which is just as effective and in some ways more damaging than a physical withdrawal can be. On the other hand, Christian organizations have become immersed in the world because of their very prosperity as organizations. Congregations which spend thousands of dollars and in some cases hundreds of thousands of dollars annually and denominations which each spend millions of dollars annually become in practice big businesses, and are run according to accepted decent business standards. This involves investment, property, the management of loans, production, especially of printed matter, and employment. At point after point Christian organization is forced into practice which is hardly distinguishable from business establishments, forced by the requirements of law and by the pressure of lay opinion. A distinctive witness in the handling of this whole enterprise becomes increasingly difficult. More damaging is the temptation to conduct other church affairs and policy on the basis of prudence. Vestries, sessions, and trustees, mindful of the demands of property and finance and position in the community, find it easier to follow the requirements of caution rather than the imperatives of the Gospel. Church organizations, sunk more and more effectively into the world by virtue of their very success as organizations, tend to become indistinguishable from the world in the essential matters of the Gospel.

The fact that Christianity has been so largely confined to specialized institutions has all but destroyed the distinctions which should mark Christians from the world they live in. Many, and especially young Christians, have caught a great vision of the Kingdom of Christ and have felt the joyous conflict which is involved in living in that Kingdom and in the midst of the world, only to be encouraged to give witness to Christ primarily in the church organization and there to discover that they were too idealistic and therefore wrong, or to discover that the weight of institutional patterns, customs, and necessities could not be changed. Many a Christian in whom the vision could be awakened never dreams that it exists because they have been taught from the Sunday school up that being religious means being active in church. Time after time in the history of the Church, it has been true that new vitality, more courageous Christian living, and more decisive Christian witness has arisen when awareness of the conflict between Christ and the world has been most acute. The static, quiescent, and dull periods have been those in which the Church comfortably accommodated itself to its surrounding world. This is what is happening now, in the sense that we struggle to build bigger and better church organizations, draining Christian energy off from the task of redeeming the world. Our problem is to set the Gospel in its proper relationship to the world—its injustice and cruelty, its cynicism and despair—thus creating the basic condition in which new power and fresh vision rise up.

There is, however, another part to the picture. Within the churches there are stirrings, acknowledgment that this situation exists and that it must be corrected. Self-criticism is widespread and in one sense at least thoroughgoing. It is thorough in the sense that there is scarcely an aspect of the life of the churches which has not undergone searching criticism, by the highest bodies and by the most influential Christian leaders. In addition, one senses a dissatisfaction on the part of the laity, an attitude of putting up with a situation which, it is somewhat dimly realized, is not good, a perhaps wistful searching for the sterner stuff of the Christian Gospel. The point of uncertainty is whether the explicit and official self-criticism of the churches and this mood among the laity ever connect with each other. Can it be that when they do connect at the point of concrete decision, the weight of institutional considerations overpowers both perspectives and renders them helpless? However that may be, the prevalent criticism of self that is current in the churches is a very hopeful sign.

Coupled with it are some experiments. These are of greater proportions and significance on the continent of Europe than in the United States. The great annual demonstration of laymen in Germany, the Kirchentag; the continuing work of the Evangelical Academies in Germany; work among different professional groups in Holland and France; the Ecumenical Institute of the World Council are all evidence of a new vision and sense of responsibility on the part of laymen in these countries. Ecclesiastically unofficial experiments in this country are very small but promising in their motives and conceptions: the Buffalo Conference on the Christian and His Daily Work, Parishfield, the Christian Faith and Life Community, Kirkridge, the East Harlem Protestant Parish, and to some extent the student Christian movements may be mentioned. On the whole, however, the massive evangelistic and laymen's movements of the churches have followed traditional lines and have not been the centers of any radically new experiment in either concept or method.

4. A THREE-WAY STRATEGY

Given this setting, it must be the strategy of the Church to reconceive the presuppositions, patterns and forms of current organized church life so that instead of weakening the distinction between the Gospel and the world, it strengthens that distinction in the heart of the believer and helps him to use it constructively in his work in the world.

We suggest that a fundamental strategy to accomplish this end must have three parts.

a. Freedom to "Run the Course"

It must be our purpose to free the Christian community from the heavy weight of institutional baggage which now impedes its action.

The Christian Gospel is very concrete. There is no room in the Gospel, as it is written out for us in the New Testament, for vague ideas about God, or about being "religious" in an indefinite way. God is a Spirit, He is Truth, He is Unseen, but these intangibles are made concrete and definitely known. Jesus Christ is the revelation of God. We are not justified in assuming that anything else belongs to the revelation of God in the same all-important way. Jesus Christ, His mind and His spirit, is the only Master of the Christian and the Christian community.

We have lost sight of this fact. It is true that verbally we do our proper homage, and in our churches we repeat together that Jesus Christ is the Lord. Nevertheless, we have somehow got it into our heads to too great a degree that we give our best service to Christ by being active and loyal to something called a church, by being known as a good church member. In other words, there is a sense in which the organized Christian church itself has been allowed to get in between a man and the mind of Christ. The Christian Gospel has been robbed of its definiteness, and in place of its single and exclusive claim that God was in Christ, we have it that God is in all that is done in church, and that here we serve Him. More than that, we do not very carefully scrutinize all that goes on in church to make sure that it does serve the Almighty God, or that it is in harmony with the mysterious and simple and terrible and tender mind of Christ. Church programs never deviate very dramatically, but there is all too frequently that subtle and devastating irrelevance of program activities to the mind of Christ which separates us from it rather than leading us deeper into it.

From this perspective we must call everything into question, regarding nothing in our contemporary church life as sacrosanct. Does our form of Holy Communion—that is, the form we uphold in our denomination—conform to the mind of Christ? Worship is "conducted" on Sunday morning and during the week in divers ways. What really happens in these worship services? This is a question which doubtless can never ultimately be fully answered, the final judgment in those deep areas belonging only to God. Yet there is a difference, as we all know, between worship in which the Spirit of Christ is moving and a worship service which is merely dormant. When the meeting of the men's group is opened with a worship service, does anything happen, and what relationship does it have to the mind of Christ? On Sunday morning, is "the worship part" the trimming for a speech, or is the Sunday morning hour a time when people are caught up together by God in Christ? It is perhaps harder to change the time-honored ways of worship of a congregation than any other part of its life. Yet one wonders, thinking of the mind of Christ, whether much in the worship habits of any local church is not so much human baggage, irrelevant to the depths of the Gospel.

Similar questions must be raised about the other parts of the church work and program, one by one, and all together. What "service" do the deacons provide? Do they serve in the hard, unyielding terms of that justice which must roll down like a mighty stream, or that love which stops when the Pharisee went by? Upon what is the "fellowship" of the church based—upon the deep feeling which is developed when one after another bears the burdens of others, laymen bearing a ministry to laymen; or upon that other type of jovial "good fellowship" which is found also in the countless men's and women's clubs to which so many belong. If anyone has a doubt about this, let him set two or three Negro families in the midst of a white congregation in which there is "good fellowship" and see what happens. How does the educational program of the church measure up? Are we sure that the things which now are taught in our prepared curricula and in our more spontaneous meetings are the things which the mind of Christ would have us teach, or that lead us deeper into that mind? Taken all together—worship, education, service, fellowship—what of this local congregation? Does it contain a light which shines in the community it lives in, and is this light the light of God reconciling men to Himself in Christ?

The answers to any such questions as these are easy to rationalize. For one thing, most of us must simply recognize that we have not lived close enough to Christ to know His mind, and that it is therefore more mysterious to us than it necessarily should be. Insecure in our own knowledge of Christ, we cling to the traditions of the fathers and of our own customs. We become afraid to let go, lest in losing this that has at least at one time proved to be good and true, we have nothing. We do not realize fully enough that once we have, as it were, cut loose and submitted ourselves to Him, we are then able to see the traditions and the customs in their true perspective and to use them with freedom. "For freedom Christ has set us free; stand fast, therefore, and do not submit again to a yoke of slavery."

This perspective is not a burdensome one, but rather light. It frees us. It sets us loose from dead weight that holds us back as we move in the world to do the will of Him who sent us. It is also a strengthening perspective, for true strength does not lie in the massiveness of our organizational paraphernalia. It is a purifying perspective.

When we place ourselves in our Churches under His judgment and in obedience to His calling and His sending, we shall know that we cannot manifest our unity and share in His fullness without being changed. Some of us who have been assured that we possess the true order and the true sacraments will find ourselves called to give its rightful place to the preaching of the Living Word. Some who have neglected the sacraments will be confronted by Him who humbled Himself in Baptism and broke bread and shared the cup to make us partakers of His passion and death. Those who have sought to show forth the glory of the Church as the Body and Bride of Christ must stand under the judgment of His simplicity and servanthood. Churches which have valued little His prayer that the oneness of His people be made manifest to men will be summoned to make His prayer their own. Churches complacent in the face of racial divisions in the Body will be brought to repentance by Him in whom bond and free, Jew and Gentile, Greek and barbarian, are one. Churches which have stressed one-sidedly that God in His Church gives Himself to men will be reminded that Christ in His humanity offered Himself to the Father. Those who are ever looking backward and have accumulated much precious ecclesiastical baggage will perhaps be shown that pilgrims must travel light and that, if we are to share at last in the great Supper, we must let go much that we treasure. Churches settled and self-assured will have to hear again the Lord's heart-broken concern for the sheep without a shepherd and know that to be His Church is to share in His world-embracing mission. Churches too much at home in the world will hear themselves called out of the world. Churches too wrapped up in their own piety or their own survival will see again Him who identified Himself with the deprived and the oppressed.—[Third World Conference on Faith and Order, Official Report]

b. The "Third Race"

We must again establish the Church as a community in the world and not a group belonging to an organization.

"So we are ambassadors of Christ, God making His appeal through us." This we would submit is the key to what the New Testament means by belonging to the Church. It is not through a professional ministry and what that ministry does, it is not through an organization, even though it be centuries old, that God makes His primary appeal. God makes His appeal through the community of believers. From the side of the believer, this means that He represents the appeal which God makes to men, the appeal to be reconciled to Him through Jesus Christ. The believer is an ambassador, stating the case wherever he is and in whatever he is doing, for the Great Act of God. In *one* sense thus the believer *is* the Church, and does not belong to it. Or, he belongs to it, insofar as he embodies it in himself.

The crucial question is whether or not this is in any sense a complete and compelling thing for Christians today. This is of course a perennial problem; we are never, as human beings feeble and frail, completely true and constant ambassadors for Christ. Yet if the main argument of this chapter is true, there is a profound perversion of our conception of ambassadorship which we must make haste to correct. There is too much evidence that for all practical and visible purposes, to be an ambassador for Christ means primarily being a member of a church, rather than that to be a member of the Church means to be an ambassador of Christ. Christians do not live and operate in the world enough as Christians; diplomatic outposts are not flung far enough into the common life. Christians do not operate a comprehensive Point Four program; they only live in the embassies.

This is the basic reason why the churches show little concern with the issues of life which desperately plague mankind. Having become captive to the spirit of specialization and allowed religion to be put into specialized institutions, Christians are content to leave it at that, developing a high degree of proficiency in building these specialized institutions up, but neglecting the weightier matters of life. Therefore, Christians lose their ability to control sex and family life; therefore, Christians lose their influence in politics; therefore, eleven o'clock Sunday morning is the most racially segregated hour of the week. To represent the work of God in Christ, and in representing it to exemplify it in one's own person, is to break through all of this. It is to take God's work into one's full life, and it is to take one's full life into God's work. The one becomes the test of the other.

This is not, however, a purely individualistic matter. The ambassador has a country behind him. So the Christian has behind him the great fellowship of believers, the community of Christ's faithful. He may be physically separated from them, when he is driving a bus or working in an office, but he is a part of that company. More than this, he must be consciously a part of that company and he must be able to prove it to himself, to them, and to others. The Christian community requires a demonstrable corporateness, something more solid than the sum total of individual members' efforts. When in the general run of church life a congregation wants a new building, there is a corporate decision and a corporate program to get it. The action of two or three is not enough. If it is so obviously necessary in such a lesser thing as a new building, is it not also obviously necessary in the weightier matters of the law? Must we not reach into the area of corporate decision concerning spiritual and moral action? This is different from the resolutions which are passed by church assemblies, whether small or great. Of these we have plenty. A corporate *decision* involves the creation of a will among the group, a determination which has the strength to carry individuals with it and to withstand pressures and temptations. This does not mean coercion which to be sure is practically impossible and morally wrong. It does, however, mean the willingness of people to allow such a will to be formed. If, as we do time and again, we allow it to be formed in relation to purely organizational affairs, why not allow it to be formed, why not work for its development, in regard to spiritual and ethical matters? If the Church is to be a community of people operating in the *world*, it must gain the power of corporate decision. For our contemporary churches, the test in this area is to become as decisive and effective in regard to the great issues of mankind as in regard to the problems of church organization.

This points to another requirement, the development of a common Christian discipline. Is it not our prevailing habit to think that anyone has a right and privilege of conferring with a minister about spiritual and ethical problems, and that the minister has some right of inquiry and of question over his congregation in these; but that the attitude is strictly *laissez faire* as between one member and another? Is it not true, in other words, that we have relinquished any claim which a common discipline may have, a discipline of Christian living to which all are committed? Discipline in this sense was in clear evidence among New Testament Christians as it has been at every time of notable power in the life of the Church since. There is reason, therefore, to conclude that it is a necessary ingredient of the corporate life of the Christian community. Early Christians spoke of the Church as a "third race," a group of people distinguishable by their devotion and the quality of their life. This is, however, not a legal matter. The development of Christian discipline should not in the first instance be the responsibility of church authorities, whether committees or individuals, to legislate. Christian discipline has more to do with the development of a common will, of which we spoke above. This is the root of all individual discipline and all public discipline. The routine of a person's life, that is to say his daily discipline, will inevitably fall into accord with his deepest will. Public laws cannot be enforced short of the consent of the public will. Discipline in the Christian community must start with the development of a corporate will, the resulting common convictions being put into a tangible discipline gladly upheld by the Christian will of the total group. It is difficult to see how the Christian community can be effective in the world without it. To urge a pure individualism in Christian living is to urge people to frustration: the world is too strong. To legislate a moral code is doomed from the start, for it omits the essence of the Gospel. But to foster and create a common will and to solidify it into a corporate discipline is to give substance to the Body which Christians are called to be.

c. Daily Work and the Gospel

It must be our purpose to make a conscious and significant connection between the Gospel and the work we are called upon to do throughout our life.

It has frequently been true that the first two lines of strategy which we have suggested have become the bulwarks of a relatively isolated sectarianism. Freedom from entangling organizational and institutional impediments, and a moral and spiritual discipline, are factors which, far from pushing the Christian community into the workaday world, can in fact be powerful incentives to withdraw from the scene, and to isolate the Christian group from surrounding life. It is possible also that these two interests might be so conceived that Christians could work in the world, without primary reference to work itself, but only with reference to their conduct on the job as disciplined Christians. If in the interests of a comprehensive ministry to a community and a nation, the Churches have tended to compromise and institutionalize their position, the sects in the interests of vigor and of moral purity have tended to withdraw from the very areas where life is the most difficult, decisions the most far reaching, and temptations the most severe. In one sense the perennial problem of Christian strategy is to combine as may be best in a given situation the comprehensive ministry of the Church, with the incisive witness of the sect. This is admittedly a counsel of perfection. Yet one suspects that the periodic need for reform stems at root from a perversion of either one of these two sides of Christian living. Either the churches have so weakened their witness as to demand a new conception of it, or the sects have become so isolated as to demand a new orientation for their mission in the world. In a peculiar way, churches in the present scene combine some elements of both of these

difficulties. On the one side, they have become specialized, institutionalized, and thus withdrawn from the world of men's affairs
much as the sects always have tended to be in Christian history.
On the other hand, they have maintained a comprehensive appeal
and vast membership and have tended to weaken the incisive-
ness of their witness.

We suggest that a conscious connection between the Christian
Gospel and the work which men do is for this present time and
scene a solution to the problem. It is in this area where current
Christian conceptions need the greatest reform. It is at this point
that comprehensiveness of approach to the current scene and clear-
cut Christian witness may be best combined. As we have been
at pains to point out earlier, there are circumstances in which
the issue of work and vocation is not the crucial issue. Yet at the
present time we suggest that it is crucial.

In Chapter III we have indicated some of the ways in which
the Gospel may be effectively connected with the work which
people do day by day and throughout their lives. It is not necessary to repeat here what was said there. One point should be
stressed. It is not sufficient to carry one's Christian discipline
merely into the surroundings of one's daily work. It is necessary
to behave in a disciplined Christian way on the job, but this is
not enough. The crucial connection is that which must be made
between work itself and the demands of the Gospel. Is the work
worthy in itself? Are the objectives of one's work in harmony
with Christian demands? Is the social effect of the work beneficial
or harmful judged by the standard of the mind of Christ? These
and other questions are all involved in the over-all and all-important question.

To deal seriously with this question is to provide a comprehensive setting to the Christian mission in the world. There is
hardly anything more universal than work. It is a part of every
man's experience. Moreover, there is hardly any area of man's
life which raises more baffling and complex problems than the
sphere of daily work. Here is involved the delicate balance of
compromise with principle which is made necessary in order to
uphold other equally worthy principles. Here is involved a whole

range of sociological issues, as we have suggested in Chapter III. Again a complex variety of psychological problems are involved. Issues relating to national policy, both domestic and foreign, are likewise a part of the scene. If the Christian community is to direct the light of the mind of Christ into the areas of human work, it is engaged on as comprehensive a mission as there is for it to undertake.

Yet it is a mission which also requires both freedom and discipline. It requires freedom because the work which men do is done everywhere; it is not, that is, done in church or in some controlled situation where it is relatively easy to be Christian. It is done amid all sorts and conditions of men and of circumstances. Only those who operate with the confident freedom of the Christian man have the spiritual independence, the flexibility and the mobility wherewith to enter into this uncharted area. By the same token, discipline is required also. The stresses are too great; the perplexities are too difficult and numerous; the temptations are too powerful for an individual to trust merely his own unsupported insights. The ambassador must have instructions, lest he fail to represent his country. The Christian especially in such a far-flung outpost as the area of daily work also needs his.

No combination of a comprehensive ministry and a decisive witness is ever automatically achieved. Merely directing the Christian Gospel to the fields of daily work will not do it. This combination must be constantly worked at, reviewed time after time, re-evaluated again and again. The temptation will arise to align the Gospel with certain kinds of work, as when Christianity and capitalism or Christianity and socialism seem to some to be identical. The temptation will arise to freeze a discipline into a permanent thing and to make acceptance of the discipline a test of the acceptance of Christ. These and other pitfalls must be constantly guarded against with that kind of Christian skepticism which knows that they can never be wholly avoided. Nevertheless, providing that the whole stands always under the judgment of Christ and is motivated by the love of Christ, we cannot avoid the clear call to inject the comprehensiveness, freedom, and discipline of the Gospel into those realms of life where men do their work.

5. LAYMEN'S COMMITMENT AND EXPERIMENT

How can it be done? There is one and only one key to the answer to that question. Who are the ambassadors? Who are the Church? The ambassadors are men and women caught by the love of Christ. A very few of these people are the professional servants of the Church. They will have their important function to perform, but it will be a behind-the-scenes function. The primary responsibility will be taken up by lay men and by lay women. We say "will be," and we do not say "ought to be." In this matter there is no "ought to be," for the plain fact is that the Christian Gospel will not get connected with daily work unless lay men and lay women do the connecting. Professional clergy, no matter how much they may want to help, simply cannot do the actual job. It is a matter of fact.

Yet with what equipment will laymen undertake this awesome task? Even a person with no more political experience than the casting of a vote and the reading of newspapers realizes something of the delicacy and complexity of ethical problems involved in work in government. So too with the work of production and distribution, and with work in area after area of our highly specialized, interdependent and complex society. The deepest knowledge of Biblical truth and Christian experience is fundamental to Christian witness in these areas. A refined sensitivity (which is not an intellectual matter) to people both individuals and en masse is a matter of necessity. A personal experience of God in Christ, so deep as to be henceforth unshakable, is a further, and the most basic, necessity of all.

Do lay people have all this? If so, well and good. If not, here is the first step to be taken. We do not dare say simply that we must overhaul our educational program; the matter is deeper than that. We do not dare suggest any comprehensive scheme; because the problem is more concrete and relevant to specific individuals than any single plan or series of comprehensive pro-

grams can probably fruitfully be. No series of suggestions is
enough. In final analysis, what is necessary is for those who are
concerned to start work on all these fronts right now. If there
is a minister who sees the problem and what in general must be
done, let him rally some laymen right away. If there are laymen
who understand what is required, let them begin to dig and to
work at what is after all peculiarly their own problem. The
places at which different people begin; the things which they will
take up; the techniques by which they do so must all vary person
by person and group by group. But let us start!

Let us also experiment. The word "experiment," especially in
ecclesiastical circles, is regarded askance, a word used by radicals
and eccentrics. In our scientific world this is a curious situation.
Actually the only concrete way of breaking out of our current
setting is to experiment. Does a congregation want a discipline
of Christian living? Start to build it. Do a group of lawyers
want to connect the Gospel with their practice of law? Let them
try, experimenting with imagination and with faith. This cannot
be worked out in advance in books, but must be hammered out
in the heat of the day. Supposing there is a blank wall: a hand-
ful of transportation workers in a vast system can see no fruitful
connection between the Gospel and what they have to do. What
then? Is it not the beginning of a solution to see the problem
for what it is, with all of its meaninglessness and frustration?
This *is* the Christian struggle in the world and there is hope in
that struggle only if one enters into it, and not if one runs away
from it. Experiment, therefore, must embrace the virtually hope-
less as well as the relatively easy. We are not dealing in these
matters with a light and easy problem. We deal with problems
which require truth, righteousness, faith; which call for the power
of spirit and the imagination of mind given to us by Christ.
We are dealing with the slow and hard process of the redemption
of the world. Therefore, "Put on the whole armour of God."

The three lines of action which we have been stressing must
be undertaken simultaneously. Almost inevitably, any one taken
up by itself is foredoomed to failure. Those who only fasten
upon the need to overhaul the organized pattern of church life

court frustration, for a commanding purpose is needed to accomplish any such formidable task as that. Those who take up the great purpose, that of connecting the Gospel with work, must also pay attention to the Christian community which will carry out that purpose. A base of thought and action is needed. And those who seize at once upon the need for new programs and new lines of experiment must consider the fundamental reorientation that is needed within the present church scene, or the new programs and promising experiments will be stifled. This is indeed the weakness of so much ingenious programming in church circles today. The programs do not fit the organization which is to carry them out, or they fit it entirely too well. Either way, it is the basic organizational and institutional pattern that is likely to triumph over even the best-planned programs. Yet it is folly to neglect the concrete action. If the new seeds are any good, they must yield new fruit.

Each part must be undertaken together with the other parts. Yet there is a center to the whole. Many factors play upon the life of the Christian and even though they are not a part of his faith, they determine much of his life. Yet it is a part of the Christian interpretation of life to say that what a man believes, he is and does. The question is, what does he *believe*? The center of our whole strategy is simple. It is to meet and understand the Lord. He animates every Christian impulse; He guides every Christian strategy; He illumines every perplexity and eases every anxiety. In not allowing Him to meet us in our work, we have allowed our work itself to be diverted from its true purpose. The point of the whole matter is again to meet Christ the Lord in our work, thus redeeming the work and in redeeming the work, contribute to the salvation of mankind.

A BIBLIOGRAPHY ON
WORK AND VOCATION

Robert S. Michaelsen
(with the assistance of Carl E. Nelson,
John H. Peatling, Jr., Masao Takenaka,
and Ursula Schuster)

I. BIBLICAL AND HISTORICAL

A. PRIMARY SOURCES:

Patristic & Medieval

Antoninus, Saint (Archbishop of Florence, 1389-1459). Ardent Thomist. Example of early Thomistic thought on the place of occupations in Thomas' social theory. See esp. his *Summa Theologica Moralis,* Pt. III

Antonius, Saint (The Great). *Epistola I.* In Migne, J. P., *Patrologia Graeca,* XL, 999-1003.

Athanasius, Saint. *The Life of Saint Antony.* Translated and annotated by R. T. Meyer. Westminster, Md., Newman Press, 1950.

Augustinus, Saint, of Hippo. "The Work of Monks," in St. Augustine, *Treatises on Various Subjects* (Vol. 16). *The Fathers of the Church.* New York, Fathers of the Church, Inc., 1952.

Basilius, Saint (The Great, Archbishop of Caesarea in Cappadocia, 4th cent.). *The Ascetic Works of Saint Basil.* Translated into English, with introduction and notes, by W. K. L. Clarke. London, Society for Promoting Christian Knowledge; New York & Toronto, The Macmillan Company, 1925.

Benedictus, Saint (Abbot of Monte Cassino). *The Rule of Saint Benedict.* Translated, with an introduction, by Cardinal Gasquet. London, Chatto, 1925.
Standard rule for Western monasticism.

Cassianus, Joannes. *De Coenobiorum Institutis,* Bks. I and IV. In *Nicene and Post-Nicene Fathers,* second series, Vol. XI, pp. 201-5, 219-33.

Clement of Alexandria (c.200). See *The Ante-Nicene Fathers,* Vol. II.

Clement of Rome. *Epistle to the Corinthians,* in *The Ante-Nicene Fathers,* Vol. I.

Diognetus, Epistle to, —, in *The Ante-Nicene Fathers,* Vol. I, pp. 26-27, 29.

Eucherius, Saint (Bishop of Lyons, A.D., 449). *Epistola De laude eremi.* In Migne, J.-P., *Patrologia Latina,* L, 701-712.

The Shepherd. *Homiliae,* IV-I.X In Migne, J.-P., *Patrologia Latina, L,* 841-56.

HERMAS., in *The Ante-Nicene Fathers,* Vol. II.

THOMAS AQUINAS, SAINT. *De perfectione vitae spiritualis.* Shows Thomas' distinct preference for the monastic (or "religious") life, to which he restricted the terms *vocare* and *vocatio.*

————. *Summa contra Gentiles,* P. III, Chaps. XXX, XXXIV, XXXVII, CXXXIII, CXXXV.

————. *Summa Theologica,* II-II, questions 55, 66, 77, 78, 179, 182, 187.

Reformation and Post-Reformation

ALLESTREE, RICHARD. *The Whole Duty of Man.* . . . First printed in 1657. Latest English ed. New York, Stanford and Swords, 1850. Important guide to the moral life. English Protestant.

BAXTER, RICHARD. *Christian Directory.* London, 1673. London, G. Bell & Sons, Ltd., 1925. A late Puritan "Summa." Shows some adaptation of the Protestant concept of vocation to the rising "spirit of capitalism."

BARROW, ISAAC. *Of Industry.* London, 1693, Anglican.

BURY, EDWARD. *The Husbandman's Companion.* London, 1677. Nonconformist.

CALVIN, JOHN. Commentaries. See especially the commentary on I Cor. 7:20. See also other entries under "vocation" or "calling."

————. *Institutes of the Christian Religion* (Definitive ed., 1559), Bk. III, Chaps. vi, vii, x, xxiv; Bk. IV, Chap. xiii.

————. *Opera.* See especially "vocatio" in the Index. Vol. LVIII, p. 223.

COTTON, JOHN. *Christ the Fountain of Life.* London, 1651.

————. *The Way of Life.* . . . London, 1641. Early American Puritan.

CROWLEY, ROBERT. "Voyce of the Last Trumpet" and "The Way to Wealth," in *The Select Works of Robert Crowley.* Ed. by J. M. Cowper. London, published for the Early English Text Society by N. Trübner & Co., Extra Series, Vol. XV, 1872. Sixteenth-century Englishman. Forerunner of Puritans.

DEFOE, DANIEL. *The Complete English Tradesman.* London, 1726. Secularized doctrine of vocation.

FLAVELL, JOHN. *Husbandry Spiritualized; or, the Heavenly Use of Earthly Things.* London, 1669, 1674—3rd ed. Late seventeenth-century English non-conformist.

HOOKER, THOMAS. *The Sovles Vocation or Effectval Calling to Christ.* London, 1638. Early American Puritan.

LATIMER, HUGH. *Seven Sermons before Edward VI.* Ed. by Edward Arber. English Reprints; London, 1868. Esp. pp. 177-81. Sixteenth-century Englishman. Forerunner of Puritans.

LEVER, THOMAS. "A Sermon Preached at Paules Crosse," in *Sermons, 1550.* Ed. by Edward Arber. English Reprints, Vol. XXV; London, 1869, pp. 101-43. Sixteenth-century Englishman. Forerunner of Puritans.

LUTHER, MARTIN. See especially his three basic treatises, the *Treatise on Good Works,* and a number of sermons on the subject of vocation or calling. (Luther did not systematically set forth his view of vocation in any one treatise.)

MATHER, COTTON. *Two Brief Discourses: One Directing a Christian in His General Calling; another Directing Him in His Personal Calling.* Boston, 1701.

————. *Essays to do Good.* . . . New York, The American Tract Society 184-?. Representative of late American Puritanism.

The New Whole Duty of Man: Containing the Faith as well as Practice of a Christian made easy for the Practice of the Present Age . . . London, 1766 (a late edition. The earliest one available in print.) Important guide to the moral life. Widely used by Protestants in the eighteenth century.

PERKINS, WILLIAM. "A Treatise of the Vocations or Callings of Men," in *Workes.* Cambridge, 1608, Vol. I, pp. 727-56. Very influential among seventeenth-century English and American Puritans.

RITSCHL, ALBRECHT. *Die Christliche Lehre von der Rechtfertigung und Versöhnung.* Bonn, 1883.

SHEPARD, THOMAS. *Certain Select Cases Resolved; Specifically tending to the right ordering of the Heart, that we may comfortably walk with God in our General and Particular Callings.* Collected by T. Shepard from the *First Principles of the Oracles of God.* Ed. by W. Adderley. London, 1648. Early American Puritan.

STEELE, RICHARD. *The Tradesman's Calling.* . . . London, 1684. See also *The Religious Trader: A New Edition of the Tradesman's Calling,* 1684. Preface, Recommendations (and alterations) by Isaac Watts. New York, 1773. Steele was an important late seventeenth-century English non-conformist.

SWINNOCK, GEORGE. *The Christian-mans Calling; or, A Treatise of Making Religion One's Business.* Edinburgh, 1868, 3 Vols. Late seventeenth-century English non-conformist.

For the creeds and confessions of the Reformation and after see:

SCHAFF, PHILIP. *The Creeds of Christendom,* Vol. III. *The Evangelical Protestant Creeds,* with translations. New York, Harper & Brothers, 1877; 1952. Index under "call," "calling," and "Election."

Triglot Concordia (The Symbolical Books of the Evangelical Lutheran Church). St. Louis, 1921. Index under "call," "callings (temporal)," and "Election."

A certain amount of material can be found in the books and manuals of discipline of some of the Protestant churches. For example, see the various editions of the Book of Discipline of the Society of Friends under the heading "Trade." See also the Book of Discipline of the Methodist Church under the heading "General Rules."

B. SECONDARY WORKS:

Biblical

BERTRAM, G., "ἔργον" (ergon), *Theologisches Wörterbuch zum Neuen Testament.* Ed. by G. Kittel. Stuttgart, 1935, Vol. II, pp. 631-49.

BORNHAUSER, KARL. *Der Christ und Seine Habe nach dem N. T.; eine sociologische Studie.* Gütersloh, Bertelsmann, 1936.

HERMANN, JOHANNES. *"Das Arbeitsethos in der biblischen Urgeschichte"* in *Glaube und Ethos. Festschrift für Wehrung*, p. 9 ff. Stuttgart, Kohlhammer, 1940.

HUSSLEIN, JOSEPH. *The Bible and Labor*. New York, The Macmillan Company, 1924.

HUTCHINSON, JOHN. "The Biblical Idea of Vocation," in *Christianity and Society*, XIII/2, Spring, 1948, pp. 9-16.

RICHARDSON, ALAN. "The Biblical Doctrine of Work," in *The Frontier*, Vol. II, No. 3, March, 1951, pp. 109-20.

————. *The Biblical Doctrine of Work*. London, S.C.M. Press, 1952.

SULZBERGER, MAYER. *The Status of Labor in Ancient Israel*. Philadelphia, The Dropsie College for Hebrew and Cognate Learning, 1923.

WALL, R. *Wealth and Poverty in New Testament Life and Teaching*. New York, 1934.

Historical

ALTHAUS, PAUL. " 'Iuxta vocationem.' Zur Lutherischen Lehre von Ordnung und Beruf," in *Luthertum Jg.*, 1936, S. 368 ff.

BETCKE, WERNER. *Luthers Sozialethik*. Gütersloh, C. Bertelsmann, 1934, pp. 119-30.

CALHOUN, ROBERT L. *God and the Common Life*. New York, Charles Scribner's Sons, 1935.

EGER, KARL. *Die Anschauungen Luthers vom Beruf; ein Beitrag zur Ethik Luthers.* . . . Giessen, J. Ricker, 1900.

FLEW, R. N. *The Idea of Perfection in Christian Theology*. London, Oxford University Press, 1934.

GEOGHEGAN, ARTHUR T. *The Attitude towards Labor in Early Christianity and Ancient Culture*. Washington, Catholic University Press, 1945.

HARKNESS, GEORGIA. *John Calvin: The Man and His Ethic*. New York, Henry Holt & Company, 1931.

HOLL, KARL. "Die Geschichte des Wortes Beruf," in *Gesammelte Aufsätze zur Kirchengeschichte*. Tübingen, Mohr, 1928. Vol. III, pp. 189-219. Brief but excellent sketch.

HOPKINS, CHARLES HOWARD. *The Rise of the Social Gospel in American Protestantism—1865-1915*. New Haven, Yale University Press, 1940. London, Humphrey Milford, Oxford University Press, 1940.

KIRK, KENNETH ESCOTT. *The Vision of God*. London and New York, Longmans, Green and Company, 1931.

LINHARDT, R. *Die Sozialprinzipen des heiligen Thomas von Aquin*. Freiburg im Breisgau, Herder & Company, 1932.

MAY, HENRY F. *Protestant Churches and Industrial America*. New York, Harper & Brothers, 1949.

MICHAELSEN, ROBERT S. "The Gospel of Work in America," in *Social Action*, Dec. 15, 1949. "Changes in the Puritan Concept of Calling or Vocation," *New England Quarterly*, Vol. XXVI, No. 3, pp. 315-36.

NIEBUHR, H. RICHARD. *Christ and Culture*. New York, Harper & Brothers, 1951.

———. *The Kingdom of God in America.* New York, Harper & Brothers, 1937.

PAULUS, NIKOL. "Die Wertung der weltlichen Berufe im Mittelalter," in *Historisches Jahrbuch,* 1911, Vol. XXXII, 725-43.

RAISTRICK, ARTHUR. *Quakers in Science and Industry.* London, The Bannisdale Press, 1950.

SOKOL, ARTHUR E. "The Concept of Calling in the German Literature of the Middle Ages," *Modern Languages Association of America, Publications,* Vol. 50, March, 1935.

TROELTSCH, ERNST. *The Social Teaching of the Christian Churches,* translated by Olive Wyon. London, Allen & Unwin, Ltd., 1931, New York, The Macmillan Company, 1931, and later editions.

WATSON, PHILIP S. "Luther's Doctrine of Vocation," in *Scottish Journal of Theology,* II, 4, Dec. 1949.

WINGREN, GUSTAF. *Luthers Lehre vom Beruf.* München, C. Kaiser Verlag, 1952.

WORKMAN, HERBERT BROOK. *The Evolution of the Monastic Ideal.* London, The Epworth Press, 1927—2nd ed.

Protestantism and Capitalism

CUNNINGHAM, WILLIAM. *Christianity and Economic Science.* London, J. Murray, 1914.

DOWDEN, EDWARD. *Puritan and Anglican: Studies in Literature.* New York, Henry Holt & Co., 1901. On the decline of the Puritan doctrine of vocation.

FANFANI, AMINTORE. *Catholicism, Protestantism and Capitalism.* London, Sheed & Ward, 1935, 1939. Mildly critical of the Weber thesis. Good use of sources.

HUDSON, WINTHROP. "Puritanism and the Spirit of Capitalism," in *Church History,* Vol. XVIII, No. 1, March, 1949.

HYMA, ALBERT. *Christianity, Capitalism and Communism.* Ann Arbor, Mich., G. Wahr, 1937.

JOHNSON, EDGER A. J. *American Economic Thought in the Seventeenth Century.* London, P. S. King & Son, Ltd., 1932. Critical of Weber thesis.

O'BRIEN, GEORGE A. T. *An Essay on the Economic Effects of the Reformation.* Westminster, Md., The Newman Bookshop, 1944.

ROBERTSON, HECTOR M. *Aspects of the Rise of Economic Individualism.* Cambridge, Cambridge University Press, 1933. Very critical of Weber.

ROUGIER, LOUIS. "La Reforme et le Capitalisme moderne," in *La Revue de Paris,* Oct. 15, 1928.

SCHLATTER, RICHARD B. *The Social Ideas of Religious Leaders, 1660-1688.* London, Oxford University Press, 1940.

SÉE, H. "Dans quelle mesure Puritains et Juifs ont-ils contribués au Progrés de la Capitalisme Moderne?" in *Revue Historique,* XLV, 1927.

SOMBART, WERNER. *The Quintessence of Capitalism.* London, T. F. Unwin, Ltd., 1915. Critical of Weber.

TAWNEY, RICHARD H. "Religion and Business, A Forgotten Chapter in

Social History," in *The Hibbert Journal*, Vol. 21, No. 1 Oct., 1922, pp. 65-80.

———. *Religion and the Rise of Capitalism*. New York, Harcourt, Brace & Co., 1926, 1937, London, J. Murray, 1929. See also Penguin Books, Inc., New York, first Pelican Bks. Ed., Nov., 1947. One of the best works on the subject.

TROELTSCH, ERNST. *The Social Teaching of the Christian Churches*. London, Allen & Unwin, 1931. Supports Weber thesis.

WEBER, MAX. *The Protestant Ethic and the Spirit of Capitalism*. London, Allen & Unwin, 1930, and New York, Charles Scribner's Sons, 1930, 1948. First clearly stated the thesis that the Protestant ethic paved the way for the development of the "spirit of capitalism." Placed much emphasis upon the doctrine of vocation.

II. CONTEMPORARY

A. THEOLOGICAL

BARTH, KARL. *Die Kirchliche Dogmatik*, III/4. Evangelischer Verlag, Zurich-Zollikon, 1951. See esp. pp. 558 ff. and pp. 683 ff.

BILLING, EINAR. *Our Calling*. Translated from Swedish by Conrad Bergendoff. Rock Island, Augustana Book Concern, 1947.

BRADLEY, FRANCIS H. *Ethical Studies*. Oxford, The Clarendon Press, 1927. See esp. Essay V on "My Station and Its Duties."

BRUNNER, H. EMIL. *Christianity and Civilization*, Pt. 2: Specific Problems. New York, Charles Scribner's Sons, 1949. See Chap. V, "Work."

———. *The Divine Imperative*. Translated by Olive Wyon. London, Lutterworth Press, 1937, Philadelphia, Westminster Press, 1947. See the section on "Vocation and Occupation."

CALHOUN, ROBERT L. *God and the Common Life*. New York, Charles Scribner's Sons, 1935.

———. *God and the Day's Work*. New York, Association Press, 1943.

———. "The Day's Work as Christian Vocation," in *Social Action*, Dec. 14, 1949.

Christians at Work. Reports of the Industrial Research Group of the Youth Department of the British Council of Churches.

CRIPPS, SIR RICHARD STAFFORD. *God in our Work; Religious Addresses*. London and New York, Thomas Nelson & Sons, 1949.

DAVIS, T. W. *Men at Work*. London, S.C.M. Press, 1946.

EDDY, SHERWOOD, and PAGE, KIRBY. *Creative Pioneers*. New York, Association Press, 1937.

ELLARD, GERALD. *The Mass of the Future*. Milwaukee, The Bruce Publishing Co., 1948.

FFORDE, SIR ARTHUR. "Encounters with Doubt," in *The Frontier*, Vol. II, No. 6, June, 1951, pp. 229-38.

FORRESTER, WILLIAM R. *Christian Vocation: Studies in Faith and Work*. London, Lutterworth Press, 1951.

HALL, C. P. *The Christian at His Daily Work*, "The Christian Meaning of Work for Today—with questions for self-examination and group discussion." New York, National Council of the Churches of Christ in the United States of America. Dept. of the Church and Economic Life. Division of Christian Life and Work, 1951.

HANDLEY, HENRY (The Bishop of Knavesborough). "Harvest Thanksgiving," in *Parish and People,* Vol. II, No. 2, Sept., 1951, pp. 1-4.

"A Holy Calling," a special number of the *Student World,* 2nd Quarter, 1950, Vol. 43, No. 2.

HOMRIGHAUSEN, ELMER G. "The Vocation of the Christian Today," in *The Gospel, the Church and the World.* Ed. by Kenneth Scott Latourette. New York, Harper & Brothers, 1946.

HORTON, DOUGLAS, LAMPE, WILLIAM BLAKEMAN, AND TITTLE, ERNEST FREMONT. *Christian Vocation.* Boston, The Pilgrim Press, 1945.

Intercollegian, Vol. 70, No. 5, Jan., 1953.

JENKINS, DANIEL THOMAS, ED. *The Doctor's Profession.* London, S.C.M. Press, 1949.

LLOYD, ROGER. *The Church and the Artisan Today.* London, Longmans, Green & Company, 1952.

LOCKHART, EARL G., ED. *My Vocation* (by eminent Americans). New York, H. W. Wilson, 1941.

Man's Work and the Christian Faith. Reports of a Conference, published by the Industrial Christian Fellowship, 1948.

The Meaning of Work. Issued by the Study Department of the World Council of Churches, July, 1950.

MERRIAM, THORNTON. *The Economic Order and Religion.* New York, Harper & Brothers, 1945.

MILLER, ALEXANDER. *Christian Faith and My Job.* New York, Association Press, 1946.

———. "Toward a Contemporary Doctrine of Vocation, in *Christian Faith and Social Action.* Ed. by John A. Hutchison. New York, 1953.

MORTON, RALPH T. *Household of Faith.* The Iona Community, 1951.

MOULD, RALPH N. *Christianity Where Men Work.* New York, Friendship Press, 1947.

MUELDER, WALTER G. *Religion and Economic Responsibility.* New York, Charles Scribner's Sons, 1953.

NALL, TORNEY O., AND DAVIS, BERT H. *Young Christians at Work.* New York, Association Press, 1949.

NELSON, JOHN OLIVER. *Every Occupation a Christian Calling.* New York, Association Press, 1951.

———. *Christian Youth and Christian Vocation.* Issued by the United Christian Youth Movement, Chicago, 1951.

OLDHAM, J. H. "The Two Orders in Which We Live," in *The Frontier,* Vol. I, No. 12, Dec. 1950, pp. 458-65.

———. "On Work," in *Christian News Letter,* No. 148.

———. *Work in Modern Society.* London, S.C.M. Press, 1950, New York, Morehouse-Gorham Company, 1950.

PIEPER, JOSEF. *Leisure the Basis of Culture.* London, Faber & Faber, 1952.

Professional Life as Christian Vocation, "A Report on Laymen's Institutes and Groups, 1947-48." Papers of the Ecumenical Institute, No. III, Oikumene, Geneva.

RAMSEY, PAUL. *Basic Christian Ethics.* New York, Charles Scribner's Sons, 1950.

ROBERTSON, JAMES ALEXANDER. *Divine Vocation in Human Life.* London, J. Clarke, 1925.

SAYERS, DOROTHY. *Why Work?* London, Methuen, 1942. See also *Creed or Chaos.* New York, Harcourt, Brace & Company, 1949, pp. 46 ff.

SCHUSTER, SIR GEORGE. *Christianity and Human Relations in Industry.* London, The Epworth Press, 1951.

SPEERS, W. C. *What on Earth Are You Doing?* New York, Harper & Brothers, 1951.

STALEY, EUGENE S., ED. *Creating an Industrial Civilization.* New York, Harper & Brothers, 1952.

STONE, DONALD C. "Government Service as a Christian Vocation," in *Motive,* March, 1951, Vol. XI, No. 6, pp. 10-12.

SYMONS, W. G. "The Layman in the Church," in *The Frontier,* Vol. III, No. 2, Feb., 1952, pp. 55-65.

———. *Work and Vocation.* London, S.C.M. Press, 1946.

TILLICH, PAUL. *The Protestant Era.* Translated, and with a concluding essay, by James L. Adams. Chicago, University of Chicago Press, 1948.

TRUEBLOOD, ELTON. *The Common Ventures of Life.* New York, Harper & Brothers, 1949.

———. *Your Other Vocation.* New York, Harper & Brothers, 1952.

TYNDALL, E. DENIS. "The Hallowing of Daily Life and Work," in Hebert, A. G., ed., *The Parish Communion.* London, Society for Promoting Christian Knowledge, 1937, reprinted, 1944, pp. 183-98.

VAN DUSEN, HENRY P. "The Problem of Work and Vocation in the Modern World," in *The Journal of Religious Thought,* Vol. IX, No. 2, Spring-Summer, 1952, pp. 113-25.

VOORHIS, HORACE JEREMIAH. *The Christian in Politics.* New York, Association Press, 1951.

See also:

Various Papal Encyclicals, such as *Rerum Novarum* and *Quadragesimo Anno.*

The files of *The Christian News-Letter, The Frontier* and *Laymen's Work.*

The first two are published in England. (*The Christian News-Letter* has now replaced *The Frontier.*) The third is published by the section for laymen's work of the World Council of Churches, 17, Route de Malagnou, Geneva, Switzerland.

Community and Small Group movements especially concerned with Christian vocation:

The Christophers. 18 E. 48th Street, New York, N. Y. *You Can Change the World! The Christopher Approach,* by James Keller, M.M., Director of the Christophers. New York, Longmans, Green & Co., 1948. See also *Careers that Change Your World.* New York, Doubleday & Co., Inc., 1950.

The Iona Community. See George Fielden MacLeod, *We Shall Re-*

Build: The Work of the Iona Community on Mainland and on Island. Kirkridge, 1945.

Jeunesse Ouvrière Chrêtienne (JOCists). See "The Young Christian Workers Movement," in *Social Justice Review*, Vol. 40, Jan.-Feb., 1948, p. 336.

Kirkridge, Bangor, Pennsylvania.

Parishfield, Brighton, Michigan. See the Parishfield Papers.

Society of Brothers, Burwarton, Shropshire, England.

B. GENERAL—WITH SPECIAL REFERENCE TO WORK IN CONTEMPORARY INDUSTRIAL SOCIETY:

ADAMS, WALTER, ED. *The Structure of American Industry.* New York, The Macmillan Company, 1950.

ADORNO, T. W., ET AL. *The Authoritarian Personality.* New York, Harper & Brothers, 1950.

BAKKE, E. WIGHT. *Bonds of Organizations.* New York, Harper & Brothers, 1950.

————. *Citizens without Work; A Study of the Effects of Unemployment upon the Worker's Social Relations and Practices.* New Haven, Yale University Press, 1940, London, H. Milford, Oxford University Press, 1940.

————. *Mutual Survival; The Goal of Union and Management.* New York, Harper & Brothers, 1946.

————. *The Unemployed Worker; A Study of the Task of Making a Living without a Job.* New Haven, Yale University Press, 1940, London, H. Milford, Oxford University Press, 1940.

————, AND KERR, CLARK. *Unions, Management and the Public.* New York, Harcourt, Brace & Co., 1949.

BARNARD, CHESTER 1. *The Function of the Executive.* Cambridge, Harvard University Press, 1938.

————. *Organization and Management.* Cambridge, Harvard University Press, 1949.

BAUM, MAURICE. *Readings in Business Ethics.* Dubuque, Iowa, Wm. C. Brown Co., 1950.

BOULDING, KENNETH E. (with commentary by Reinhold Niebuhr). *The Organizational Revolution; A Study in the Ethics of Economic Organization.* New York, Harper & Brothers, 1953.

BOWEN, HOWARD R. (with commentary by F. Ernest Johnson). *Social Responsibilities of the Businessman.* New York, Harper & Brothers, 1953.

BRADY, ROBERT A. *Business as a System of Power.* New York, Columbia University Press, 1943.

BROOKS, ROBERT. R. R. *Unions of Their Own Choosing. An account of The National Labor Relations Board and Its Work.* New Haven, Yale University Press, 1944.

BROWN, A. B. *The Machine and the Worker.* London, Ivor Nicholson & Watson, 1934.

CHAMBERLAIN, NEIL W. *Collective Bargaining Procedures*. Washington, J. Douglas Brown, 1944.

——. *The Union Challenge to Management Control*. New York, Harper & Brothers, 1948.

CHASE, STUART. *Men and Machines*. New York, The Macmillan Company, 1929.

——. *Men at Work; Some Democratic Methods for the Power Age*. New York, Harcourt, Brace, 1945.

——, AND TYLER, MARIAN. *Roads to Agreement; Successful Methods in Human Relations*. New York, Harper & Brothers, 1951.

Code of Ethics and Procedural Standards of Labor-Management Arbitration. Prepared by the American Arbitration Association and the National Academy of Arbitrators and approved by the Federal Mediation and Conciliation Service. New York, American Arbitration Association.

DAUGHERTY, CARROLL R., AND PARRISH, JOHN B. *Labor Problems of American Society*. Boston, Houghton, Mifflin Co., 1952.

DRUCKER, PETER F. *The End of Economic Man*. New York, The John Day Co., 1939.

——. *Concept of the Corporation*. New York, The John Day Co., 1946.

——. *The Future of Industrial Man*. New York, The John Day Co., 1942.

——. *The New Society: The Anatomy of the Industrial Order*. New York, Harper & Brothers, 1950.

ELLSWORTH, JOHN S., JR. *Factory Folkways; A Study of Institutional Structure and Change*. New Haven, Yale University Press, 1952.

GARDNER, BURLEIGH B., AND MOORE, D. G. *Human Relations in Industry*. Chicago, Richard D. Irwin, Inc., 1949.

GINZBERG, ELI, ET AL. *Occupational Choice*. New York, Columbia University Press, 1951.

GLOVER, JOHN DESMOND, AND HOWER, RALPH M. *The Administrator, Cases on Human Relations in Business*. Chicago, Richard D. Irwin, Inc., 1949.

GOLDEN, CLINTON S., AND RUTTENBERG, HAROLD J. *The Dynamics of Industrial Democracy*. New York, Harper & Brothers, 1942.

HALSEY, GEORGE D. *Supervising People*. New York, Harper & Brothers, 1946.

HERON, ALEXANDER R. *Why Men Work*. Stanford, Stanford University Press, 1948.

HOPPOCK, ROBERT. *Job Satisfaction*. New York, Harper & Brothers, 1935.

LESTER, RICHARD A. *Labor and Industrial Relations*. New York, The Macmillan Company, 1951.

LEYS, WAYNE A. R. *Ethics and Social Policy*. New York, Prentice-Hall, Inc., 1941.

——. *Ethics for Policy Decisions*. New York, Prentice-Hall, Inc., 1952.

LINDBLOM, CHARLES E. *Unions and Capitalism*. New Haven, Yale University Press, 1949.

Lynd, Robert S., and Lynd, Helen Merrell. *Middletown; A Study in Contemporary American Culture*. New York, Harcourt, Brace & Co., 1929.

———. *Middletown in Transition; A Study in Cultural Conflicts*. New York, Harcourt, Brace & Co., 1937.

Lytle, Charles Walter. *Wage Incentive Methods*. New York, The Ronald Press Co., 1938.

Mathewson, Stanley. *Restriction of Output Among Unorganized Workers*. New York, The Viking Press, 1931.

Mayo, Elton. "The Human Effect of Mechanization," in *American Economic Review*, XX, 1930, pp. 156-76.

———. *The Human Problems of an Industrial Civilization*. New York, The Macmillan Co., 1933; Boston, Division of Research, Graduate School of Business Administration, Harvard University, 1946.

———. *The Social Problems of an Industrial Civilization*. Boston, Division of Research, Graduate School of Business Administration, Harvard University, 1945.

Millis, Harry A., and Montgomery, Royal B. *Organized Labor*, Vol. 3 in *Economics of Labor*, New York, McGraw-Hill Co., 1945.

Mills, C. Wright, and Schneider, Helen. *The New Men of Power*. New York, Harcourt, Brace & Co., 1948.

Mills, C. Wright. *White Collar; the American Middle Classes*. Oxford, Toronto, Canada, 1951.

Moore, Wilbert Ellis. *Industrial Relations and the Social Order*. New York, The Macmillan Company, 1946.

———. *Industrialization and Labor*, Ithaca, Cornell University Press, 1951.

Myers, Charles A., and Schultz, George P. *The Dynamics of a Labor Market*. New York, Prentice-Hall, Inc., 1951.

Perlman, Selig. *A Theory of the Labor Movement*. New York, The Macmillan Company, 1928.

Person, H. S., ed. *Scientific Management in American Industry*. New York, Harper & Brothers, 1929.

Pigors, Paul, and Myers, Charles A. *Personnel Administration; A Point of View and a Method*. New York, McGraw-Hill Book Co., Inc., 1947.

Pope, Liston. *Millhands and Preachers; A Study of Gastonia*. New Haven, Yale University Press, 1942.

Reynolds, Lloyd G. *Labor Economics and Labor Relations*. New York, Prentice-Hall, 1950.

———, and Shister, Joseph. *Job Horizons; A Study of Job Satisfactions and Labor Mobility*. New York, Harper & Brothers, 1949.

Riegel, John W. *Management, Labor and Technological Change*. Ann Arbor, University of Michigan Press, 1942.

Riesman, David. *Faces in the Crowd*. New Haven, Yale University Press, 1952.

———. *The Lonely Crowd*. New Haven, Yale University Press, 1950.

Roethlisberger, Fritz Jules. *Management and Morale*. Cambridge, Harvard University Press, 1943.

————, AND DICKSON, WILLIAM J. *Management and the Worker.* Cambridge, Harvard University Press, 1939.

SCHULTZ, THEODORE W. *Production and Welfare of Agriculture.* New York, the Macmillan Company, 1949.

SCOTT, WALTER DILL, ET AL. *Personnel Management.* New York, McGraw-Hill Book Co., Inc., 1941.

SLICHTER, SUMNER H. *Union Policies and Industrial Management.* Washington, D. C., The Brookings Institute, 1941.

STEIN, HAROLD, ED. *Public Administration and Policy Development: A Case Book.* New York, Harcourt, Brace & Co., 1952.

TANNENBAUM, FRANK. *A Philosophy of Labor.* New York, Knopf, 1951.

TEAD, ORDWAY. *The Art of Administration.* New York, McGraw-Hill Book Co., Inc., 1951.

————. *The Art of Leadership.* New York, McGraw-Hill Book Co., Inc., 1935, London, Whittelsey House, Inc., 1935.

————. *Human Nature and Management.* New York, McGraw-Hill Book Co., 1929.

————, AND METCALFE, HENRY C. *Personnel Administration.* New York, McGraw-Hill Book Co., Inc., 1933.

TODD, ARTHUR JAMES. *Industry and Society.* New York, Henry Holt & Co., 1933.

VEBLEN, THORSTEIN. *The Engineer and the Price System.* New York, B. W. Huebsch, Inc., 1921.

————. *The Instinct of Workmanship and the Status of the Industrial Arts.* New York, The Macmillan Company, 1914, New York, B. W. Huebsch, Inc., 1922.

WALKER, CHARLES R. *Steeltown.* New York, Harper & Brothers, 1950.

WARD, ALFRED DUDLEY, ED. *Goals of Economic Life.* New York, Harper & Brothers, 1953.

WARNER, WILLIAM LLOYD, AND LOW, J. O. *The Social System of the Modern Factory.* Yankee City Series, Vol. IV, New Haven, Yale University Press, 1947.

WHITEHEAD, THOMAS N. *The Industrial Worker.* Cambridge, Harvard University Press, 1938.

————. *Leadership in a Free Society.* Cambridge, Harvard University Press, 1936.

WHYTE, F. *Industry and Society.* New York, McGraw-Hill Book Co., 1946.

WILLIAMS, WHITING. *Mainsprings of Men.* New York, Charles Scribner's Sons, 1925.

Women's Jobs; Advance and Growth (232). *Women in Higher-Level Positions* (236). *Handbook of Facts on Women Workers* (237). Washington, D.C., Dept. of Labor, Women's Bureau.

WRIGHT, DAVID McCORD, ED. *The Impact of the Union.* New York, Harcourt, Brace & Co., 1951.

YODER, DALE. *Personnel Management and Industrial Relations.* New York, Prentice-Hall, Inc., 1946.